CARYL PHILLIPS

A New World Order

Caryl Phillips was born in St. Kitts, West Indies. Brought up in England, he has written for television, radio, theater, and film. He is the author of two previous books of nonfiction, *The European Tribe* and *The Atlantic Sound,* and six novels, *The Final Passage, A State of Independence, Higher Ground, Cambridge, Crossing the River,* and *The Nature of Blood,* and has edited two anthologies, *Extravagant Strangers* and *The Right Set.* His awards include the Martin Luther King Memorial Prize, a Guggenheim Fellowship, and the James Tait Black Memorial Prize. Phillips lives in New York.

INTERNATIONAL

ALSO BY CARYL PHILLIPS

FICTION

The Final Passage

A State of Independence

Higher Ground

Cambridge

Crossing the River

The Nature of Blood

NONFICTION

The European Tribe

The Atlantic Sound

ANTHOLOGIES

Extravagant Strangers

The Right Set

A New World Order

Essays

CARYL PHILLIPS

Vintage International
Vintage Books
A Division of Random House, Inc.
New York

A VINTAGE INTERNATIONAL ORIGINAL, MAY 2002

Published in the United States by Vintage Books, a division of Random House, Inc., New York, and in Canada by Random House of Canada Limited, Toronto. Originally published in hardcover in Great Britain by Secker & Warburg, an imprint of Random House UK Ltd., London, in 2001.

Library of Congress Cataloging-in-Publication Data
Phillips, Caryl.
A new world order: essays / Caryl Phillips.
p. cm.
ISBN: 0-375-71403-0
PR9275.S263 P47647 2002
824'.914—dc21
2002020104

www.vintagebooks.com

Printed in the United States of America
10 9 8 7 6 5 4 3 2 1

For my father

Acknowledgments

Over the years I have been blessed with fine editors, but I owe particular thanks to Leon Wieseltier of the *New Republic.* I am also grateful to Sonny Mehta and Geoff Mulligan. I would like to acknowledge the input of Vrinda Condillac, whose close reading of the text and many insightful suggestions often sent me back to my desk to rethink or recast not only individual essays, but whole sections of the book. Finally, I remain indebted to Sari Globerman. Without her good-natured assistance the process would have been infinitely less rewarding.

Contents

Not from Here

You were not born here
my child
not here.

You saw daylight
among our islands
the sun was always there.

None could tap the light
from your eyes
or dictate roofs into space
for your colour.

There in the middle of a hemisphere
you and I were born
down there.

We were not in the exodus,
there was no Moses
and this was no promised land.

You may not know this yet
my son;
I sense that you sense it.

Yet what we leave
we carry.
It is no mud
we dry
on our boots.

The saliva we swallow
must ever dwell
down there.

John La Rose

Introduction: A New World Order

The airport terminal is a circus of activity. I have arrived. Although this is my first visit to sub-Saharan Africa, I know instinctively where I am. I offer up my vaccination certificates and then my passport. And now my journey begins. Through the crowded customs area, out into the cloying heat of the night. The flurry of hands and the press of sweating bodies. The cacophony of noise and shouting. I am met by a British Council official in a khaki suit. He stands with his African driver. 'Welcome to Africa. I believe that it's your first time with us.' I smile, but the driver looks away. I try to catch his eye, but he is cleverer than I am. A porter attempts to take my bags from me. I hold on to one bag, but I relinquish the other. We clamber into the jeep and my bag is safely loaded. The bearer stands with proffered hand and my British host rewards him with enthusiasm. As the grateful fellow scampers off, my host smiles at me. He is eager to make sure that I have witnessed the transaction. I understand. And then the engine roars to life and the headlights cut through the darkness, illuminating a hundred shiny faces. Arms bend at right angles to shield eyes from this sudden glare. The jeep kicks up dust and we pass through the military checkpoint. My British host gives a respectful wave and he receives a fatigued half-salute in return. We are now hurtling through the night, thundering past shanty towns and people. On the outskirts of the city I meet Africa, and the feeling is one of familiarity. I am thirty-two. I recognise the place, I feel at home here, but I don't belong. I am of, and not of, this place.

I have never before been in an aeroplane. I step from the

jetway and into the cabin. I am amazed. There are seats everywhere. I feel as though I have stepped into a narrow, tubular cinema. I locate my seat. Everyone around me seems so sure of himself. It is a new world. There are seat belts to be fastened. There is a pocket in the seat in front of me stuffed with reading matter. The seats are narrow, but I am comfortable. And then one by one every seat is taken. People begin to push luggage into bins above my head. They shove it under the seat in front of them. Suddenly the atmosphere is cramped and uncomfortable. And then the engines start and, after a long sleep on the tarmac, the animal roars to life. I look all around, but everybody seems to be taking this terrifying noise in his stride. I am twenty. I am going to America, to New York. And eight hours later I have survived my first aeroplane journey. I have eaten the food. I have watched the film. I have read the magazines in the seat pocket in front of me. I have drunk the free drinks. I have stood in line to get into the narrow room that is the toilet. I have arrived in New York City on a hot, Saturday night, with no idea of how to get to the apartment of a friend of a friend on the Upper East Side of Manhattan. I have no idea how to find the Upper East Side. The flight has arrived ten hours late so the friend of a friend will no doubt be wondering what has happened to me. Or will she? I step out of the terminal building. The night is stiflingly humid. Bright neon lights, raucous voices, the constant blaring of car horns. Saturday night in New York City. I stand with my bags and look all around me. I am in the new American world. I should be frightened and disorientated. But I am not. I recognise the place, I feel at home here, but I don't belong. I am of, and not of, this place.

The plane journey from London to Antigua passes in near silence. My mother and I read, and watch the film, but there is no discussion of any sort. Time is our friend. And now we are changing planes in Antigua. We watch, from the primitive construction that passes for a terminal, as the British Airways jumbo jet soars high and into the distance towards Barbados. And now we board the small, turbo-propped plane that will take us to St Kitts. Our birthplace. The place that neither of us has seen for twenty-two years. Time is now our enemy. My mother begins to talk. I look out of the window as the parched soil of Antigua slides away and is replaced by the impossibly deep blue of the Caribbean Sea. The water is still, like the surface of a mirror. My mother is trying to compress everything into one short flight. How can she explain a whole life in twenty minutes? She tries to repair inaccuracies, give information, to confess. And now she abandons her quest with the same confluence of grace and panic that marked the onset of this short conversational storm. The plane is descending to the past. I look out of the window. Tall sugar cane sways in the breeze. I note a thousand different shades of green. Roads snake carefully between neat, manicured fields. Cars trickle. A church. A town square. A cluster of houses carelessly thrown together. A child's play town. I look across at my mother. There is much history still dammed up inside of her. Eventually the plane taxis to a halt. The ground staff opens the door and a hot blast of air rushes into the plane. I unbuckle my seat belt and prepare to stand. My mother remains seated, as though reluctant to take these final few steps. I am eager. I peer out of the window at the arrivals hall. Behind the glass there are anxious relatives who are keen to greet me. Relatives whom I had never heard of until a few minutes ago. I left this island twenty-two years ago as a four-month-old infant. I look now at the island of my birth. I recognise the place, I feel at home here, but I don't belong. I am of, and not of, this place.

I am seven years old and everything is happening too fast. I kiss a girl outside school. On the cheek. A light kiss, but nevertheless the kind of kiss that seven-year-olds should not know about. A cluster of parents stand by and look on with horror. I am aware of the girl's sudden surprise, of the parents' outrage, but I walk past the parents. My sooty touch on their tiny Desdemona in the working-class streets of Leeds. I walk slowly, daring them to comment. And then, some few weeks later, I am walking down this same street and a dog notices me. I run. The dog runs after me. I run faster, and the dog runs faster, and I shout to the dog and to myself, 'I am not a chocolate biscuit,' and my legs continue to pound out hectic miniature strides. Eventually I run into the arms of an old lady doing her shopping. I am hysterical with fear and exhaustion and I blurt out the words, 'A dog bit me.' The woman knows I am making this up. There is no dog in sight. I am not a chocolate biscuit. The puzzled woman sees me for what I am. And then later, in the cinema, I sit by myself during the children's matinée. Above the cinema there is a dance studio. Some weeks earlier my mother had enrolled me, but she was forced to withdraw her stubborn son when I refused to dance with girls. Now she is happy to give me sixpence so that I can walk down the hill and go to the cinema and sit by myself in the dark and watch whatever adventure or cartoon is being screened. And so I sit in the dark and imagine, for my imagination is my only true childhood friend. I like to write. I have fallen in love with adjectives; 'glisten', 'glimmer' and 'glitter' are my favourite words. And I love stories. At the end of the screening, I stand while the national anthem is played. I stand, a seven-year-old boy in a cinema at the bottom of a hill in Leeds, and I listen to the turgid tones of 'God Save the Queen'. And then I step back into the streets and prepare to walk up the hill to my 'home'. It is winter. My bare knees are cold, and I start to run, all the while keeping a wary eye out for dogs. Buses roar past me. On the pavement people move with heads bowed, shoulders hunched, pulling at cigarettes. I dance in and out of their footsteps. As they breathe their breath clouds. I am seven years old in the north of England; too late to be coloured, but too soon to be British. I recognise the place, I feel at home here, but I don't belong. I am of, and not of, this place. History dealt me four cards; an ambiguous hand.

A life lived along the twin rails of reading and writing. The one act informing the other. And all the while a particular interest in the work of those who have been dealt the same ambiguous hand. Who am I? How do I explain who I am? How do I come to be here? Frantz Fanon lying in the shallow stony soil of Algeria. Ignatius Sancho standing behind the counter of his Mayfair grocer's shop. On a hot summer's day in St Paul de Vence, a grinning James Baldwin threads his way through the Frenchmen playing petanque and sits at 'his' table outside the café. The puzzled anxiety on the brow of a young John Coetzee in 'white' South Africa. All of them writing about their condition. Reading about their condition and then writing about my own. Developing a passion for literature. Developing a passion for transgression. A confused fifteen-year-old boy is confronted with the reality of Anne Frank and realises that he is not alone. He begins to recognise the laborious certainties of the old order. A life lived along the twin rails of reading and writing. The one informing the other. A passion for literature. Travelling furiously across borders and boundaries.

I am running near my home in New York City. I like to pass through Battery Park as the light is fading and look out towards the Statue of Liberty. As I run into the park I notice two slightly menacing young men in scruffy jackets and jeans walking towards me. I stop running and begin to walk. But they ignore me. They stop by the harbour wall. Then they both fall to their knees and begin to pray to the Statue of Liberty. As I walk by them, I recognise their football shirts. They are from Croatia. They are both of, and not of, this place. I sit on a bench at a civil distance from them and watch as they remain on their knees. The New World. A twenty-first-century world. A world in which it is impossible to resist the claims of the migrant, the asylum seeker, or the refugee. I watch them. The old static order in which one people speaks down to another, lesser, people is dead. The colonial, or postcolonial, model has collapsed. In its place we have a new world order in which there will soon be one global conversation with limited participation open to all, and full participation available to none. In this new world order nobody will feel fully at home. And then they both stand, cross themselves and walk off as though in search of a bar. I remain seated and watch others come and go. None kneels in prayer, but many stand and gaze at the Statue of Liberty. I too stand.

I am in West Africa. It is a bleak, yet beautiful dawn. I sit on a stone wall which forms the outer perimeter of my hotel, and I watch the Atlantic Ocean breaking over rocks some twenty yards away. I contemplate the long, painful journeys that the slave ships made across the Atlantic from this very shore. Daniel, a waiter from the hotel, understands my routine. He appears, as though from nowhere, and hands me a cup of black coffee. And then he speaks. 'I am so sorry to hear about your princess. You must be very upset.' I am puzzled, but I am soon informed that Daniel has been watching the CNN coverage of the news of the death of Princess Diana in Paris, an event that took place during the night. The new global conversational babble. These days we are all unmoored. Our identities are fluid. Belonging is a contested state. Home is a place riddled with vexing questions. My Croatian brothers on their knees in Battery Park. I encourage Daniel to sit with me and gaze upon the ocean. I want to tell Daniel that the seven-year-old boy who fell in love with adjectives has grown up. I want to tell Daniel that this boy has had to understand the Africa of his ancestry, the Caribbean of his birth, the Britain of his upbringing, and the United States, where he now resides, as one harmonious entity. He has tried to write in the face of a late-twentieth-century world that has sought to reduce identity to unpalatable clichés of nationality or race. He has learnt to accept his transgressive nature. But he knows that the world is changing. In this new world order of the twenty-first century we are all being dealt an ambiguous hand, one which may eventually help us to accept the dignity which informs the limited participation of the migrant, the asylum-seeker, or the refugee. As the laborious certainties of the old order continue to fade, and the volume of the global conversation increases, ambiguity embraces us. I want to tell all of this to Daniel. But Daniel sits for a while and then stands. He asks to be excused. Daniel beats a respectful retreat. He leaves his brother to grieve for his princess.

The United States

Introduction: The Burden of Race

It is over a decade now since I followed the austerely dressed young Ghanaian man around the W.E.B. Du Bois centre in Accra. He showed me Du Bois's study, his books, his living area and then of course Du Bois's final resting place in the grounds of the centre. A local film crew arrived to interview me as I sat in the shadow of the tomb. They were anxious to hear my first impressions of Ghana and they were equally keen that I speculate upon how their country might have appeared to Du Bois upon his arrival back in 1961. Surely he loved it on sight, which is why he renounced his American citizenship and took a Ghanaian passport? It must be the case that he fell in love with Africa, yes? My interviewer was a beautifully dressed woman in her middle years who, as the interview progressed, appeared to be increasingly perplexed by my reluctance to imagine myself into Du Bois's state of mind upon his arrival in Ghana. The fact was, I was more concerned with Du Bois's state of mind as he departed from the United States.

So many disillusioned African-American intellectuals and artists have, during the course of the past century, left their homeland with a one-way ticket tucked into their back pocket. I imagined that in 1961, as Du Bois stood on the deck of his ship and looked back at his country, he probably wondered about that most prophetic of his statements: in 1903 he had declared 'that the problem of the twentieth century is the problem of the colour line'. I wondered if the Africa-bound Du Bois felt that the problem had finally defeated him and forced him into exile. My interviewer lost patience and wound up the interview, but by now my mind was elsewhere entirely. As I speculated about the United States, I knew that 'the colour line' was a problem that was going to endure well into the twenty-first century. I imagined that, from the vantage-point of his ship, W.E.B. Du Bois could already see the degree to which the United States was sailing towards the kind of racial polarity, in thought and action, that would make it impossible to usher in an age in which sons of slaves and sons of former slave masters might sit down at the same table. In fact, the United States was in danger of drifting towards a situation in which there was a tacit understanding that a permanent division existed between the races.

Five years after my failed interview at the W.E.B. Du Bois centre, I sat in leafy Massachusetts, where I was teaching at the time, and along with the rest of the nation I watched as the football player turned media pitch-man O.J. Simpson was found not guilty of murdering his wife and the waiter Ron Goldman. Delivery of judicial decisions that are clouded by race is part of the American tradition; in fact, as recently as 1991 four white members of the Los Angeles Police Department were videotaped beating the black truck driver Rodney King. Incredibly enough, they were acquitted by a jury of ten whites, one Asian and one Hispanic, whose collective decision provoked serious rioting in Los Angeles. At the time of these riots I was on vacation in Florida. An elderly white man approached me as I read the newspaper by the pool of my Orlando hotel. 'Excuse me,' he said, 'but I just want you to know how disgusted I am by that verdict.' I nodded, and would have asked him to sit and offered to buy him a drink, but he did a fair impression of an elderly Caucasian Carl Lewis as he scampered from sight. I smiled. At least he had tried to communicate. A few years later the verdict in the O.J. Simpson trial seemed to offer no such potential for the crossing of racial lines.

My white faculty colleagues, my white students, in fact the white populace of the Massachusetts college town appeared to believe one thing, and the black people I spoke with believed something entirely different. It was clear that two distinctly different narratives were being spun out of the same facts and the indecorous media circus which surrounded the trial encouraged this idea. The journalists mixed the three ingredients of race, violence and miscegenation into a cocktail familiar to any student of American history, and Johnnie Cochran merely stirred the concoction when he reminded the courtroom of the Scottsboro Boys, who, back in the 1930s, were falsely accused of rape by two white women. But other hands had stirred before him. His invocation of the spectre of Emmett Till, the young black boy brutally mutilated and killed for talking to a young white girl, and his reference to the much-televised beating of Rodney King were in accord with the prevailing climate. All the participants – lawyers, defendants, witnesses and family – debased themselves as they scrambled to construct their racially centripetal narratives.

Feeling both of, and not of, the nation is a cripplingly anxious condition that has long existed in American life. W.E.B. Du Bois eloquently outlined the problem in *The Souls of Black Folk* in the following terms: 'One ever feels his twoness – an American, a Negro; two souls, two thoughts, two unreconciled strivings; two warring ideals in one dark body, whose dogged strength alone keeps it from being torn asunder.' However, the problems associated with this feeling of 'twoness' have ranged far beyond the African-American world. How to be both an American and oneself is a vexed question which has troubled wave after wave of migrants. From the mid-nineteenth century until the middle part of the twentieth century, so-called 'white' migrants found themselves trapped in vicious stereotypes which threatened totally to undermine their sense of self. During their passage across the Atlantic they revelled in the 'fact' that a life beyond Europe meant that the stigma of their birthright of common blood and low class would soon no longer restrict their ability to achieve. However, upon arrival they discovered that prejudice had already marked them out as lazy, filthy, lascivious, thieving, drunken, criminal brutes, with deeply flawed characters, who as such would be denied access to full participation in this new

American society. They would be barred from schools, clubs, neighbourhoods and certain jobs. However, as time passed, Poles, Irish, Italians, Jews and other immigrants would, by dint of achievement and persistence, rise above this prejudice and take their place in American life as 'white' people. Their status as Americans would be confirmed behind the hyphen: they would be Polish-Americans, or Italian-Americans, or Jewish-Americans. Their 'twoness' would be acceptable. It has never been so straightforward for African-Americans who, until very recently, were 'coloureds' or 'negroes' or worse.

Given the African-American's unique position in American life – his involuntary migration, his unrewarded labour, the longevity of his sojourn on American soil, his huge cultural contribution across the centuries – the continued existence of his sense of 'twoness' is surprising. However, the factor that is unique to African-American life is, of course, virulent racism. Institutionalised racism, in fact, so that white presidents, churchmen, professors, doctors, lawyers, felt they were exercising their moral duty when they insisted that African-Americans be recognised as constitutionally inferior. Thomas Jefferson, a man who fathered children with a slave, had no doubts about the matter. 'It appears to me that in memory they are equal to whites. In reason much inferior and in imagination they are dull, tasteless, and anomalous.' Theodore Roosevelt was equally clear: 'A perfectly stupid race can never rise to a very high plane; the Negro for instance has been kept down as much by lack of intellectual development as anything else.' But despite their well-documented history of contempt, expressed verbally and physically, whites have always been fascinated by African-American life.

For much of the past century white interest in African-American life was regarded as an exotic pastime – perhaps a night-time trip to the Cotton Club, or secretly watching black boxers (as depicted in the opening scenes of Ralph Ellison's *Invisible Man*), or furtive sexual encounters. However, these days whites no longer have to 'slum it' to participate, for the African-American contribution is mainstream in music, sport and the arts. Whitney Houston and Michael Jordan are many things, but 'exotic' is not one of them. Sadly, the movement of African-American culture from the periphery to the centre has not ushered in an era of racial tolerance. The whites cry, 'They're taking over our sports', 'They're taking over the music scene', 'They're even taking over golf and tennis', while the African-American achievers, sensing continued patronage and racism, adopt an 'in your face' attitude fuelled by the vast sums of money they are making and informed by a keen sense of historical injustice. In the past the 'white man' was able to close the door on careers like those of Nat King Cole or Paul Robeson; today, modern capitalism decrees that Latrell Sprewell plays on, and who is going to stop Puff Daddy from recording? There is a stand-off; racial posturing is part of the cultural armour of today's America.

In the past decade the discordant clamour of racial entitlement has increased in volume. The 'Y'all gonna give it up or am I gonna have to kick your ass and take it' school has grown in direct proportion to white intransigence. The more abrasive and imbued with 'attitude' African-Americans become, the more irritated and resentful whites become, which in turn serves to justify the initial African-American hostility. American whites are increasingly being asked to deal with racial guilt, while African-Americans continue to stoop under the weight of racial fatigue, and both sides are angry. The black anger is assumed to be 'articulated' by gansta rappers, who in one generation have debased a black aesthetic form which used to proclaim 'Ain't No Mountain High Enough' and dragged it down the slopes and into the gutter where 'Bitchez Ain't Shit but Hoes and Tricks'. These self-styled spokesmen of black disaffection glamorise violence, irresponsibility and sexism, chanting 'Fuck the Police' and 'Slap the Bitches'. They root their discordant, self-loathing message in the white American consciousness as being one that has sprung from the well of African-American culture. Unfortunately, nearly two-thirds of rap music is bought by whites who can enjoy the freak show before scurrying off to graduate school or Wall Street. The fact is, of course, that gansta rappers bear no more relationship to African-American life than the Mafia does to Italian-American life, or flat-footed policemen do to Irish-American life. However, the association is encouraged and rewarded by capitalists, both black and white, who encourage these young men to turn their anger and violence on themselves, to flaunt authority, embrace indiscipline and vulgarity, taunt homosexuals and disrespect women, and the more they do so the more they will be rewarded because, after all, they are just being true to their primitive bad selves.

It is not only the world of rap music that is imbued with the crotch-clutching swagger of racial posturing. The 'sister/girlfriend' school of black women's literature seems determined to tell Miss White Thang where to get off. The films of Spike Lee bray a not too subtle message, and there are a whole roster of television sit-coms which purport to reflect contemporary African-American life but which, in fact, do little more than make *Amos 'n' Andy* look positively progressive. But it is not just the artists who are embracing an 'aesthetic' defined by race. Inside the academy we now have 'progressive scholars of color', as they often like to style themselves, with highly paid sinecures who earn fat appearance fees for delivering lectures with variations on titles such as 'I'll kick your ass, Whitey, but you'll feel good while I'm doing so'. In New York City one tenured 'professor of color' still teaches his students that black people are sun people, and white people are colder, ice people, all the while masquerading as some form of multiculturalist while in essence he is little more than a monoculturalist buffoon. The sad fact is that students are expected to plough themselves into debt to listen to this nonsense, while the universities appear to be powerless to remove such people. Wherever one turns, the retreat to black essentialism is justified by the continued existence of white racism, as if the latter fact, as undeniably deeply rooted as it is, somehow justifies the former. The fact is it does not.

Racism is as American as Mom's apple pie. The country was plagued with it in the 1940s when Richard Wright and James Baldwin left for France, and it was still endemic a decade later when W.E.B. Du Bois left for Ghana. These African-Americans, and countless others like them, left because they knew that as soon as the creative mind becomes infested with the politics of race, then the creative mind is no longer creative. At different times during the twentieth century Claude McKay, Langston Hughes, Countee Cullen, Alain Locke, William Gardener Smith, Frank Yerby, Chester Himes and others all sought some kind of temporary refuge away from the essentialising politics of race which plague the United States. By its very nature art anneals and looks for connections, not divisions. It revels in contradiction and ambiguity. However, to be an African-American artist in a country in which black and white find it difficult to speak to each other means that one is constantly being placed in the role of conversational supplicant. Either one explains oneself, which is more therapy than art, or one shouts. This has been, and to some extent continues to be, the environment in which the African-American artist is expected to create. In such a situation one either endures or escapes. These days the rappers have shown us a third option, which involves making capital out of this 'stand-off'. And for some white artists there is also the opportunity for *them* to profit from this divide. The white rapper Eminem seems to suggest a final ironic twist; the white appropriation of the black appropriation of black disaffection. Racial posturing comes full circle.

Ralph Ellison always used to claim that he wrote out of a tradition that stretched from Twain to Melville to Faulkner. He described it as an American tradition, but insisted that it was part Negro and that for him there was no contradiction. His 'twoness' was easily resolved by viewing himself as black, which for him meant being wedded to a distinct experience which cherished discipline, eloquence, grace and good manners. However, he also knew himself to be intrinsically a part of the larger culture. As such, when Ellison looked into the American mirror he did not see racial types, he viewed cultural achievement. For him identity politics, as practised in the academy, or nationalist politics, as practised in the street, were not only narrow by definition, but were tinged with the taint of victim studies and skirted dangerously close to arguing for an oppression-based mode of thinking. Ellison's philosophy was clear. He understood that for African-Americans life beyond the auction block was blighted by racism, but this fact alone could neither encapsulate nor limit their humanity.

> I would not counsel giving up the struggle against racism, you have to do that to stay alive . . . but the American-ness, along with the African-ness of the Americans is a far greater challenge . . . I want to throw my hands up in the air every time somebody reduces a complex question of culture to a matter of race.

Perhaps it is as well for Mr Ellison that he is no longer around to witness the present confusion. Race is scientifically a matter of a few physical characteristics that bear no relationship to intelligence or behaviour, despite the furtive attempts of some to prove otherwise. In fact, the genetic material that is responsible for our racial make-up accounts for less than 0.1 per cent of our human genetic map. However, while other parts of the African diasporan world begin to embrace fusion and hybridity, and recognise it as our quintessential human condition, Americans continue to ignore their cultural commonality and snipe at each other across the fence of race. Race posturing in the United States is now the national sport. There is money to be made from speaking the race dozens, from declaring 'I am somebody' as opposed to wondering who the other person is. Former President Clinton was right when he declared that 'it sometimes feels like two nations, one black, one white'. But, as ever in a time of crisis, it is not going to be the task of politicians to solve this conundrum; that responsibility will fall on the shoulders of the artists. More than ever before, the United States needs a William Faulkner or a Ralph Ellison. It needs individuals whose vision is inclusive, culturally based, and who vigorously reject the self-righteous discourse of racial entitlement. Race matters. Sure it does, but not that much.

Native Son by Richard Wright

The year was 1978. I was a twenty-year-old, denim-clad backpacker who had just made his way across the United States by Greyhound bus. In common with others of my generation I was living cheaply, moving erratically from one place to the next, and I was hungry for experience. By the time my fatigued body reached the West Coast of the United States I was ready to sit down and reflect. I had ten days or so before I had to return to England, and Oxford, where I had one more year of studying before being set loose upon the world, hopefully clutching a bachelor's degree in English. One Californian afternoon I wandered into a bookshop and bought a copy of *Native Son* by Richard Wright. I had heard of neither the author nor the novel, but, as I recalled in the introduction to my book *The European Tribe* (1987), my encounter with Wright had a profound – in fact, seminal – effect upon me.

> The next morning I woke early. I walked down to the beach with the Richard Wright book, and pointed my deck chair towards the Pacific. It was a warm, but not hot, early October day. The atmosphere was a little muggy, barely holding the heat. When I rose from the deck chair it was dark and I had finished my reading by moonlight. I felt as if an explosion had taken place inside my head. If I had to point to any one moment that seemed crucial in my desire to be a writer, it was then, as the Pacific surf began to wash up around the deck chair. The emotional anguish of the hero, Bigger Thomas, the uncompromising

> prosodic muscle of Wright, his deeply felt sense of social indignation, provided not so much a model but a possibility of how I might be able to express the conundrum of my own existence ... I had decided that I wanted to try to become a writer.

In short, it was the novel *Native Son* which led me to my vocation.

Two years before the appearance of *Native Son* (1940) Richard Wright published his first book, *Uncle Tom's Children,* a collection of five stories which illuminate the miserable social and economic conditions that ensnared most African-American lives in the middle part of the twentieth century. Although the collection sold well and earned the author a reputation as a talent to watch, Wright was unhappy with the book's reception. *Uncle Tom's Children* evoked both pity and sympathy from its white readership, but Wright worried that by stirring up such emotions he had allowed white readers to assume that they were not in any way responsible for the situation that African-Americans found themselves in. As Wright states in his essay 'How "Bigger" was Born', he had 'written a book which even bankers' daughters could read and weep over and feel good about'. Richard Wright was a writer who, more than most writers, sat down at his desk with a clear political and social agenda in mind. To his way of thinking, the evocation of pity was both useless and dangerous. Wright decided that the 'mistake' of this first book would be rectified with the publication of his second. In his debut novel he would not offer his white readers the opportunity of an escape into either pity or sympathy. Wright was determined that he would make them face the difficult facts of African-American life for themselves and encourage them to accept their complicity in the misery of this American underclass. His novel would be 'hard and deep', and the narrative would move swiftly to its conclusion 'without the consolation of tears'.

Richard Wright was born in Natchez, Mississippi in 1908,

the first son of Nathan and Ella. There would soon be a brother, Leon (b. 1910), and the two boys were largely brought up by their mother, who struggled to keep them clothed and fed. Their father left home when Richard and Leon were young, and Ella and the boys travelled between Tennessee, Arkansas and Mississippi in search of food and shelter. The poverty, the abandonment by his father, and the peripatetic wandering left young Richard deeply scarred and cognizant of the fact that his life lacked any coherent structure or form. As though this were not humiliating enough, Wright's childhood also involved his having to learn to negotiate the demeaning 'rules' and conventions of black/white relations in the South. In 1927, when he was nineteen, he left Memphis, Tennessee and moved north to Chicago in search of a better life, but big-city life proved to be just as problematic as life in the South. Wright arrived in Chicago at a time when the whole country had been plunged deep into the Depression and jobs were scarce. For a while Wright had no choice but to apply for temporary assistance, but all the time he continued to read assiduously and develop the habit of writing. Perhaps the most important aspect of Wright's move to Chicago was the opportunity it afforded him to fall in with people who might help a poor Mississippi boy in his deeply-held desire to transform himself into a full-time writer.

Once in Chicago Richard Wright became active in the Communist Party, which was, at that time, one of the few groups of people who seemed to have the interests of African-Americans at heart. It was while Wright was under their 'influence' that he wrote *Native Son*, although he subsequently fell out with his 'comrades' and came to regard Communism as being largely antithetical to the African-American cause. Much of Wright's subsequent personal and professional life involved his experimentation with various alternative philosophical frameworks within which he could think and act in order that he might address the problems of non-white peoples, not only in the United States, but in a pan-African and ultimately global context. However, in the 1930s it was the ideology of Communism that captured the young writer's imagination and *Native Son* would be written with the controversial shadow of the 'red' brotherhood cast broadly across his desk. Wright's beliefs certainly did not hurt the book's reception or sales. *Native Son* was published on 1 March 1940 and it was the first novel by a black author to be chosen for the Book of the Month Club. Within the first three weeks the book had sold a sensational quarter of a million copies; within five months it had sold half a million copies and its author had become one of the most famous writers in America.

Six years later, in 1946, and shortly after the successful publication of his autobiographical memoir *Black Boy*, Richard Wright and his wife left the United States and visited France as official guests of the French government. In 1947 they returned to France, where they settled permanently. It has often been suggested that the difficulties which Wright experienced trying to buy a house in supposedly 'liberal' Greenwich Village, New York led directly to his eventual departure. These difficulties were not helped by the fact that Wright's wife, Ellen, was white. However, the reasons for Richard Wright's departure cannot be tied to any single incident. He was a man who felt, like many African-Americans before and since, that he would find it easier to develop and flourish as an artist if he placed himself beyond the tempestuous racial climate of the United States. Wright believed that a change of perspective might aid him in his attempts to slip the restrictive noose of the label 'negro' artist and in his efforts to achieve recognition as a 'universal' artist. He also felt that his wife and six-year-old daughter might be safer, and enjoy a better family life, once clear of the racism and violence of the United States.

For the remaining thirteen years of his life, Richard Wright based himself in Paris, where he continued to write both fiction and non-fiction. He became the leading figure in the African-American expatriate community in Paris in the 1950s, a community which at various times included Quincy Jones, James

Baldwin, Beauford Delaney, Josephine Baker, Chester Himes and many others. He befriended Jean-Paul Sartre, Simone de Beauvoir, André Malraux and André Gide, and for a while he was the darling of the French literary establishment. Wright also travelled extensively, producing works set against the backdrop of Spain, West Africa and the Far East. However, his writing never again achieved the commercial or critical success of the work he had produced in the United States between 1938 and 1947. In the early 1950s Ralph Ellison and James Baldwin began to publish; it became clear that a new generation of writers was emerging who seemed to be rejecting much of the polemical thrust of *Native Son* and Wright's other work, in favour of a more self-conscious literary product. James Baldwin's influential essay 'Everybody's Protest Novel' (1949) yokes *Native Son* together with *Uncle Tom's Cabin,* and Baldwin goes on to castigate both novels for reducing human complexity to stereotype.

The basic point behind Baldwin's attack was that he viewed *Native Son* as more political tract than novel. According to Baldwin, the novel was conceived of not by dwelling upon character and letting a concern with character drive and determine the plot. To Baldwin's mind it is a novel with an agenda which the author has somewhat clumsily imposed upon his characters, and by extension his readers, from the lofty vantage-point of his ideological ivory tower. In fact, many critics believe the plot of *Native Son* to be too schematic, the central character too all-knowing and the melodramatic conclusion to be essentially unconvincing. However, whatever structural or ideological weaknesses may exist in the novel, these cannot diminish the power of the remarkable spell which *Native Son* has managed to cast over successive generations of readers, nor can these perceived 'weaknesses' undermine the almost unbearable narrative tension which Richard Wright manages to achieve.

The central character in *Native Son* is a twenty-year-old black man named Bigger Thomas. He lives in a single cramped room on the South Side of Chicago with his mother, his younger sister and his brother, Buddy. Bigger and Buddy share a bed.

The room is rat-infested, money is tight, there is no allowance for privacy, arguments are rife and the rent is high. Bigger's mother finds some solace in her religion, but for the sister and younger brother it is clear that their future is gloomy. For Bigger it is already too late. Bigger keeps a gun and a knife and he has already carried out a series of robberies with his gang friends. Now the gang are contemplating the unthinkable; 'crossing over' the colour line and robbing a white man.

At the outset of the novel Bigger provokes an argument with, and then viciously attacks, one of his best friends. He then takes his knife to a pool table and slashes it in a manner that suggests he is hell-bent on destruction; put simply, he is out of control. It would appear that resorting to violence is the only way in which Bigger is able to articulate his despair at the racially charged inequity which daily threatens to consume his life. Bigger is offered a job as a chauffeur by a Mr Dalton, the head of a wealthy white family who have given over five million dollars' worth of philanthropic donations in an effort to 'help' the negroes. However, the generosity of the Dalton family makes Bigger feel uneasy. The ambiguities that envelop their charitable contributions become clear when we discover that the Dalton family owns the over-priced slum room in which Bigger and his family live. In fact, the Daltons have made their money by being slum landlords to the African-American community on the South Side of Chicago.

Mary Dalton, the pretty young daughter of the family, is presently associating with Communists, much to the distress of her parents. She and her 'red' boyfriend, Jan, attempt to befriend Bigger. They make Bigger take them to a black restaurant so they can eat chicken with 'authentic' blacks, but their gestures of 'friendship' only arouse in Bigger deep feelings of anger and violence, for he feels that he is being patronised. While it is clear to Bigger that the hostile whites do not understand him, and never wish to do so, the supposedly liberal whites appear to Bigger to be equally myopic in their understanding of 'his' problems. If anything, his feelings of hostility towards the liberals are more urgently felt than his feelings of fear towards the bigots. Eventually Bigger descends to violence of the most perverse kind as he allows himself to be consumed by the hate, anger and frustration which have been daily gnawing away at his young life.

Clearly there is a huge dichotomy between the morally unspeakable actions of Wright's hero, Bigger Thomas, and the sympathy that we nevertheless feel for him. Wright's ability to have us empathise with this man in his loneliness, and his skill in enabling us to understand what has motivated Bigger's brutality, is the great achievement of the novel. Wright has written a novel about an outlaw who undoubtedly derives some degree of pleasure and relief from killing, yet the reader gradually learns to recognise some glimmer of truth in the cliché 'society's to blame'. In his first book Wright had worried that pity would be the overwhelming emotion the reader would be left with. In *Native Son* there is no such danger. Bigger Thomas conforms to the worst stereotype of the black murderer and rapist. He may be a victim of his circumstances, but Bigger is proactive and he relishes the destructive force that he unleashes, for he grows to understand that whites cannot control it. In other words, Bigger Thomas makes the unsettling discovery that it is the act of violence itself that, in fact, sets him free. The reader is horrified and outraged by the events and revelations of the novel, but held captive by a narrative which suggests that *both* blacks and whites are likely to be ensnared in a nightmare of savagery and physical and emotional pain unless somebody addresses the problems of American racism.

The novel's first section, 'Fear', and the second section, 'Flight', both move with the speed and compulsion of a thriller. However, the final section, 'Fate', is riddled with unlikely setpieces behind which one can clearly hear the voice of the author. As has already been established, Richard Wright had a political point to make, and as he tries to make his point the structure of the novel becomes aesthetically clumsy and increasingly burdened with improbability. Bigger Thomas, now incarcerated and facing the death penalty, is represented by Boris Max, a Jewish Communist lawyer who understands and sympathises with African-American people. Bigger is not only hostile towards Max, he is hostile towards Jan, Mary's Communist boyfriend, whom Bigger has unsuccessfully tried to frame for murder. Jan forgives him, but Bigger's hostility towards all things white encompasses these two 'good' men who are trying to save him from execution. When, at the conclusion of the novel, it becomes clear that Bigger will die, he somewhat unconvincingly recognises the goodness of both Max and Jan. Suddenly this angry, violent, young man 'understands' that there are good white people as well as bad ones. It all rings somewhat untrue.

The immediate and enduring power of *Native Son* is obviously tied, both then and now, to the drama of race in America. Two groups of people face each other. One group is black and one group is white. One group's path to economic, social and political power remains largely blocked. One group of people dominates the other and some among this dominant group continue to invoke all manner of vague historical reasoning to justify their privileged position. In the pages of *Native Son* Richard Wright reminds us that the dominated group will continue to seize upon the 'moral' authority of violence as the only means of true expression unless both groups begin voluntarily to overhaul this lamentable system. Until this happens many lives will be destroyed and much suffering will be engendered. Wright's novel is a plea for the system to be dismantled by the kind of 'mature' communication which Bigger and Max eventually achieve; black and white fighting together for the same end against an unjust system. However, being the political animal that he was, and possessing an unquenchable ambition to be recognised as a 'universal' as opposed to a 'negro' artist, Wright was never going to be content to view the 'struggle' in purely racial terms. In his essay 'How "Bigger" was Born' Wright attempts to place Bigger in a larger context.

> The difference between Bigger's tensity and the German variety is that Bigger's, due to America's educational restrictions on the bulk of her Negro population, is in a nascent state, not yet articulate. And the difference between Bigger's longing for self-identification and the Russian principle of self-determination is that Bigger's, due to the effects of American oppression, which has not allowed for the forming of deep ideas of solidarity among Negroes, is still in a state of individual anger and hatred.

Mercifully, the text of *Native Son* remains unencumbered by such pedantry.

In December 1960 Richard Wright died of a heart attack. He was still a relatively young man of fifty-six. Although there was immediately some controversy about his death, and speculation as to whether or not it involved foul play, what was tragically clear was that one of the most important American literary careers of the twentieth century had come to a premature end. Most of the obituaries, while commenting on his literary exile in Paris, and his poor beginnings in Mississippi, began their analysis of his writing by referring to his masterwork, *Native Son*. Today, some forty years after his death, some fifty years after Baldwin's famous essay, and sixty years after the novel was first published, Wright's critics and commentators still joust over the aesthetics of this problematic novel. One thing, however, that nobody ever seems to disagree about is the novel's extraordinary narrative power. This is what attracted readers back in 1940 and transformed *Native Son* into one of the great literary bestsellers of all time, even though the subject-matter was, to say the least, disturbing for both black and white readers alike.

I have never returned to the California beach where, over twenty years ago, Richard Wright's *Native Son* fuelled my ambition to be a writer. I have, however, regularly visited Paris and sought out Wright's final resting place in Père Lachaise cemetery where his ashes are interred. I have also regularly walked past 14 rue Monsieur le Prince where Wright lived during his years in Paris. These small pilgrimages have helped me to remain close to an author to whom I will be forever indebted. The final irony, of course, is that I now live in Greenwich Village, only a few short blocks from Charles Street where, back in the mid-1940s, the great American writer Richard Wright endured much difficulty and unspeakable humiliation trying to live and write as a free man in the country of his birth. With chin held high, Richard Wright chose to leave for France; this 'native son' was not going to allow the United States to turn him into a 'Bigger Thomas'.

2000

Giovanni's Room by James Baldwin

In the autumn of 1956, when the novel *Giovanni's Room* was published, James Baldwin was a thirty-two-year-old black American writer living in Paris. He had spent much of the previous eight years in Europe, principally in Paris, escaping what he perceived to be the restricted opportunities which his homeland offered to him. He was, in one sense, just another in a well-established tradition of twentieth-century African-American artists who had chosen to leave the United States for what they hoped would be the less racially oppressive air of Europe. Sidney Bechet, Paul Robeson and Josephine Baker were among those who had preceded him, and in 1948 Baldwin simply packed his bags and followed in their wake.

Baldwin arrived in Paris with forty dollars to his name. He was the author of numerous reviews and essays, principally for the *New Leader*, *Commentary* and the *Partisan Review*, but he had no book to his name. Predictably, he was soon plunged into the type of unromantic poverty that can quickly overtake the life of an innocent abroad. Baldwin was a gregarious and charismatic young man, and although times were tough (so much so that at one point he was imprisoned), he managed to beg and borrow from friends and eventually complete a first novel, *Go Tell It on the Mountain*. The novel was published in May 1953 by Alfred A. Knopf, one of America's most established publishing houses, and it attracted generally favourable reviews. The *New York Herald Tribune* described it as a work of 'insight and authoritative realism', although the *New York Times* found that its religious themes rendered it 'almost as remote as a historical novel about the Hebrew patriarchs and prophets'. However, although Baldwin's career appeared to be successfully launched, he now faced the problem of what to do about a second novel.

James Baldwin was born on 2 August 1924 in Harlem, New York. He was the eldest of six children, although the man whom the children called 'father' was not actually Baldwin's father. His mother had given birth to her first child by a man who had soon disappeared from both of their lives. The man whom Baldwin knew as 'father' was a fierce, Bible-thumping disciplinarian who appeared to have little time for his wife's eldest child. The poverty that bedevilled their family life only served to increase Baldwin's father's antipathy towards the world. He was particularly harsh to the increasingly intelligent and precocious child, whose presence he grew to resent. Young James sought refuge in reading and in visits to the cinema. Soon he was writing and he quickly gained a schoolboy reputation as a 'man of letters'.

In the summer of 1941 Baldwin left school and began a series of menial jobs. He had harboured a hope that he might go on to college, but his grades were not particularly good and the family needed him as a breadwinner. However, at this point, the largest trauma in his life was his decision to break with the church. The travails of his upbringing in Harlem, his coming of age in the church, and his subsequent abandoning of the pulpit, are recorded and depicted in *Go Tell It on the Mountain*. Having left the church, the young Baldwin moved to Greenwich Village, where he supported himself in a variety of jobs including railroad hand, dishwasher, waiter and elevator boy. He became part of a more eclectic and artistic community and during these years he befriended the painter Beauford Delaney and the author Richard Wright, who would soon leave for Paris. Wright recognised that the strangely intense young man had talent and, before leaving for Paris, he helped to secure a fellowship for the cash-strapped fledgling. Later, when Baldwin first arrived in Paris in 1948, Wright extended the hand of welcome, but the friendship between them never fully recovered after Baldwin's publication, in 1949, of an essay entitled 'Everybody's Protest Novel'. The essay was highly critical of Wright's famous novel, *Native Son,* and to Wright's mind, the master had been betrayed by the pupil.

By 1953 James Baldwin had a fast-developing literary reputation and editors were aware of the young negro author. However, the label 'negro author' was one which Baldwin never warmed to. He had no desire to be thought of as just another negro limited to writing only on 'negro' topics. He saw his talent as universal, and he was determined that he should be free to write about anything or anybody he pleased. As he contemplated a new novel, he naturally looked to the world in which he had been living for the past few years: Paris. One of the defining characteristics of *Go Tell It on the Mountain* is that it is a novel that essentially contains no white characters, aside from a man whom the young hero accidentally bumps into in Central Park. In this sense it was a 'safe' novel for a negro author to write. James Baldwin would not be playing it 'safe' again.

Giovanni's Room opens in the south of France with David, a young white American already in his second year in Paris, casting his mind back over the events of the previous few months. David had arrived in Paris determined to break from the United States and the troubling spectre of his father. He meets Hella, a young American woman, and they become engaged. When Hella goes on an extended vacation to Spain, David encounters Giovanni, a proud and handsome Italian waiter, and he falls in love with him. Through late winter and an entire spring they conduct their affair. When, in early summer, Hella returns to Paris, David abandons Giovanni and resumes his life with Hella, which causes Giovanni to suffer painful feelings of rejection. Eventually a distraught Giovanni returns to his old job working for Guillaume, a seedy and exploitative man described in the novel as 'a disgusting old fairy'. Guillaume constantly taunts a depressed and abandoned Giovanni, who eventually 'snaps' and, in a fit of rage, murders Guillaume. On receiving this news,

David, who has by this time removed himself to the south of France, is plunged into despair. Hella eventually discovers the nature of David's sexuality and leaves him. A distressed David is left alone in the south of France contemplating the imminent execution of Giovanni and musing on the chaos that has ensnared his life.

Giovanni's Room is, by any standards, an audacious second novel. A novel by a young African-American writer containing no black characters and dealing with the taboo subject of homosexuality. There had been other attempts by black writers to write novels without any black characters. This 'raceless' writing had been pioneered by Charles Chesnutt and Paul Laurence Dunbar at the turn of the century. Other work in this tradition includes Ann Petry's *Country Place* (1947) and William Gardener Smith's *Anger at Innocence* (1950). There had also been attempts by African-American novelists to write on homosexuality, including Chester Himes's *Cast the First Stone* (1952), a novel which introduces us to a handsome white hero who, while in prison, first resists then succumbs to a sexual relationship with a younger, darker man. However, to attempt to put the two together, and write a 'raceless' homosexual novel, and to do so at the inception of a promising career, suggests either calculation or an admirable recklessness of spirit, or both. In retrospect, it is clear that James Baldwin knew exactly what he was doing.

Some years later, in a reply to an interviewer's question, James Baldwin made plain his feelings about the connectivity between race and sexuality: 'The sexual question and the racial question have always been entwined, you know. If Americans can mature on the level of racism, then they have to mature on the level of sexuality.' In other words, for Baldwin the journey from *Go Tell It on the Mountain* to *Giovanni's Room* was neither discontinuous nor disruptive. The themes of race and sexuality are unified, one feeding the other. Although *Giovanni's Room* appeared to some critics to be a professional suicide note, as far as Baldwin was concerned the novel was a logical successor to *Go Tell It on the Mountain*. The uncloseting of sexual desire was to be viewed as just another step on the path towards the uncloseting of the racially prejudiced mind. Baldwin challenges us with a question: 'How, in fact, *can* one write about race without writing about sexuality?'

But *Giovanni's Room* is also about freedom, the same kind of freedom that Baldwin sought to discover by leaving the United States and relocating in France. Some years later Baldwin memorably described his flight to Paris as 'a leap into visibility'. During the course of *Giovanni's Room* David admits that 'nothing is more unbearable, once one has it, than freedom. I suppose this was why I asked her to marry me: to give myself something to be moored to.' In Paris David is free to live the 'dangerous' bohemian life, but he is frightened of life. Hella is also frightened. While she is in Spain considering David's proposal of marriage, she writes to her fiancé, 'I'm really not the emancipated girl I try to be at all. I guess I just want a man to come home to every night . . . I want to start having babies. In a way it's really all I'm good for.' For Baldwin the narrow, unexamined life, to which the American couple wish to retreat, is a lamentable existence. Sadly, both David and Hella appear to have accepted the stereotype of the roles assigned to them by American society. David bleats on about his fears of not being a 'real' man. He longs to be safe, 'with my manhood unquestioned, watching my woman putting my children to bed'. Meanwhile, Giovanni, who has embraced risk and led a life unchecked by society's hypocritical 'rules', is in despair. When Hella returns, David imagines that he can leave Giovanni and return to the 'purity' of his restricted world. This, of course, proves to be impossible.

When Baldwin delivered the manuscript to his publishers, Knopf, they suggested that he change the title of the book and make it about a woman. Baldwin refused. Having rejected the iron collar of assigned identity in his personal life, Baldwin felt that he had no choice but to do so in his professional life. When the Knopf editorial team continued to urge him either to adapt or abandon the novel, and instead come up with another 'negro' novel, Baldwin chose instead to leave his publisher and move to the smaller, less prestigious, Dial Press. The book would be published just as Baldwin had written it and *Giovanni's Room* immediately elicited the kind of responses that one might have predicted.

Although white critics praised aspects of the book – its construction, its lyricism, its daring – their response was in the main muted. The *New York Times* was typical, its reviewer regarding *Giovanni's Room* as a novel written with 'dignity and intensity'. A notable exception was the response of the writer Nelson Algren, who in the *Nation* went out of his way to welcome Baldwin's second novel. 'This novel', he insisted, 'is more than another report on homosexuality. It is a story of a man who could not make up his mind, one who could not say yes to life. It is a glimpse into the special hell of Genet, told with a driving intensity and horror sustained all the way.'

African-American critics, on the other hand, both publicly and privately, were dismayed and baffled. Langston Hughes (with reference to *Go Tell It on the Mountain*) was already on record as having suggested that Baldwin 'over-writes and over-poeticizes in images way over the heads of the folks supposedly thinking them'. He described the young writer's first novel as 'a low-down story in a velvet bag – and a Knopf binding'. Even before the appearance of *Giovanni's Room,* Hughes had suggested that Baldwin had not only a racial and cultural identity crisis but a personal identity crisis too. The 'evidence' of *Giovanni's Room* served only to 'confirm' Hughes's worst suspicions, although on this occasion the 'dean' of negro writers chose to hold his tongue.

Later African-American critics, notably Eldridge Cleaver and Amiri Baraka, were not only hostile, their responses to Baldwin's sexual agenda reeked of homophobia and envy. In his essay on Baldwin, 'Notes on a Native Son', Cleaver describes homosexuality as a 'sickness' on a level with 'baby-rape'. In an essay on

Baldwin by Baraka the author suggests that Baldwin is so anti-black that if he were 'turned white . . . there would be no more noise from [him]'. Baldwin, however, in his public utterances on identity politics and the relationship between sexuality and race, refused to grant those such as Cleaver and Baraka any ground. He remained stubbornly defiant. 'People invent categories in order to feel safe. White people invented black people to give white people identity . . . Straight cats invent faggots so they can sleep with them without becoming faggots themselves.'

Baldwin's third novel, *Another Country* (1960), built upon the sexual themes of *Giovanni's Room*, but it was set in New York City and contained a multi-racial cast. In fact, after *Giovanni's Room* Baldwin never again wrote a novel with an exclusively white cast. His career did, however, continue to resist narrow categorisation, and he continued to redraw literary and socio-political boundaries. Easy connections and casual prejudice were anathema to Baldwin's moral world and the remarkable *Giovanni's Room* makes an early and unforgettable declaration of the author's future intentions.

Since its publication the novel has become a foundation text for gay culture, but the appeal of *Giovanni's Room* is decidedly broader than this. Baldwin understood this, even as those around him faltered in their support and insisted that publication would wreck his career. 'They said I was a negro writer and I would reach a very special audience . . . And I would be dead if I alienated that audience. That, in effect, nobody would accept that book coming from me . . . My agent told me to burn it.' Mercifully, the young James Baldwin had already cultivated a necessary stubbornness. He fired his agent. He refused to allow anybody to curtail his freedom, or dictate the terms of his own life, both personally and professionally. *Giovanni's Room* is an elegant and courageous second novel in a literary career which would soon develop into one of the most remarkable of the second half of the twentieth century.

2000

Marvin Gaye

Imagine the scene. We are in the late eighteenth century and attending a slave auction in Charleston, or Barbados, or Savannah. One by one the captives are ushered on to the auction block, prodded, inspected, examined for venereal taint, and then the bidding opens. The most prized specimens are the young males who are able to perform one vital task beyond the physical drudgery which will blight all these African lives. Young males can be used as 'studs' and therefore to produce new slaves for free. African-American males remain the only migrant group in the American world whose social standing upon arrival was deeply wedded to their ability to perform sexually. To the white American plantocracy, the more priapic, virile and sexually robust the man, the greater his value. Sadly, soon after their arrival, this is how African-American men began to think of themselves.

The writings of James Baldwin, Richard Wright and Ralph Ellison were the subject of a special study during my last year as a student at Oxford. I was standing on the verge of graduating into a Britain that was being torn apart by 'race riots', yet there was no discourse about race in British society and certainly no black writers. Paradoxically, I looked to the United States, and to the African-American writers who had taken their place in the American literary tradition, to aid me in my attempts to understand contemporary Britain. Richard Wright's *Native Son* seemed to me accurately to reflect the anger and frustration that I could sense in the Britain of the late 1970s. Perhaps even more powerfully, the solitary brooding nature of Ralph Ellison's hero in *Invisible Man* was suggestive of the isolated and confusing condition that many second-generation black Britons found themselves in during this period; particularly those, like myself, who were trapped in an academic ivory tower while all around Britain was burning.

As my research progressed, I was surprised to discover that a great number of African-American writers and artists, including James Baldwin and Richard Wright, had left the United States and chosen to live in what they considered to be the racially liberating climate of Europe. This concerned me, for while their insights appeared to be clear and penetrating on issues connected with American racism, their vision became cloudy when faced with the realities of European racism. In their rush to escape the bigotry and discrimination of their homeland, these writers seemed to be content to overlook the treatment of both colonial and economic migrants in Paris, Berlin, Amsterdam and London. They also appeared to be indifferent to the disturbing and undeniable spectre of the Holocaust. What kind of a Europe did these writers imagine they were running to?

Beyond the writers, the American artists I most admired were the musicians, particularly Stevie Wonder, Curtis Mayfield and most importantly Marvin Gaye. Their ability to transform pain into art, and to create incisive narratives that spoke to both blacks and whites with clarity and passion, excited the young writer in me. I listened endlessly to Stevie Wonder's 'Living for the City' and to Curtis Mayfield's 'Darker than Blue' and 'Back to the World'. These songs were as important to me as any novels or plays, for they fearlessly addressed injustice. However, the musician I admired above all others was Marvin Gaye. He had arguably made the most important musical statement of all with his brilliantly original suite of songs on the album *What's Going On*, but he had also displayed, in this and other work, a deep connectivity to the word 'love'. Stevie Wonder, Curtis Mayfield and other socially committed soul musicians had also written love songs, and great ones at that, but there seemed to me to be a particularly passionate vulnerability to Marvin Gaye's love songs. While recognising the problems of drugs, violence and racism, Gaye seemed to be insisting that if we could all just learn to open our hearts and love each other then many of these social problems would be solved without our having to resort to political or legislative solutions. An admittedly romantic thesis, but it was one that appealed to me, for I felt that a true understanding of the word 'love' was all too often absent from the work of many African-American artists, including Richard Wright and Ralph Ellison.

In June 1981 I finally had the opportunity to see Marvin Gaye perform live at London's Apollo Theatre, but it was a disturbing performance which made me wonder about the direction that his career was taking. Here was a Motown artist whose finest recordings suggested both a hard political edge and great personal sensitivity, yet onstage in London he seemed content to strut around and present himself as little more than 'Mr Sex Machine'. I had waited a long time to see my 'hero' and my sense of disappointment was profound. A belief in the power of 'love' seemed to have given way to a simplistic desire to be loved. The Marvin Gaye whom I was presented with not only lacked sensitivity, he lacked subtlety. If one could imagine the stage of London's Apollo Theatre to be an American auction block, then this Marvin Gaye would have fetched top dollar. Why was this consummate black artist, a man who had written 'Save the Children' and 'Mercy, Mercy Me (the Ecology)', settling for the demeaning role of throwing sweat-stained handkerchiefs at screaming English women? And why was such a man living in Europe – in Belgium, of all places?

David Ritz's wife slows the car to a halt outside the two-storey house on Gramercy Place. We are in the predominantly black, middle-class Crenshaw district of Los Angeles. It is a large house with a mock Tudor façade. To the left of the house a smaller property lies within the same fencing. Although it is night, and the sky is moonless, I can see that both houses have fallen into a state of disrepair. The windows are bare and an indifferent assortment of clumsy signs announces that the property is for sale. David Ritz twists around in the passenger seat and states the obvious. 'I guess nobody wants to buy.' He does not have to suggest why. On the morning of Sunday 1 April 1984, in the larger of the two houses, Marvin Gaye's father walked into his eldest son's bedroom and shot him twice with a handgun. He then marched downstairs and on to the front porch, where he threw his handgun on the lawn and took up a seat. He waited for the police to arrive.

Marvin Pentz Gay Senior was the third of thirteen children. He was born on a farm in Jessamine County, Kentucky on 1 October 1914 and named Pentz after the German doctor who delivered him. Gay's parents were sharecroppers, but they differed from the rest of the community, for his mother was a member of an eccentric Pentecostal church – the House of God. The church espoused adherence to a mixture of Orthodox Judaism and Pentecostal Christianity in which women followers were required to dress in white with Stars of David visible on their garb. Gay followed his mother into the church and in 1934 he met his wife to be, Alberta, in Washington DC, where he had gone to preach. The following year they were married and they settled in the south-west projects of the capital city, where Gay held services in their small, cramped house.

Marvin Pentz Gay Junior (he later added the 'e') was born at Freedman's Hospital, Washington DC on 2 April 1939, the second child and the first son. Soon there would be another sister and a brother, Frankie, but the atmosphere in the household was always strained. Gay was a strict father who drilled his children on the Bible and kept Sabbath on a Saturday. Never formally ordained, Reverend Gay was regarded in the neighbourhood as an uncompromising man of God. In his own house he was a man to be feared and he would not flinch from inflicting harsh physical punishment. Marvin told his biographer David Ritz in 1982:

By the time I was twelve, there wasn't an inch of my body

> that hadn't been bruised and beaten by him ... Living with Father was something like living with a king, a very peculiar, changeable, cruel, and all-powerful king. You were supposed to tiptoe around his moods. You were supposed to do anything to win his favor. I never did. Even though winning his love was the ultimate goal of my childhood, I defied him. I hated his attitude.

By the mid-1950s Gay had become disenchanted with the church. Another member of the congregation had been named chief apostle over Gay and this bruised Gay's ego. For the greater part of Marvin's childhood his father had been a spiritually possessed, Bible-fearing patriarch, but by the time Marvin reached his teens his unemployed father seemed to have lost his purpose in life. He had worked for short periods at Western Union and at the Post Office, but it was now his wife's labour as a domestic that supported the family. The tension between Marvin and his increasingly embittered father was exacerbated by the fact that as Marvin was growing into adolescence his father's life suddenly appeared to be directionless. Furthermore, Gay was now openly exposing another side of his character, one that had been inadequately disguised for much of Marvin's childhood.

Marvin Gay Senior was an openly effeminate man, both in terms of his manner and his clothing. This caused Marvin to be the target of relentless teasing about his 'sissy' father. In 1982 he told David Ritz, 'My father likes to wear women's clothing. As you well know, that doesn't mean he's homosexual. In fact, my father was always known as a ladies' man. He simply likes to dress up. What he does in private, I really don't know – nor do I care to know.' Shortly before her death in 1986, Ritz asked Alberta Gay if her husband was homosexual. She replied, 'I'm not certain. I do know that five of his siblings were homosexual. And it's true that he liked soft clothing. Soft things of all kinds attracted him. He liked to wear my panties, my shoes, my gowns, even my nylon hose. Marvin would see him like that sometimes.'

Dave Simmons, a long-time friend of Marvin's, remembers Marvin telling him how difficult it was going to church on a Saturday and having a father who had the reputation of walking around in women's clothes. I sat with fifty-eight-year-old Simmons in the lobby of a Los Angeles hotel. Tall and muscular, and dressed casually in T-shirt, jeans and baseball cap, Simmons bears a striking resemblance to Marvin. He shook his head as he told me, 'Marvin added the "e" in a hurry. He was worried about the gay thing.' Then Simmons tipped his hat back and idly rubbed his bald head. 'You know, Marvin was ashamed of his father.' He paused. 'It was a serious problem.'

As a young boy Marvin used to sing in his father's church, but at fifteen he stopped singing at the altar and began to enjoy 'sinful' secular music. After a brief spell in the United States Air Force, Marvin moved to Detroit, partly to escape his father, who disapproved of his singing 'devilish music', and partly to try to become involved in the emerging Motown scene. Marvin began as a session drummer and he played on early hits by Smokey Robinson and the Miracles, but in 1962 he recorded two songs, 'Stubborn Kind of Fellow' and 'Hitch Hike', which both entered the charts. Marvin's career as a singer with Motown was launched, but Marvin was not happy.

Marvin Gaye disliked dancing, a 'failure' which regularly brought him into conflict with the head of Motown records, Berry Gordy. Motown was built upon the notion of 'hot' rhythm and blues that would cross over from black to white audiences, all of whom would be swept up in colour-free gyration. Marvin, however, wanted to be a balladeer. He wanted to combine Perry Como's relaxed presentation with Billie Holiday's pain, and he declared his intent from the very beginning of his career. His first album, *The Soulful Moods of Marvin Gaye* (1961), featured ballads which Marvin felt could 'express the deepest secrets of the soul'. However, Berry Gordy was not interested in such music, nor could he provide the polished musical arrangements and elaborate strings which might transform Marvin's tracks into the Perry Como sound that Marvin craved for. When Marvin's debut album failed, he was encouraged by Gordy to concentrate on the hip-shaking, 'sexy', rhythm and blues songs which eventually resulted in Marvin's brace of hits in 1962.

In 1965 Marvin returned to love ballads with two albums, *A Tribute to the Great Nat King Cole* and *Hello Broadway,* both of which failed commercially because Motown was still not fully equipped to produce such music. Furthermore, the public did not associate a Motown artist with the polished, understated elegance that Marvin was trying to project. They wanted sweat and hot sexuality, but Marvin was determined that he should be allowed to wear a tuxedo, sit on a stool and sing love songs. At a packed San Francisco nightclub in 1966 Berry Gordy turned up to see Motown's number-one sex symbol. However, when Marvin made his entrance he did so with a single spotlight upon him, popping his fingers and singing 'Me and My Shadow'. He had on a hat and carried a cane and there followed a whole set comprised of such numbers. A furious Gordy berated his singer, but Marvin had made his point. Shaking his behind like all the other Motown acts might be commercially rewarding, but Marvin found its blatant appeal to sexuality both cheap and easy. Furthermore, as Marvin told Gordy, he was unhappy with the manner in which Motown expected its singers to record.

The idea of an album being two hits and ten pieces of filler had never satisfied Marvin. He thought of himself as more artist than singer, and as somebody who could think thematically and compose orchestrally. Marvin sought to convince Berry Gordy that he should be allowed to produce his own 'concept' album, but Gordy had a formula that worked and a highly valuable commodity to protect in Marvin Gaye. However, after a long stand-off between these two stubborn men, Marvin got his way and in 1971 he released *What's Going On.* It was an immediate success, and unusually for a popular record, *Time* magazine accorded it a two-column review, describing it as 'a vast, melodically deft symphonic pop suite ... The overall style ...

is so lush and becalming that the words – which in themselves are often merely simplistic – come at the listener like dots from a Seurat landscape.'

Despite the artistic and commercial success of *What's Going On*, Berry Gordy was still not happy with Marvin recording what he perceived to be 'protest' albums. However, he need not have worried, for Marvin's next album, *Let's Get It On* (1973), was a suite of songs about the pleasures and dangers of loveless sex, which both pleased his fans and satisfied Berry Gordy. The album that followed, *I Want You* (1976), was even more graphic in content and little more than a fully fledged celebration of sexual carnality. On this album Marvin can be heard promising to perform oral sex and boasting about doing it 'three times a day'. In performance Marvin Gaye was now beginning to project himself as an 'all-night-long lover', and thrusting his pelvis with the best of them. As he confessed to David Ritz, 'I . . . saw that pleasing women meant pleasing your bank account. Sex and money and music were all tied up together. I thought I was cool, I thought I could handle anything, but, oh, man, I didn't know what I was in for.'

During the 1970s Marvin settled into the role of 'sex god', even though he still yearned to sing his ballads and do thematically important work in the tradition of *What's Going On*. Like so many artists before him, he imagined that he could moonlight in the commercial gutter for a while, and then return to his 'art'. However, Marvin underestimated the price that he would have to pay for making a temporary peace with sexual vulgarity. He was an insecure man who had lost his virginity to a prostitute while in the Air Force, and thereafter he had continued to make extensive use of prostitutes. However, he rarely had sex with them, preferring to talk about sex, or make them parade naked in front of him. A great connoisseur of pornography, he feared intimacy, disliked kissing and viewed women as dangerous. For a man whose religious upbringing encouraged him to regard sex as an extremely powerful force, it was reckless of Marvin to submit to a vision of himself as a sexual ring-master when, in fact, nothing could be further from the truth.

In the late 1970s Marvin's troubled personal life began seriously to disrupt his work. His first marriage to Anna Gordy, a woman seventeen years his senior, and the sister of Berry Gordy, was over. In October 1977 Marvin finally married his girlfriend, Janis Hunter, who was seventeen years his junior and had already borne him two children, Nona and Frankie (known to everyone as Bubby). However, by 1979, his marriage to Janis had effectively ended and much hostility existed between Marvin and his ex-wives. A 1978 album, *Here My Dear,* based upon his marriage to Anna, had been a commercial and critical failure and there was no doubt that Marvin's artistic reputation was waning. Meanwhile his drug habit was beginning to grow out of control and he was running from the IRS and a horde of other debtors. In late 1979 Marvin Gaye fled the mainland United States for Hawaii, a forty-year-old bankrupt.

Between late 1979 and the early summer of 1980 Marvin lived an eccentric life in Hawaii. For much of the time he slept in a bread van, existing on bananas and pineapples; at one point he tried to kill himself by ingesting more than an ounce of pure cocaine in less than an hour. He wrote letters to friends on the mainland asking for help, which they duly offered in the form of cash and occasional visits. Marvin hoped for some kind of reconciliation with Janis, but when she eventually turned up in Hawaii they quarrelled so badly that Marvin held a knife to her heart and by his own admission came close to killing her. He was afraid to return to Los Angeles, where his affairs were in the hands of receivers, his studio had been closed up and he now owed well over a million dollars in taxes. However, his life in Hawaii was becoming increasingly poverty-stricken and Marvin knew that the simplest way out of this mess would be for him to tour abroad and make some money. Having learned of Marvin's situation, the British promoter Jeffrey Kruger arranged a tour of Britain, in the hope that Marvin might begin to address his financial problems and gain some perspective on his life at home in the United States.

The British tour was a drab affair. Few venues sold out and the concerts themselves were unsatisfactory, with Marvin doing little more than pace about the stage and encourage the women in the audience to 'come get to this'. The drugs and limousines interested Marvin more than the performances and the tour ended in fiasco when he refused at the last minute to perform at a Royal Gala charity event in the presence of Princess Margaret. Marvin's royal 'snub' became headline news in Britain, but at this stage of his life he cared little about what the press thought of him. The tour over, Marvin now faced the unappealing prospect of leaving Europe and returning to the United States, where he would have to face up to his responsibilities. He chose instead to remain in London.

Professionally Marvin was facing a crisis. Motown had already invested over a million dollars in the recording of a new album, but he was reluctant to return to the studio and complete the project. He had no 'concept' in mind, and the working title of the album, *Love Man,* only pointed to the heart of the problem. Marvin found himself trapped by the 'all-night-long lover' image that was now synonymous with his success, and although he resented its crassness he had no idea of how to move beyond it. The days when he could write and perform socially committed, yet heart-wrenchingly sensitive work seemed to have receded into the distant past. Eventually a frustrated Berry Gordy made the decision simply to use what material Motown already had. He instructed his engineers in Los Angeles to do a final mix of the album, which, in January 1981, he released under the title *In Our Lifetime.* Alone in London, and heavily indulging in drugs, Marvin was outraged. The music was incomplete and at least one of the tracks ('Far Cry') was little more than a 'guide track', the musical equivalent of a writer's first jottings. After twenty years as a central player in the Motown success story, Marvin vowed never again to record for Motown and he remained true to his word.

* * *

Early images of African-American people in literature, theatre and film all concentrate on sexually neutering the black male and presenting him as either a child, or a buffoon, or both. Mark Twain's Jim in *Huckleberry Finn* is a sexually arrested man whose emotional development stops at the level of playing with a white boy. The minstrels of the theatre and the early 'Rastus' figures in the American cinema are caricatures of black men whose clownish make-up and clumsy gestures are deliberately designed to be as sexually unalluring as possible. Usually named 'Smoke' or 'Molasses', the characters of these black men generally develop no further than grasping at white men's property and lusting after white women.

White American society placed so much emphasis upon black male sexuality that it created for itself an imaginary nightmare. A fear was engendered in white America's soul that somehow African-Americans were more highly sexed and therefore likely to be both a threat to white females and a source of comparative embarrassment to white males. With the advent of slavery a system of laws was introduced which forbade miscegenation; the very *idea* of a black man being caught with a white woman was enough to cause white men to reach for their shotguns, and should a black man be 'difficult' it was usually not enough simply to punish the black man, he was often castrated too.

In the middle part of the twentieth century Harry Belafonte couldn't kiss a white girl, Sidney Poitier couldn't marry one and Nat King Cole couldn't sing with one. As recently as 1967 it was still illegal to marry across the colour line in Virginia and, even when all such laws had vanished, for a black man to attempt such an audacious act was still regarded as 'headstrong' at best, 'foolish' at worst. However, with the advent of the Civil Rights movement, and the emergence of the 1960s' dashiki generation, black people's confidence grew. Cassius Clay told white America how pretty he was. Furthermore, he insisted that he was not going to fight in a white man's war, and he then reinvented himself in his own image as Muhammad Ali. His was a dignified transformation, but for most black males, whose self-image had been long blighted by white America's notions of black sexuality, the growth in confidence simply heralded a movement from stereotype to stereotype. In essence, from sambo to superspade, with rampant sexuality as the undignified barometer of black men's changing status.

In the 1969 film *100 Rifles* a bulked-up, handsome Jim Brown pinned a semi-clad and willing Raquel Welch to a bed. In *Sweet Sweetback's Badasssss Song* (1971), Melvin Van Peebles won a 'sex contest' with a white woman. These and countless other acts of cinematic transgression were supposed to signify the black male's declaration of independence. His most potent 'weapon' was to be neither the gun nor the brain, it was to be the penis. The mythical 'weapon' that the white man prized him for was now being unsheathed and turned loose in the heart of the white man's world. As Eldridge Cleaver wrote in *Soul on Ice* (1968), the black man knew full well that 'the black man's penis was the monkey wrench in the white man's perfect machine'.

In the world of music James Brown boldy declared himself a 'sex machine', while Isaac Hayes whispered in our ear that John Shaft was everything a woman could desire. The movie's advertising slogan reminded us that 'Shaft's his name, shaft's his game'. Images of hyper-potent male sexuality continue to underpin black music down to the present, so that while Puff Daddy and Babyface choose to present themselves as responsible young fathers and husbands, the values they celebrate are still those connected to the notion of the black man as sexually dynamic and keen to please. New players on the block such as D'Angelo, whose antics on stage and video make Michael Jackson's crotch-grabbing seem passé, have taken the notion of hyper-sexuality to a new level, while gay singers like Luther Vandross continue to indulge the fantasies of their female audiences with promises of satisfying them in ways that no other man has been able to satisfy them.

The 'superspade' image endures far beyond the world of music. What was Clarence Thomas thinking of when, as Anita

Hill claimed, he boasted about his size and ability? The former basketball star Wilt Chamberlain claims to have bedded over 10,000 women, declaring his 'stats' as though they qualify him to enter a sexual hall of fame. And one only needs to watch any black television situation comedy for evidence of how closely sexual prowess continues to be connected to black male 'achievement' and 'desirability'. Where, in all of this, one might wonder, is there room for ambivalence? For doubt? For love? Where is there room for an African-American man to choose to measure his worth in the American world by standards other than his hyper-sexuality?

Freddy Cousaert is built like a prizefighter and he makes large gestures as he speaks. In the early 1960s Cousaert opened a nightclub in Ostend called 'The Groove', and he was largely responsible for introducing black American music into Belgium. His nightclub grew in size and reputation and by the 1970s he was promoting soul and reggae concerts all over Europe. In September 1980 Cousaert found himself in Britain on one of his many business trips. A fellow promoter informed him that, having finished the Jeffrey Kruger tour, Marvin Gaye was now living in London and would soon be performing in a small West End club. He asked if Cousaert would like to meet Marvin and naturally Cousaert was thrilled. Two days later he met a stoned Marvin in an unkempt apartment in London's Knightsbridge. He tentatively suggested a European tour and to his surprise Marvin appeared interested. As Cousaert remembers it, 'Marvin tried to talk a little about capacities and merchandising, and to make it sound like he knew what was going on. But he didn't. In the end we exchanged addresses and chatted about basketball.'

Liliane, Cousaert's wife of thirty years, pours us coffee and then switches on a low light. Cousaert looks tired, but determined. This story of how he 'saved' Marvin Gaye is central to his life and he wants to get it right. Cousaert sent Marvin a formal proposal for a concert tour and a few weeks later an anxious Marvin called Belgium. Cousaert told me, 'Marvin asked for an advance. I sent him a cheque to London, without any security, even though I knew he was wasting his time there. In December 1980 Marvin went to Brighton to the sea for a few days with his five-year-old son Bubby and his Dutch girlfriend Eugenie. He called me and told me that he liked wind and rain, so I said he should come over here. I said we've got plenty in Belgium and Marvin said he'd come after Christmas for a few weeks. He planned to come in February 1981 and we got an apartment ready for the first week. But I didn't hear from him, so I called London and found that he had changed apartments. He was no longer living in Knightsbridge. It turned out that he had moved to a flat in a hotel near Marble Arch.'

Cousaert tracked Marvin down and spoke to him on the telephone. Marvin assured a somewhat irritated Cousaert that he was packed and ready to leave for Belgium whenever Cousaert arrived, so Cousaert departed immediately. However, when he arrived in London, he was appalled by what he found. 'The flat was awful. Bubby was crying, it was a mess. There were about five hangers-on in the bedroom and Marvin was high from snorting coke. I pointed to the car and told Marvin, "I borrowed it and I have to have it back in Belgium tomorrow. If you're not ready at eight in the morning, forget it." The next morning Marvin, Eugenie and Bubby were the only ones left in the apartment, and they were ready. But Marvin did not know where he was at all. Also the folks at reception were watching every move because they suspected that Marvin had no money to pay the bill.' Cousaert paid the bill and in February 1981 he drove Marvin Gaye out of London and in the direction of Ostend in Belgium.

Ostend is a windswept, somewhat lonely outpost of 80,000 people on Belgium's North Sea coast. It boasts a quarter-mile-wide expanse of beach, which eventually gives way to the rough, grey sea. Beyond the sea there is no horizon. The swelling blanket of water simply meets the thick canvas of sky and forms one heavy, seamless curtain. As I looked through my hotel window, I saw a flotilla of floodlit oil tankers sliding slowly by. On the beach a lonely stick-like figure leant into the wind, while overhead a single gull wheeled lazily. Shortly after Marvin's arrival in Ostend, Freddy Cousaert arranged for a half-hour documentary to be shot on location. The film is called, appropriately enough, *Transit Ostend.*

In one scene Marvin enters a working-class bar which is full of Belgian workers enjoying a beer at the end of the day. They look quizzically at this American black man, and ask him if he's from Paraguay. Marvin confesses to being a singer from Los Angeles and they laugh at him. Then Marvin attempts to play darts. He is not very good and again they laugh at him. In another scene Marvin, resplendent in red and white tracksuit, first jogs along the beach, then works out in a gym. As he does so he announces that his next fight is going to be with his wife: 'fifteen rounds for all the property'. He looks confused and worried. The Marvin Gaye of *Transit Ostend* is a man at a crossroads in his life. He has entered unfamiliar territory in terms of language, race and culture, but he is attempting to maintain good grace and manners. Here, in Belgium, Marvin is neither a star nor is he an American. He has no viable role to play, not even the role of black American sex symbol which he considers so demeaning. The creases of worry on his forehead suggest that he knows what he is in Belgium. He is simply a black man.

Between February 1981 and October 1982 the Cousaerts welcomed Marvin into their world. Cousaert arranged for Marvin to live with Eugenie and Bubby at 77 rue Promenade in a small fifth-floor apartment overlooking the North Sea. In early 1981 Larkin Arnold, then a senior vice-president of CBS records, flew to Belgium in the hope that he might sign Marvin Gaye to his label. These days Larkin Arnold still maintains some relationship to the music business, although he is primarily a lawyer and businessman. The walls of his Beverly Hills offices are decorated with the gold and platinum discs of the many artists he has worked with over the years. When I mention his visit to Marvin in Belgium he arches his eyebrows and leans back into his chair. 'I found him as positive as one could be in that desolate city. I was surprised, for he was in a cold, one-bedroom apartment overlooking the North Sea, not much bigger than my office. A couch, a bed and a synthesiser were all there was. He was glad to see me, another black man, in town and we talked because there wasn't anything else to do. But I was surprised at his situation.'

Soon after Arnold's departure a deal was struck which necessitated the delivery of an album by the summer of 1982. Arnold, together with Marvin's lawyer Curtis Shaw, also set about paying off Motown (approximately $2 million), establishing a 'reasonable' payment schedule with the IRS, and arranging for the IRS's criminal charges against Marvin to be dropped. In his capacity as Marvin's business partner, Cousaert received Marvin's $50,000 advance on the album, which he banked in Switzerland. He then negotiated a further $25,000, which was spent on musical equipment for Marvin. Cousaert attempted to encourage Marvin to forget his latest idea of a money-spinning tour and to begin work on the album, but Marvin remained stubborn. Cousaert knew that without a new album Marvin's career was not going to develop. 'I told Marvin in September 1981, no tour, we record. But Marvin told me, "Stop, you're not my father, Freddy. I left my father when I was sixteen." But I wasn't treating him like a father. He was behaving like a spoiled kid.'

Cousaert's relationship with Marvin deteriorated further in July 1982 when Marvin's visa problems necessitated his leaving Belgium for three months. A hurt Cousaert was not invited to accompany Marvin, although Marvin (who did not have a driving licence) took their company car and the master tapes of the album. Between July and September 1982 Marvin moved erratically between France, Switzerland and Munich, in Germany, where, in August, he eventually finished recording his most unashamedly commercial album, which he had now entitled *Midnight Love*. Meanwhile, back in Belgium, financial problems were mounting around Marvin's affairs and Cousaert knew that he would have to track Marvin down. He did so and in late September he arranged to meet Marvin in Geneva, where, after an unpleasant encounter in which Marvin accused Cousaert of embezzling his money, Marvin provided Cousaert with the necessary signatures which both released Marvin's $50,000 advance and effectively terminated their business relationship. Shortly thereafter *Midnight Love* was released. Marvin's album notes do not acknowledge Freddy Cousaert or any member of his family. After their frosty meeting in Switzerland, Cousaert never saw Marvin again.

'Sexual Healing' was written in Ostend, with the basic rhythm track laid down by Odell Brown and a title suggested by Marvin's biographer, David Ritz. Back in Los Angeles I sat with Ritz, a small bald man with earrings in both ears and tattoos the full length of his arms, who rocked back and forth in his chair as he spoke. His comfortable Los Angeles study is decorated with posters and photographs of his musical heroes, many of whom (including Smokey Robinson, Etta James and Ray Charles) he has written books about. Shortly before Marvin's death, Ritz sued Marvin and CBS in order to establish that he held part of the copyright of 'Sexual Healing'. On the album Ritz received no songwriting credit, but Ritz claims that one night in Ostend, having seen all the sado-masochistic pornographic material littered about Marvin's apartment, he told Marvin that what he needed was 'sexual healing'. Thereafter Ritz claims that they penned the song together. His suit was settled out of court and Ritz is now listed as co-writer of the song, along with Marvin and Odell Brown.

Marvin's attitude towards sex veered wildly between the puritanical and the pornographic, a fact easily discerned by listening to the music that he produced after *What's Going On*. For instance, the album *Let's Get It On* features an exquisite paean to the purity of love and longing, 'If I Should Die Tonight', but, a few tracks later, there is the unmistakable coarseness of a song entitled 'You Sure Love to Ball'. When

I asked about Marvin's own sexuality, Ritz was candid. 'Marvin had performance anxiety, premature ejaculation and impotence. He also liked to wear little frilly things, blouses and so on. He did it with guilt and confusion. He never said, "I cross-dress," but he'd say, "I like to wear frilly things from time to time and get wild." It didn't surprise me because he was intrigued with his dad.' Ritz then pointed to a passage in a book by Tony Turner entitled *Deliver Us from Temptation* (1992). Turner is a former dresser for the Temptations and Diana Ross, and Ritz explained that had the book been published before he wrote his own biography of Marvin he could have, and would have, expanded upon Turner's observations, for he felt 'Turner got him right and it [the passage] has all the earmarks of truth'. Turner met Marvin in London shortly before Freddy Cousaert took Marvin to Belgium. Turner remembers the singer asking him to make a wig.

> He liked the experience of a woman's wig on his head, all rolled up – but he didn't want it styled on a wig head, he wanted me to roll it on him, like he was in a beauty shop and this was his own hair. Some days I would do two or three styles for him! Then he would get himself dressed up. Marvin had found a nice selection of clothes over there in the cross-dressing shops. He had the cross-sex undergarments and everything. He wasn't that interested in make-up. What he really liked were the bras, corsets, garter belts, and negligées that he would wear around the apartment with nothing else on top – just a wig on his head with rollers in it like any old housewife. Later, when Marvin's father shot him dead in 1984 and the whole story of their troubled relationship came out, I discovered that the Reverend Gay was into wigs too.

A great deal of Marvin's time in Europe was spent exploring the personal nature of his relationship to 'masculinity', and slowly coming to terms with the tragic fact that he had no idea how to escape the burdensome public role of 'Sex God'. His fear of being unable to perform adequately, both on stage and in bed, was temporarily alleviated by his continued use of female prostitutes for purposes of voyeurism and domination. Their willingness to adopt a submissive role boosted Marvin's fragile sense of himself as a 'real' man. However, what Marvin really needed was not so much 'sexual healing' as some kind of armistice which might release him from what he perceived to be his personal and professional obligation to be 'the baddest buck on the block'. But a man who has largely made his name and fortune by encouraging women to 'get it on', cannot expect suddenly to sing 'Fly Me to the Moon' and be taken seriously.

Marvin fully understood that the ability to be a 'real' man in a sexual sense is a key element of being a black male in the United States, but he regarded this as crass. At the same time Marvin did not want to be like his father. In Marvin's eyes, his cross-dressing, effeminate father had failed as a man and caused him untold shame and humiliation. Beyond his use of prostitutes, and his own cross-dressing experiments, the only forum available to Marvin to work out these problems in was his music. The fade-out lyrics on 'Sexual Healing' are 'Baby, please don't procrastinate, if you do I'll have to masturbate'. Unreleased tracks at the time of his death included songs with such titles as 'Sanctified Pussy' and 'Dem Niggers Are Savage in the Sack', the latter being a bleakly comic investigation of the myth of a black man's supposedly limitless sexual powers. Marvin was struggling to banish his problems with irony, but alone and isolated in Europe he was retreating further into a world of sexual experimentation and drugs.

In October 1982, his visa problems now resolved, Marvin travelled to Holland from Paris. CBS Records, in the person of Larkin Arnold, were trying hard to persuade Marvin to return to the United States in order that he might do promotional work for the *Midnight Love* album and eventually tour. Despite his insecure yearnings for the fame and fortune which only the United States could provide, Marvin remained ambivalent about returning home. By remaining in Europe he could continue to avoid the marital and financial problems that he had spent the past three years running from and he could also indulge his sexual fantasies. Furthermore, like American artists before him, he was able to enjoy the freedom of not feeling any responsibility to comment on European society, including its racism. He was lonely, but in a peculiar way he was also liberated. Then one night Marvin received a phone call from home informing him that his mother had been taken seriously ill with kidney problems and subsequently hospitalised. A reluctant Marvin knew that he now had no choice but to leave Europe and return to Los Angeles.

Dave Simmons remembers picking Marvin up at Los Angeles airport and taking him straight to the Cedars-Sinai Medical Center to see his mother, who by this stage was in intensive care. Simmons severely chastised Marvin for leaving his mother in the care of his father, who had clearly done nothing for her. In fact, when Marvin arrived, Gay was not even in Los Angeles; he was on an extended visit to Washington DC. His father's negligence angered Marvin but, familial problems aside, Marvin's professional life was in the ascendance. 'Sexual Healing' was by now a huge international hit, but after three years of European exile Marvin was finding it difficult to cope with the pressure of constant media attention. He began free-basing, as opposed to simply snorting, cocaine and inevitably his physical and mental health began to suffer. The situation was not helped by the embarrassing and semi-pornographic promotional video for 'Sexual Healing', which was recorded soon after his return to the United States. It features a 'helpless' Marvin being examined by a scantily clad female doctor who causes his blood to boil, and his temperature to rise, as she administers 'Sexual Healing'.

In January 1983 Marvin Gay Senior returned to Los Angeles from Washington and moved back into his bedroom in the Gramercy Place house, which Marvin had been sharing with his mother. The unbearable tension in the family home, compounded by excessive drug use and serious financial problems, continued to wreak a terrible toll on Marvin. In April 1983 Marvin set out on a five-month-long national tour, but by this stage he was a mere shadow of the physically healthy man who had arrived back from Europe. Most people thought that Marvin would never complete the 'Sexual Healing' tour, but – as stubborn as ever – he was determined to prove his detractors wrong. The tour featured a dramatic and sad illustration of Marvin's continued confusion about the disparity between his image as a potent sexual god and the reality of his sexual inadequacy. At one point in the show he would drop his pants and, clad only in briefs, his waistline bulging, his head hung low, he would pose somewhat pathetically before his audience. It was clear that this sad, disturbed man had finally submitted to the power of the stereotype.

The tour ended in August 1983 and Marvin returned to Los Angeles, where he moved into a friend's apartment. The tour had been a financial, as well as an artistic, disaster and because Marvin had been ignoring his new schedule of payments to the IRS, he was now indebted to the agency to the tune of nearly four million dollars. In November 1983 Marvin moved back into the family's Gramercy Place house and isolated himself in his bedroom, where he took to long solitary bouts of smoking dope, free-basing cocaine, and reading the Bible. Alberta Gay occupied the bedroom next to Marvin's and beyond hers was the Reverend Gay's bedroom, where he spent much of his time drinking vodka.

According to Alberta Gay, on the morning of Sunday 1 April 1984 she and Marvin were upstairs talking in his bedroom. They heard an angry shout from downstairs. The words were indistinct, but mother and son both knew it was seventy-year-old Marvin Gay Senior. Gay was frustrated because he could not find some letters pertaining to an insurance policy. Marvin shouted to his father that he should behave in a more civil manner and come upstairs if he had something to say.

Moments later Gay appeared at the door and began to berate seventy-one-year-old Alberta Gay. An angry Marvin raised his voice and told his father to leave the room. 'You can't talk to my mother that way,' he said. When his father refused to leave the bedroom Marvin pushed him out into the corridor, where the argument continued until Alberta intervened. Marvin then returned to his bedroom and comforted his agitated mother. Moments later Gay appeared at the door, this time armed with a 38mm revolver which Marvin had given to him some months earlier. He took aim and fired from a distance of about six feet. A bullet ripped into forty-four-year-old Marvin's heart and he fell to the ground. Alberta Gay began to scream as her husband took a few steps forward, lined up his pistol and fired again, this time into his son's left shoulder. Then, without saying a word, he calmly turned around and walked downstairs, where he threw the gun on the front lawn and took a seat on the porch. He sat impassively and waited for the police to arrive.

Gay remembered a different version of events. He claimed that on the morning of Sunday 1 April, he and his son began arguing in Gay's upstairs bedroom. The quarrel then escalated into a physical fight. 'He grabbed me and he slung me to the floor and he started beating me, kicking me,' said Gay in an interview with the *Los Angeles Herald Examiner* shortly after the incident. 'He kicked me everywhere he could kick me. He knocked me on the bed and when I fell my hand happened to feel the little gun under the pillow.' Gay claimed that having got to his feet his son knocked him to the ground again. 'I laid there and tried to get my poor self together.' According to Gay, Marvin then stormed out of his father's bedroom and into the hallway, where Alberta Gay was crying and pleading with her son to stop the beating. Gay said that at this point Marvin turned on him and threatened him with the question, 'Oh, you want some more, do you?' Gay admitted pulling the trigger twice, but he claimed that he thought he was firing blanks. 'I didn't know any bullets was in the gun,' he said. 'I thought it was loaded with blanks or BBs [ball bearings]. The first one didn't seem to bother him. He put his hand up to his face like he'd been hit with a BB. And then I fired again. This time I heard him say, "Oh," and I saw him going down.' Gay remembered that as soon as the bullets were discharged his wife came to him and said, '"Marvin's bleeding." I went down the hall and looked. "Babe," I said, "call the paramedics."' Gay told the journalist that it was hours later when he heard from a detective that his son was dead. 'I just didn't believe it,' claimed Gay. 'I thought he was kidding me. I said, "Oh, God of mercy. Oh. Oh. Oh!" It shocked me. I just went to pieces . . .' Few people, including the Los Angeles Police Department, believed Gay's account. They charged him with first-degree murder. His wife began divorce proceedings.

Marvin Gay Senior was a source of disappointment to his son, for he was not a man in the way that Marvin wished him and needed him to be. He was neither capable of, nor interested in, providing for his own family. Instead, he ruled his household by fear, beat his wife, abused his children and engendered confusion in the soul of Marvin by flaunting his ambivalent sexuality and continually attempting to undermine the confidence of his handsome and talented son. For much of his life Marvin had tried to win the approval and affection of this jealous, egotistical man, but Gay refused to show his son that he cared for him. As Marvin sank further into the world of drugs, he became obsessed with the idea – quite probably biblically inspired – of punishing his father for failing as a man, and punishing himself for failing – in his own eyes – as an artist, a lover, a husband and a father. Marvin felt that the sins of one generation were being passed on to the next generation and he could not bear this. When he looked at his father he saw an addictive, sexually confused, emotionally unstable failure of a man. Marvin grew to loathe his father because so much of what he saw in his father eventually reminded him of himself.

I asked Dave Simmons about the morning that Marvin was shot. He sighed deeply and shook his head. His eyes began to fill with tears. 'You know, Marvin knew what he was doing. He wanted to die, but he also wanted to punish his father. The shooting was his way of committing suicide. What better way of doing it than putting it on his father? Make him live with it for the rest of his life.' Marvin's eldest sister, Jeanne, is also convinced that her brother carefully provoked their father. Shortly after the funeral she told David Ritz, 'This way he accomplished three things. He put himself out of misery. He brought relief to Mother by finally getting her husband out of her life. And he punished Father, by making certain that the rest of his life would be miserable. I do believe that Marvin was very crazed and disturbed but, even at that point, in his own way, my brother knew just what he was doing.'

Larkin Arnold is also convinced that Marvin knew what he was doing, but he is less sure that Marvin achieved his desired aim. He told me, 'Marvin must have planned the end, but the waste, the tragedy is that the father learned nothing from it. He is in a home now and he's the meanest son of a bitch.' In 1984 a *Los Angeles Herald Examiner* reporter, Mitchell Fink, interviewed Gay in jail, where he was being held awaiting trial. The reporter stared directly into Gay's eyes and asked him if he loved his son. An unblinking Gay replied, 'Let's say that I didn't dislike him.' In 1999 an apparently unrepentant Marvin Gay Senior passed away.

Dave Simmons remembers meeting a flamboyantly dressed Gay shortly after the murder. The charges against him had been reduced from first-degree murder to voluntary manslaughter and Gay had been given a six-year suspended sentence and five years' probation. After her son's murder, Alberta Gay began formal divorce proceedings, but while she moved out and went to live with her daughter Jeanne, Gay moved right back into his room in the Gramercy Place house. Simmons recalls going to visit Alberta Gay at Jeanne's house and being somewhat taken aback to see Gay sitting by himself on a sofa with nobody talking to him. 'What made the scene even more surreal', remembered Simmons, 'was the fact that there was a video on the television of Marvin singing.' When Simmons was ready to leave he offered Gay a ride home. As fate would have it, as they were driving along one of Marvin's songs came on the radio. It was then that Simmons remembers Gay turning to him and asking coldly, 'Do you know who gets the money from these songs?' I asked Simmons if Gay showed remorse, at this or any other time. 'None,' he said. 'None whatsoever.' Simmons went on, 'You know the old biblical saying. "I brought you into this world and I'll take you out." Well, that's pretty much how Father Gay felt.'

Imagine the scene. A small church in Ostend. A disorientated Marvin walks into the church and looks around. There is nobody in sight. His mind drifts back to his childhood when he used to sing in his father's storefront church. And then Marvin begins to sing 'The Lord's Prayer'. He sings like he has never done before, his glorious tenor echoing around the small Belgian church. When he finishes his dull eyes stare into mid-air. The scene is from the film *Transit Ostend.* Marvin looks around himself. He is alone in Europe. In Belgium. A long way from home. It is far too late to sing gospel in order that he might please his father. It is too late to sing the ballads that he loves so much. It is too late to set aside the image of Marvin Gaye, 'Lover Man'. Marvin understands that he must play the part that has been assigned to him, the part that he thought he could pick up and put down at will. A Mephistophelean pact. But meanwhile, in a small church in Belgium.

2000

Fatheralong by John Edgar Wideman

John Wideman occupies a unique place in American letters. His seven novels, three collections of stories and his memoir, *Brothers and Keepers,* explore the realities of urban African-American life with a critical intelligence and a Faulknerian restlessness of form unmatched by any of his contemporaries. *Fatheralong,* his second memoir – described as *A Meditation on Fathers and Sons, Race and Society* – is perhaps his most ambitious and important work to date. Structured as six essays, the book reflects upon the journey that Wideman and his family have made from rural South Carolina, to blue-collar Pittsburgh, to affluent Amherst, where he is now a professor of English, all the while maintaining a tight focus on the troubled relationship between African-American fathers and sons. The condition of African-American men's lives has long been one of Wideman's central themes, and in *Fatheralong* this theme is most commonly revisited in a tone of thinly veiled anger.

> Ideas of manhood, true and transforming, grow out of private, personal exchanges between fathers and sons. Yet for generations of black men in America this privacy, this privilege, has been systematically breached in a most shameful and public way. Not only breached, but brutally usurped, mediated by murder, mayhem, misinformation. Generation after generation of black men, deprived of the voices of their fathers, are for all intents and purposes born semi-orphans. Mama's baby. Daddy's maybe. Fathers in exile, in hiding, on the run, anonymous, undetermined, dead.

> The lost fathers cannot claim their sons, speak to them about growing up, until the fathers claim their own manhood. Speak first to themselves, then unambiguously to their sons. Arrayed against the possibility of conversation between fathers and sons is the country they inhabit, everywhere proclaiming the inadequacy of black fathers, their lack of manhood in almost every sense the term's understood here in America. The power to speak, father to son, is mediated or withheld, white men, and the reality they subscribe to, stand in the way. Whites own the country, run the country, and in this world where possessions count more than people, where law values property more than person, the material reality speaks plainly to anyone who's paying attention, especially black boys who own nothing, whose fathers, relegated to the margins, are empty-handed ghosts.

Born in 1941, John Wideman spent his early formative years in the Homewood section of Pittsburgh, which is predominantly African-American. He grew up in a poor, but nonetheless self-supporting family presided over by the often silent spectre of his father, who at different times worked as both a waiter and a welder. When he reached junior-high-school age, the family moved to Shayside, which was a better neighbourhood, and young John Wideman excelled at basketball in an integrated environment. His academic work also prospered, and after attending the University of Pennsylvania on a basketball scholarship, Wideman became only the second African-American in fifty years to win a Rhodes Scholarship to Oxford. On returning to the United States he became the first tenured African-American professor at the University of Pennsylvania, and thereafter he began his writing career. His three early novels, *A Glance Away* (1967), *Hurry Home* (1970) and *The Lynchers* (1973), are modernist in structure and tone and heavily influenced by the work of T.S. Eliot, among others. At this stage of his career Wideman was careful to distance himself from the cultural nationalism of writers like Amiri Baraka, and those involved in the Black Arts Movement. However, by the time he came to write the Homewood Trilogy – *Hiding Place* (1981), *Damballah* (1981) and *Sent for You Yesterday* (1983) – Wideman was embracing folklore and displaying an awareness of a distinct African-American literary tradition. This process of refracting African-American subject-matter through the refining lens of modernism continued in *Reuben* (1987) and *Philadelphia Fire* (1990), and is clearly evident in *Fever and Other Stories* (1989). During the course of his career, John Wideman has travelled a long way beyond his quietly reflective early work, to a place where these days one sometimes senses that he has one foot on the soapbox. His ire has been ignited by that most American of catalysts, race; an absurd man-made contrivance which John Wideman firmly believes has conspired to not only keep us separate from each other, but also apart from our true selves.

Wideman is hardly the first African-American author to feel imprisoned by his country's obsession with race – in 1956 James Baldwin published *Giovanni's Room*, a novel in which there are no black people. To a certain extent, this was Baldwin's attempt to reject what Wideman calls 'the paradigm of race'. In fact, the more one reads of *Fatheralong* the clearer it becomes that Wideman not only shares a subjective thesis with Baldwin, but in this book he has appropriated a literary form – personal literary nonfiction – of which Baldwin was the master. And, of course, much of Baldwin's nonfiction concerned that most chequered of relationships, fathers and sons. However, Wideman's stridency clearly marks him off as separate from his literary antecedent. When Wideman imagines black fathers looking through nursery windows at their newborn, and speculating on the future traumas of racism that these children will have to endure, he does so in a secular tone that is altogether different from Baldwin's biblically inspired musings.

> And we ain't talking here about middle-class angst cause no taxis stop for your black ass in Rockefeller Center.

> Nor existential maundering when you ride the commuter train in from Scarsdale and the only seat white people ain't occupying is the one next to your brown ass. All that's part of the problem, but the bedrock issue raised by the paradigm of race ... is whether you can be someone other than a white person in this society and stay healthy, stay alive.

The book is curiously structured, moving backwards and forwards in time as though deliberately trying to mirror the linear disruption that blights African-American familial narrative. Early in the book Wideman and his father Edgar travel to 'Promised Land', a small black community in South Carolina to which the Wideman family can trace their roots. Edgar is a tough, independent-minded man in his seventies, who has endured much personal despair and social abuse without ever allowing himself to be humiliated or defeated. But Wideman's feelings about his father are ambivalent, for he barely knows the man beneath the mask. The two of them journey together in search of family history and while 'on the road' Wideman's meditations range from his thoughts on the novelist Richard Wright to his admiration for Nelson Mandela. However, Wideman's main concern, and the central pillar around which the book revolves, remains the gap which race creates between African-American men and their sons:

> You are your son's biological link to past and future. Are you also his burden. To claim you, say yes to you, must he also accept the stigma of race. Does your dark face doom him to be an outsider.

In this case the dark face belongs to Edgar Wideman.

John Wideman soon realises that he truly does not know this stranger who, unlike his much-loved mother, never gave himself over to his son. What *does* he know? He knows that his father likes the Yankees, that he has another set of children, that he did multiple jobs to support his family. But his father is a man of few emotions, who creates distance and alienation all around him. In fact, the title of the book is a wordplay which suggests the tragic depths of this situation. As a child, Wideman thought that the hymn 'Farther Along' was called 'Fatheralong', the reference being to a distant father who stood alone, proudly isolated and stubbornly self-reliant. This posture not only deprives the child, in this case John Wideman, of physical and emotional warmth, but it also negates the creation of a strong familial unit that is built up around stories which are passed on from father to son. The author argues that without this narrative baton-passing, African-American identity will never achieve dignity and resilience.

The darkly comic essay 'Picking up My Father at the Springfield Station' allows one to breathe out after the tension of the preceding pages. Wideman senior not only manages to miss his ride from Springfield to Amherst, but, once at Amherst, he also manages to miss his ride from the motel to his grandson Danny's wedding. Three generations of Wideman men, Edgar, John and John's son, Danny, form the narrative spinal cord of *Fatheralong,* and we eavesdrop on their attempts to communicate. However, the book is written with the brooding presence of two 'lost' Wideman males hovering in the background. In his earlier memoir, *Brothers and Keepers* (1984), Wideman examined the relationship between himself and his brother, Robby, ten years his junior, who is serving a life sentence for murder. Shortly after the publication of this first memoir, Wideman had to suffer the tragedy of his own son, Jake, being convicted of a similar crime. It is only when one reaches the final essay, 'Father Stories', addressed to Jake, that one understands the true impulse behind this book: 'A love story finally, love of you, your brother and sister, since no word except love makes sense of the everpresent narrative our days unfold.'

African-American writers and artists, as far back as Frederick Douglass and William Wells Brown, have grappled with the legacy of father deprivation. Wideman regards Richard Wright's *Black Boy* as the key text of this genre, which continues, beyond Wright, through to Claude Brown's *Manchild in the Promised Land*

and Alex Haley's *The Autobiography of Malcolm X*. Of late the problem of African-American fatherhood has once again come under the microscope in film, with John Singleton's *Boyz 'N the Hood,* and Matty Rich's *Straight out of Brooklyn,* and in print in a spate of autobiographical first books including Nathan McCall's *Makes Me Wanna Holler* and Brent Staples's *Parallel Time.* Wideman's *Fatheralong* is the latest dispatch from this frontline, but for all its eloquence and passion, its compelling digressions and exhortations, one troubling question lies near its heart; what effect has having a father who was always 'alone, alone, alone' had on Wideman the father?

We know what effect it has had on Wideman the man, for he tells us that, as he grew into manhood, he decided that he would take neither the warm, inclusive path of his mother, nor the cold, aloof one of his father. 'Neither Father's son nor Mother's son, betraying them both as I became myself. My mother's open arms. My father's arms crossed on his chest.' However, the love letter to his son Jake, imprisoned in Arizona for the killing of a young friend, is racked with a quality of pain and guilt that perhaps renders the question rhetorical. Modern American society's continued attempts to emasculate the African-American male only encourages such men to flaunt self-reliance and emotional independence. These are the only viable tools at their disposal and they utilise them to stake out their territory as men. Inevitably, in the process, they become mute. The real stories of everyday humiliations and racial belittling are deemed to be narratives not worthy of generational transfer; to retell these tales of human indignity would serve only to stoke the fires of anger and indignation. Unfortunately, proud silence will not help the son. Particularly the son who will one day become a father.

1995

James Baldwin: The Lure of Hollywood

I knew long before I met James Baldwin that he wanted to be involved in the movies. I don't believe that I ever heard him mention in any interview that he harboured such a desire, but through the public window of his life I espied a man who positively adored the attention of the media. He could, in the early sixties, claim to be one of the most photographed, and certainly one of the most recognisable, men in the world. He peered darkly and mysteriously into the lens of any proffered camera. His face had adorned the cover of *Time* magazine and his eyes beamed out from the dust jackets of his widely translated, best-selling books. But there is a special celebrity which only the movies can bestow and it seemed to me that Baldwin positively yearned for it.

Baldwin never sought to sublimate his love for the performing arts by engaging exclusively with literature. Quite the reverse. He seemed determined to synthesise the ambiguities and anarchy of the life of a performer – whether jazz musician or actor – into the heart of both his writing and his own life. As a young man, in the Greenwich Village of the 1940s, Baldwin let it be known that he was interested in painting and acting as well as writing. Some few years later, having abandoned the United States for the 'fresh air' of Europe, he was billed to open as a night-club singer in the Arab quarter of Paris. Almost forty years later at his funeral in New York, I was not at all surprised to hear a tape of Baldwin singing – and singing with some style. The *New York Times Book Review* once asked him to comment on his literary technique. Baldwin chose to draw comparisons with a jazz musician and a blues singer: 'I would like to think that some of the people who liked *Another Country* responded to it in the way they respond when Miles [Davis] and Ray [Charles] are blowing.'

Baldwin's writing is riddled with many covert and overt meditations upon the performer's art. John, the boy preacher of his first novel, *Go Tell It on the Mountain,* is a performer. The leading characters of his third novel, *Another Country,* are caught up in the bohemian world of New York City in the 1950s. The novel features a jazz drummer, a singer and an actor. Baldwin's final novel, *Just Above My Head,* introduces us to Arthur Montana, a famous gospel singer whose story is narrated by Hall, his elder brother and manager. The play *The Amen Corner* is perhaps Baldwin's most dramatically successful exploration of the performer's art. It not only mirrors a dilemma at the heart of Baldwin's own life, it also sheds light on a problem which Baldwin perceived to be at the centre of the black American experience: the relationship between the sacred and the profane, the religious and the secular, with all the concomitant guilt and confusion that are ushered in when an individual finds himself oscillating between these two extremes.

However, the evidence of Baldwin's writing, in both fiction and nonfiction, suggests a special love for the cinema. There is the 1960 *Esquire* essay, 'The Northern Protestant', in which an excited Baldwin flies to Stockholm to interview the Swedish director Ingmar Bergman. The meeting encourages Baldwin to cogitate upon an idea for a film of his own: 'My film would begin with slaves, boarding the good ship Jesus: a white ship, on a dark sea, with masters as white as the sails of their ships, and slaves as black as the ocean.' Baldwin's much under-rated book on film, *The Devil Finds Work,* makes it clear that Baldwin's love for the cinema was almost as intense as his love for words. In fact, Baldwin discovered the cinema before he discovered books, and he never forgot the impact that these early movies had upon him.

I am fascinated by the movement on, and off, the screen, that movement which is something like the heaving and swelling of the sea (though I have not yet been to the sea): and which is also something like the light which moves on, and especially beneath, the water.

I am about seven. I am with my mother, or my aunt. The movie is *Dance, Fools, Dance.*

Sadly, Baldwin was never able to consummate his love for the silver screen in the way in which he most desired. In other words, by seeing his books filmed, to his screenplays, and starring the actors whom he considered to be friends. Perhaps the closest Baldwin ever came to fulfilling his dreams of a career in the cinema, was in his often stormy relationship to the theatre. He studied with Elia Kazan, befriended Lorraine Hansberry and participated in numerous workshops with the leading actors, directors and writers of the 1950s and 1960s. The Actors Studio production of his play *Blues for Mr Charlie* premièred on Broadway in 1964 under the direction of Burgess Meredith. This play, along with his other dramatic work, *The Amen Corner,* was often revived. Towards the end of his life, Baldwin gained great satisfaction from seeing a successful London production of *The Amen Corner,* a production which compensated for the failure of a musical version on Broadway. When he died, Baldwin left behind the finished manuscript of a new play, *The Welcome Table.* Not surprisingly, the ninety-eight-page manuscript features the story of Edith, a Creole woman from New Orleans described by the author as 'an actress and singer/star'. However, much as Baldwin loved the theatre and working with actors, the stage could never be a substitute for either the on-screen or off-screen drama of his first love, the cinema.

I first met James Baldwin in the early 1980s at his home in the south of France. My task was to try to persuade him to participate in a major documentary about his life and work, which would be filmed in the United States, France, Turkey and Britain. Jimmy (it was impossible to address him as James

– in fact, he would not hear of it) looked across at me and his eyes lit up. 'The movies, baby. So we're gonna make a picture.' In fact, we never made the 'picture'. Some months later we filmed a twenty-minute interview for BBC TV. We then spent the next three days tape-recording our conversations, the results of which were eventually edited down into a BBC radio documentary. It was during the course of this hot Provençal summer that I discovered both the extent of Jimmy's boundless generosity and the fact that my initial hunch was correct. Indeed, Jimmy did want to be in the movies. And, although almost sixty by then, he continued to nurture a long-held desire to see his work on the cinema screen.

Jimmy grew up in the 1920s and 1930s in Harlem. In common with other American children of this period, he was a child whose dominant cultural fix was provided by the cinema. In fact, his poverty-stricken childhood seemed to be relieved only by his voracious appetite for the cinema.

> Tom Mix, on his white horse. Actually, it was Tom Mix's hat, a shadow in the shadow of that hat, a kind of rocky background (which, again, was always moving) and the white horse. *Tom Mix* was a serial. Every Saturday, then, if memory serves, we left Tom Mix and some bleakly interchangeable girl in the most dreadful danger – or, rather, we left the hat and the shadow of the hat and the white horse: for the horse was not interchangeable and the serial could not have existed without it.

The young Baldwin watched an enormous number of films, which varied wildly in quality and content. From *The Birth of a Nation* to *20,000 Years in Sing Sing*, from *A Tale of Two Cities* to *I Shall Spit on Your Graves*. What I find consistently surprising in Baldwin's film writing, on these films and others, is that no matter how much he loathes a film, he always manages to retain a sense of irony and often humour. He never betrays, even in his most vitriolic moods, his love for, and profound understanding of, the medium.

On *The Exorcist*: '*The Exorcist* has absolutely nothing going for it, except Satan, who is certainly the star: I can only say that Satan was never like that when he crossed my path (for one thing, the evil one never so rudely underestimated me). His concerns were more various, and his methods more subtle.'

On *Lady Sings the Blues*: *Lady Sings the Blues* is related to the black American experience in about the same way, and to the same extent, that Princess Grace Kelly is related to the Irish potato famine; by courtesy.'

On *Guess Who's Coming to Dinner*: 'The film's high polish does not entirely succeed in blinding us to a kind of incipient reality suggested by those two [Katharine Hepburn and Bea Richards]. Though they come, principally, out of a Hollywood scriptwriter's imagination, they unexpectedly resist being manipulated into total irrelevance – or, in other words, it proved somewhat difficult to find a place for them in this so briefly troubled Eden.'

In 1968 (despite the reservations of his friends and family) Baldwin, by now a best-selling and much respected author, answered the Hollywood call. He was engaged by Columbia Pictures to write the screenplay of Alex Haley's *The Autobiography of Malcolm X*. In *The Devil Finds Work* Baldwin writes about the difficulties he encountered with the studios and almost inevitably with the FBI. That the eventual screenplay, *One Day When I Was Lost*, never reached the screen is hardly a surprise and not altogether Baldwin's fault, given Hollywood's attitude towards black subject-matter. But one did detect in Jimmy's writing about this period an unhealthy preoccupation with the trappings of Hollywood, and an unwillingness to make the compromises necessary to succeed as a writer in the film world. Perhaps Baldwin ought to be applauded for adopting the latter position, but I wonder what effect he was trying to create by informing us that he heard of Martin Luther King's death while relaxing beside a Hollywood pool with Billy Dee Williams.

Jimmy was never happier than when he found himself in the company of other 'stars', particularly actors. His friends included Richard Burton, Burt Lancaster, Marlon Brando, Sidney Poitier and Yves Montand, to name but a handful. He talked constantly of helping his younger brother David to 'make it' as an actor, and to this end he even announced that he would be 'adapting' *Othello* so that David might take the starring role. But David, not Jimmy. The older brother was by this time a different type of actor; the type that the American media creates out of sportsmen, politicians and, of course, writers. He was a star, which involved being in possession of and cultivating all the skills of an actor, in timing, posture and delivery. And in this Jimmy was a natural. There was much his actor friends might have learned from him.

Almost the first subject Jimmy brought up with me when we met in France was *Giovanni's Room*. He referred to the fact that the German director Rainer Werner Fassbinder had wanted to make *Giovanni's Room* into a movie. He ushered me out of the main house and downstairs into his study. Once there, Jimmy pointed to the screenplay of the movie, a huge pile of typed manuscript. He had written it himself. 'They'll make it. One day they'll see that *Giovanni* 's really a movie. And they'll use my script.' I looked at Jimmy. I could see that it really mattered to him that 'they' make his second novel into a movie. It seriously concerned him that this book in particular should reach the screen.

However, Jimmy had a chaotic attitude to minor details such as contracts. He had little patience for the convoluted machinery of the publishing industry, let alone the legal chicanery and double-speak of the film world. I knew that the London-based film director Michael Raeburn and the Trinidadian director Horace Ove were both under the impression that they would be making the film of *Giovanni's Room*. In fact, I once met Horace Ove at Nice airport. He was arriving to 'finalise details' with Jimmy. I asked Horace about Jimmy's agents and lawyers? Shouldn't they be controlling these matters? Horace shrugged his shoulders. The truth was Jimmy changed his agents and lawyers with alarming rapidity. His laissez-faire attitude to business – admirable as it was in that it placed great emphasis on the import of informal friendship – made life difficult for anybody trying to do something as complex as a movie deal with him. Until the very end Horace Ove continued to negotiate with Jimmy, but Jimmy's healthy suspicion of contract law proved an insurmountable hurdle.

During the final years of his life, the years when I got to know him, Jimmy's conversation was littered with anecdotes about film. He spoke to me about the time Louis Farrakhan threatened him physically if he were not cast to play Malcolm X in the film of *One Day When I Was Lost*. He spoke about his friend Simone Signoret ('Do you know Simone?'). About his neighbour Donald Pleasence ('Nice man.'). About Marlon Brando ('Marlon and I were never lovers. We should have been, but we never were.'). He loved to tell anecdotes about his movie friends, some of which I already knew from the film essay, *The Devil Finds Work*:

> My buddy Ava Gardner once asked me if I thought she could play Billie Holiday. I had to tell her that, though she was certainly 'down' enough for it – courageous and honest and beautiful enough for it – she would almost certainly not be allowed to get away with it, since Billie Holiday had been widely rumoured to be black, and she, Ava Gardner, was widely rumoured to be white.

He once declared to me that his book *The Evidence of Things not Seen* (a book which proved to be his last original publication) would be his 'comeback'. I looked at him. 'Your comeback, Jimmy?' 'My comeback, baby.' And then, on another occasion – or indeed it may have been on the same occasion – we sat together and watched a French television screening of a terrible disaster movie entitled (I believe) *Airport* 77. I was clearly bored, but Jimmy read the film as one might read a Dickens novel.

'That woman there, she wants him, baby.' Pause. 'And you know what, she's going to get him.' When I asked him what he thought of the film *Round Midnight,* Jimmy was more wistful. 'It told it like it happened.' He paused. The film was about Jimmy's Paris, the Paris of the 1950s. He knew the people, he knew the places. He certainly knew the jazz scene at the heart of the film. He continued: 'Except they would never have let the brother [Dexter Gordon] go down like that. Not on his own.' He sighed. A romantic nostalgia tinged his voice. 'Cats looked out for one another. No matter how hard things got, you looked out for one another.'

Jimmy died before the advent of Spike Lee. He died before Hollywood finally abandoned the notion of the token black actor. He died before Denzel Washington, Morgan Freeman and Danny Glover were recognised as bankable, and not mutually exclusive, stars. Raising capital for films such as *Glory* would have been difficult, if not impossible, in the 1970s and early 1980s. It has been argued that Hollywood has stumbled forward half a century in the space of a few years in terms of its depiction of black people, but I often wonder what Jimmy would have made of these 'advances'. Would he, like Public Enemy, have simply cried – indeed continued to cry – 'Burn Hollywood, Burn.' What on earth would he have made of *Mississippi Burning* or *Driving Miss Daisy*?

Jimmy did have the pleasure of seeing his first novel, *Go Tell It on the Mountain,* filmed for American television. One night we were sitting in Horace Ove's house in London's Kentish Town. The phone rang. Horace answered. It was for Jimmy. A surprised Jimmy took the call and grinned. It was his sister, Paula. He spoke for some minutes and then put down the receiver and expressed astonishment that she had managed to track him down. He was, after all, staying at a hotel in the West End. Then Jimmy could no longer contain himself. *Mountain* (as he called it) was to be screened on Sunday. We all raised a toast. Jimmy beamed. 'And we've got the cover of *TV Guide.*' Things like this mattered to Jimmy.

And now Jimmy is gone and the world that is Hollywood is finally clamouring to make Jimmy's books into films. The time is right, but not for Jimmy. To see his two loves, movies and books, fused together was, I believe, one of the great ambitions of his life. I'm sure that if pressed Jimmy would have admitted that he craved an Oscar almost as much as he did a Pulitzer. Yet he found a way to participate vicariously in the cinema and he certainly found a way to live the glamorous lifestyle of its leading actors. But – and this is to his great credit – despite his many frustrations and disappointments, not all of which, by any means, could be attributed to his disdain for legal paperwork, Jimmy never lost his innocent pleasure in the cinema.

Perhaps my warmest memory of Jimmy is lunching with him at the Colombe d'Or in St Paul de Vence. It was a beautiful Provençal afternoon. Heads turned as Jimmy walked into the restaurant. We took a table on the terrace. The waitress approached. She knew Jimmy well. After all, he was a local celebrity and this was his regular 'hang-out'. But she had been asked to put a question to Jimmy, a question which – as it transpired – was being asked by two women seated some tables away, two women who were the highly visible wives of two movie stars. Clearly they were taken with Jimmy. The waitress cleared her throat. She was embarrassed, but she was also trying not to laugh. 'The two ladies, they would like to know if you are the gentleman who played piano in *Casablanca*.' Jimmy smiled broadly. 'Tell them, yes.'

1991

Amistad

When I ask Steven Spielberg what kind of books he likes to read a smile spreads across his face. 'History,' he says. 'I don't read fiction unless it's connected to a movie. I like to read about wartime. Historical figures from the past. Benjamin Franklin. Paul Revere. You know, those guys.' Then his attention is again seized by the first assistant director. Spielberg is directing a cut-away of a scene in which Tom Hanks asks a group of bloodied American soldiers if anybody has seen a 'Private Ryan from Iowa'. Hanks's voice becomes desperate, his tones increasingly shrill, then almost imperceptibly Spielberg leans across me, picks up a megaphone and shouts, 'Cut! Print it!' He puts down the megaphone and repeats the last sentence. 'You know, those guys.'

Spielberg is on location in Hertfordshire in England. This is the fourth week of a twelve-week shoot on a Second World War drama starring Tom Hanks entitled *Saving Private Ryan*. In the evening Spielberg is doing the final edit of *Amistad*, a gruelling workload but one which mirrors his workload in Poland in 1993. By day he shot *Schindler's List* and in the evenings he edited *Jurassic Park*. 'The kind of directors I admire are a Michael Curtiz or a Victor Fleming. The chameleons, guys who can change costumes inside of a production meeting.' He arches his eyebrows as though enquiring whether I have understood, then turns away and addresses the assistant sound recordist. He points to the playback on one of the screens before him and shows the sound recordist where the boom is casting a shadow. Then Spielberg swivels around to face me, relights his cigar and says, 'You know, I've never had any problems regularising that internal adjustment from heart to wallet.'

I had suggested to Spielberg that it must be impossible always to relate fully to his subject-matter, veering wildly as it does between the sublime and the riduculous. After all, he has already produced one of the year's biggest money-makers in *The Lost World: Jurassic Park*, a film not distinguished by its cerebral content. In a twenty-five-year career he has been responsible for three films which could claim to be, shortly after their releases, the highest grossing movies in cinematic history: *Jaws* (1975), *E.T.* (1982), and the current champ, *Jurassic Park* (1993). Having, in 1994, created his own studio, Dreamworks SKG (together with Jeffrey Katzenberg and David Geffen), Spielberg is now in the enviable position of being able to direct or produce whatever takes his fancy. However, true to his unpredictable nature, his new film is 'serious' and revisits familiar ground in that it is rooted in history (like *Schindler's List*) and deals largely with the African-American world (like *The Color Purple*). *Amistad* is about a rebellion which occurred on board a slave ship and the subsequent trial, in New Haven, of the Africans who were involved.

The film is based on fact: in 1839, on board a Cuban slave ship named the *Amistad*, fifty-three African captives, under the leadership of a proud captive named Cinque, broke free of their chains and slaughtered the crew. They kept two crew members alive in the hope that these men might help them navigate the ship back to Sierra Leone. However, the Cubans directed the ship towards the United States, where it came ashore at New York's Long Island. Eventually the Africans were tried for the murder of the Cubans and in the subsequent courtroom drama the former President John Quincy Adams came out of retirement to champion the Africans' cause all the way to the Supreme Court. The *Amistad* mutiny has passed into American history as a centrally important episode of African-American resistance to institutionalised racism, and Cinque ranks alongside men such as Denmark Vesey and

Frederick Douglass as a charismatic and inspirational leader of his people. Indeed, many African-American literary and artistic ventures have utilised the potency of the name *Amistad*, and the name of Cinque has been bestowed upon (or appropriated by) many African-American males, including the brother of the film-maker Spike Lee.

We can safely assume that the outcome of Spielberg's *Amistad* will be 'happy'. After all, nobody, including Dreamworks SKG, would spend $40 million to make a film with a downbeat ending. However, I was not allowed to see a print of the film, nor was I allowed to read the script. When I brought this up with Spielberg he cast me a helpless look and then pressed on to another point. In fact, trying to organise the meeting with Spielberg was akin to being involved in a minor production. At various times we were to meet in Los Angeles, then in Ireland and we finally met in England. The sheer effort involved in his trying to find time to sit and talk freely for a couple of hours led me to wonder about his ability to concentrate fully on his many projects. I had no doubt that he wanted to make 'serious' films. He confirmed this to me early in our meeting. 'I want to make movies that get into somebody else's head. When I see movies I don't just want to see fantasy.' However, making serious films requires a certain commitment, not just to the mechanics of filming, but to the project as a whole. Spielberg just didn't seem to have time.

Spielberg's career has involved much movement back and forth between what he terms 'entertainments' and what he describes as 'socially conscious' films. However, this commuting has been fraught with problems. Before *Schindler's List* (1994) his attempts to be 'serious' were generally regarded as critical failures. The responses to *The Color Purple* (1985), *Empire of the Sun* (1987) and *Always* (1989) fell somewhere between grudging admiration ('nice cinematography', 'good costumes') and flippant dismissal. Referring to *The Color Purple*, David Anson in *Newsweek* described the pairing of subject-matter to director as being 'as improbable as, say, Antonioni directing a James Bond movie . . . Early on I had the disorientating sensation that I was watching the first Disney movie about incest.'

The Academy of Motion Picture Arts and Sciences bestowed only a handful of Oscars on these films, although none for *The Color Purple* and none for Spielberg. After these adventures in the 'real' world Spielberg rapidly returned to the world that his critics assumed he knew best – the world of 'make-believe'. It was as though he was only acceptable when directing films such as the Indiana Jones trilogy, or producing films such as *Gremlins* and *The Goonies*. And then came *Schindler's List*. The film was greeted as though it were a public coming of age at which we could all marvel at the sight of little Steven defying Hollywood's casting of him as a kid for life. Some critics began casually to employ the term 'masterpiece' and his colleagues – including those in the Academy – fell over themselves in the rush to praise his new-found 'maturity'.

It was an absurd time, for what was being lost in this 'lovefest' was the subject-matter. The Holocaust and the death of six million innocent Jews. This obfuscation was certainly not the fault of Spielberg, who throughout this 'hoopla' behaved with characteristic dignity, but we are talking about Hollywood here, a place which has never been slow to utilise its ability to reduce the most elevated subject-matter to hitherto unimagined depths of vulgarity. Many Hollywood 'insiders' simply failed to see that there *are* problems with *Schindler's List*, particularly with reference to the periodic outbursts of sentimentality and the many unresolved ambiguities which surround the troubling character of Schindler himself. However, hyperbole and inappropriate analogies remained the order of the day, and the following words from Spielberg's soon-to-be partner Jeffrey Katzenberg (who was at the time chairman of Walt Disney studios) typified the film industry's pleasure with itself:

> It [*Schindler's List*] will affect how people on this planet think and act. At a moment in time, it is going to remind us about the dark side, and do it in a way in which, whenever that little

green monster is lurking somewhere, this movie is going to press it down again. I don't want to burden the movie too much, but I think it will bring peace on earth, good will to men. Enough of the right people will see it that it will actually set the course of world affairs.

Earlier this year *The Lost World: Jurassic Park,* Spielberg's first film since *Schindler's List,* performed predictably both at the box office and on the pages of the arts reviews. 'Could not be more trite or less witty if it tried, which it doesn't . . . claptrap,' was the response of the normally sober (London) *Times Literary Supplement.* Why, I wondered, would a man who had finally wriggled out from under the burden of being perceived of as an immensely talented director hampered by a decidedly adolescent vision, return to such glib material? And why, given the undoubtedly controversial nature of his new film's subject-matter, would he choose to re-enter the post-adolescent world with *Amistad*?

When I first walked on to the set of *Saving Private Ryan,* Steven Spielberg was standing to one side talking with a khaki-clad, hyper-ventilating Tom Hanks. The director was dressed predictably: ill-fitting blue jeans, battered sneakers, T-shirt, fully open check shirt, faded grey baseball cap, shades, cigar. He made the crew look like Armani models. After talking with him for a few minutes one thing became clear instantly. I was in the presence of a man who is comfortable with himself. I asked him when he stopped listening to other people. 'They used to whisper in my ear,' he says. 'Telling me to let Francis or Marty do the personal films. I was the circus master, I should just stay in the ring, in my space. It used to frighten me. After all, I got such a bollocking for *The Color Purple* I thought I'll never do that again. But when I realised that I had to do *Schindler's List* – that I was going to do it – that the whole thing was overwhelming my reason, then I stopped listening. And I haven't listened since.' He laughed heartily, as though somebody had told him a good joke, and then he waved a greeting to some of the extras.

Americans have always confused artistic talent with the ability to make money. This is true in literature, music, theatre, as well as film. You direct or star in a movie that makes $100 million and you can be absolutely sure there will be some 'executive' comparing you to Shakespeare or Laurence Olivier and beating down your door with one hand, while clutching in the other hand a blank cheque that he will be all too eager to wave under your nose. Steven Spielberg *is* hugely talented *and* he can make money, but is his artistic talent best suited to the 'socially conscious' movies that he wishes to make? He has, after all, spent the greater part of his career honing his skills with narratives which do not depend on character and whose historical backcloth is either irrelevant or make-believe, yet he continues to try to be something other, not only because he cares – which he does – but because he can. As he said about *Schindler's List,* 'Nobody else could have gotten any studio to say yes to this project.' And as Debbie Allen, the producer of *Amistad,* noted about this latest film, before Spielberg 'nobody else would touch it'. Spielberg can afford to pick up 'dead' history projects and breathe life into them. The riskier the subject-matter, the less likely the project is to be made and the more of a philanthropist it makes of Spielberg when he 'rescues' it. And, however 'hokey' the final print, at least the film was made. Right?

If the question is still can Steven Spielberg make a decent job of a 'serious' film, then I would argue that the jury remains out – although *Schindler's List* has enough about it to suggest that given the right script and the right circumstances he can. Might that film be *Amistad*? There is no reason as yet to subscribe to the Hollywood cynicism which already has it pegged as another of Spielberg's 'Close Encounters with the Third World'. There are, of course, those who would prefer that Spielberg simply stay well away from historically important material. Gerald Early, for instance, when talking about *The Color Purple* describes it as 'protest art that moves an audience without disturbing it, the most dangerous kind of narcotic art'. And *Schindler's List* attracted criticism from diverse quarters, including

J. Hoberman, in the *Village Voice*, who saw the Jews in the film as 'relegated to supporting parts in their own cataclysm, hang[ing] around the Krakow ghetto ... making Jewish jokes'. Perhaps Danielle Meymann in *Le Monde* best summed up Spielberg's Hollywood-isation of the Holocaust, when she noted that, in *Schindler's List*, 'We see smoke and it's not a crematorium, it's a train. We see the showers and they spout not gas but water. All the cadavers we see we don't know and all the people we identify with are saved. And that's not how history goes.' However, it remains a risky business to try and tell an artist what he or she should or should not be doing, particularly when they are already in mid-career – and a pretty successful mid-career at that.

In an age in which kids of all backgrounds are growing up with precious little understanding of the Civil Rights Movement, to say nothing of the slave trade, the abolition, or the great migration to the north, a feature film can be a valuable corrective to this historical myopia. 'None of my children and none of their friends know about it,' says Spielberg, referring to the *Amistad* mutiny. 'They need to hear it.' (Two of his six children are African-American, although he does not tell me this.) I look at him and for a moment we say nothing. 'I'm interested in history,' he says. This time he sounds as though he is trying to convince me of something. 'I'm interested in recording the growing pains inside of America. The strife and conflict. The revolutionary war, the civil war, reconstruction.' I ask him which character most interests him in *Amistad*. 'Cinque, the slave leader.' I suggest to him that he is interested in Cinque because this character is lonely, like many of Spielberg's main characters. 'Yeah. Lonely. All my movies are about lonely people.' All? 'The ones where I'm a film-maker. In the rest I'm a movie director. An overseer of suspense and adventure. It doesn't take a lot of personal identity. I just spend a lot of time thinking about how the audience will respond.' Now I'm exasperated. But why do it? I ask. Why waste your time on these 'entertainments' if what you really want to do are 'serious' films? 'Because I'm entertaining myself, of course.' Spielberg seems surprised by my question. Then he catches himself. 'But I'm more natural to myself as a film-maker in my serious films.'

Whichever way I look at it, Steven Spielberg on the *Amistad* mutiny seems to be a mis-match. Recording the 'growing pains inside of America' is an unconvincing reason to want to make a film about this crucial moment in African and American history, a moment when the issue of whether people were property was placed before the Supreme Court and ultimately resolved in favour of the Africans. In the American psyche, both black and white, Africans remain an exoticised, primitive 'other', semi-clad representatives of a 'backward' continent, who babble in a strange tongue and in whose persons violence lurks just beneath the surface. The events at the heart of this story suggest that for a moment there was some transcendence of this notion and the shackles of stereotype were temporarily cast to one side. But only for a moment. How and why this happened are huge and complicated questions. After all, at the time of the *Amistad* case, the Chief Justice of the United States Supreme Court, Roger Taney, was able to say, '[Blacks] are beings of an inferior order, and altogether unfit to associate with the white race, either in social or political relations; and so far inferior that they had no rights which the white man was bound to respect.' In other words, the *Amistad* 'judgment' was made in the face of considerable personal opposition. Clearly the *Amistad* story has something remarkable to tell us about the individual human heart and mind, and individual man's capacity to walk into the face of history and convention. It is, like all great stories, first and foremost a story of personal endeavour. However, it does worry me that in the time we spent together, aside from Cinque, Spielberg did not mention the name of a single character.

1997

Postscript

Last summer I interviewed Steven Spielberg while he was on

location in Hertfordshire. During the day he was shooting his new film, *Saving Private Ryan,* and in the evening he was finishing the editing of his upcoming movie, *Amistad.* The first question I asked him was, 'What do you read?' He looked momentarily puzzled, then told me that he reads 'mainly history'. 'Fiction?' I asked. 'If it's connected with a movie I'm making.' He took another pull on his cigar. 'But otherwise, no.' I thought this was significant then, and having now seen *Amistad* I'm convinced of this.

A few weeks ago I sat in a New York cinema and watched the film. A middle-aged white woman to my left wept passionately throughout most of the film. *Amistad,* however, failed me in three respects. First, the language. This film is set in the first half of the nineteenth century, and while extensive efforts have been made to replicate the costumes and manners of the period, the language is not grounded in period. At one point John Quincy Adams (Anthony Hopkins) asks the translator what Cinque (Djimon Hounsou) is saying. The translator, feigning ignorance, says that he 'didn't quite catch' the words. There are numerous other examples of this sloppiness.

Second, Cinque will keep taking his clothes off. At moments I had to ask myself if this was a serious dramatic reconstruction of slavery or a black gay porno flick. There is something vaguely obscene about the way in which Spielberg's camera exoticises the black male form. Mapplethorpe does the Middle Passage? Furthermore, would any captive who had endured the horrors of an Atlantic crossing, which included malnourishment, beatings, exposure to contagious diseases, and many other deprivations of an unimaginable nature, really have emerged looking like an Olympic decathlete?

Finally, there is a character named Theodore Joadson (Morgan Freeman) who not only did not exist historically, but has no viable role in this film other than that of 'honorary negro'. This is not only a waste of one of the finest actors in Hollywood, it makes a nonsense of black involvement in the abolition. African-Americans did not stand by looking handsome but indignant, and simply wait for the white man to free them. They participated fully in their own emancipation, as writers, educators, and agitators, and fought and died for their freedom. They had names, lives, wives, husbands and families, just like John Quincy Adams.

A healthy history is one that is open to debate and interpretation, to re-evaluation and reinterpretation. A history that is grounded in 'authenticity' is dangerous. *Amistad* is being used by the United States government for 'educational' purposes overseas. But, most disturbingly, a study guide has been sent out with copies of the film into schools. This study guide suggests that the fictionalised events in the film – including the character of Joadson and the imaginary meeting between Cinque and John Quincy Adams – are actually based on fact. Let us be clear. This is one director's view of a single historical incident. An imaginative reconstruction, subject to factual errors, to decisions that had to be made to heighten the drama, to scene-shifting, to acts of invention. This is precisely what should happen in drama. The idea that this film in itself redresses a historical imbalance and tells 'the truth' is nonsense, and this claim on the part of the film's producers has been a controversial part of the whole enterprise.

Spielberg told me that he reads history, not fiction. This is clear in *Amistad*, for its largest failing of all is that there are no real characters in the film. Nobody seems to grow, or be changed by the events, or to have survived their own personal crisis and thereafter directed the course of history. The issues have been imposed upon the characters, like the shark was imposed upon an earlier cast, the extra-terrestrials upon a later cast and the dinosaurs upon a more recent gathering. Character is not Spielberg's strong suit, yet character is precisely the stuff of fiction. Character should also be the bedrock upon which dramatic reinterpretations of history are built.

The current crop of Hollywood directors, be they Oliver Stone (*J.F.K*, *Nixon*), Spike Lee (*Malcolm X*), and, of course, Spielberg, are free to present their versions of history. The danger is that in the current cultural climate there is great pressure to market these versions of history as factual; the American audience wants to 'know', they don't want to 'think'. If they can 'know' and 'feel', all the better, as the woman to my left in the cinema will attest to. I fear that soon we will all come to depend on issue-led cinema and television drama for our knowledge of history, in the same way that we have already come to depend on media-based purveyors of 'truth' for our knowledge of politics and the news. History, however, speaks to the very essence of who we are. The content and marketing of *Amistad* invites us to slide further down the slippery slope.

1998

Africa

Introduction: Dispatches from Africa

Some years ago the African-American writer Eddy Harris travelled to Africa in order that he might discover the extent to which being an African-American meant that he had some natural affinity with the continent of his ancestors. He wrote a book about his travels entitled *Native Stranger*. Once on African soil, Harris's journey can be divided into four parts. First, he finds himself in Islamic Africa, north of the Sahara, which he describes as a 'Desert awakening'. Here the Middle East seems to have bled across the waters. It is a land of Ramadan, of excessive heat, of Berbers and thinly veiled racism towards people, like him, of a darker hue. He is among Africans who have over the years systematically enslaved their 'brothers' to the south.

The second part of Harris's journey takes him to sub-Saharan Africa. As he enters Senegal, something stirs in his soul. His chapter is headed 'The Beginnings of Brotherhood'. But sadly he could not be further from the truth. He is deported from Mauritania, cheated in Senegal, arrested in Liberia; he is appalled by African hygiene, poverty and corruption. At every turn he is reminded, in both small and large ways, that he is not of this place. By the time Harris embarks upon the third stage of his journey in Burkina Faso, Nigeria, Zaire and half a dozen other countries – a stage that he calls 'At the Mercy of Gods and Men' – he is almost a broken traveller. His health is beginning to collapse and eventually his body gives way to malaria. When he recovers he meets white American Peace Corps workers and European and Australian travellers. Although ambivalent about sharing their company and food, he cannot help himself. He is tiring, both physically and mentally.

As his body stumbles, so does the narrative. His chapters become shorter and less patient. Although it contains a quarter of Africa's population, Harris has little time for Nigeria. It is a place 'I never wanted to visit again'. He devotes just eight pages to this large and complex country. The final part of Harris's journey finds him at home in Zimbabwe and South Africa, countries with the Western infrastructure which he has occasionally yearned for. Here the author seems prepared to suspend some of his critical judgement in order to enjoy a respite from the nightmare that has been his journey. He visits Soweto: 'They eat. They work. They drive expensive German cars. Many live in fairly nice homes. But they cannot vote. I guess I'm not the best judge.'

Native Stranger is in the tradition of African-American texts in which the African-Americans use Africa as a laboratory, while casting themselves as experimental subjects. At the head of this tradition of racial return and experimentation are Alexander Crummell and Edward Blyden, who, in the second half of the nineteenth century, settled in Liberia. Both have been spoken of as the 'Father of Pan-Africanism', for they both believed that Africa was the true home of the negro and that a return to the land of the fathers was the only way for the negro to advance himself. However, they both shared a profound distaste for African traditions, cultures and languages. According to Crummell, 'Darkness covers the land and gross darkness the people ...' Their Africa was an Africa in which one was encouraged to look beyond the inconvenience of people's lives and hopes, their weaknesses and strengths, their essential humanity, and focus on the idea of Africa. Pan-Africanism and racial salvation were to be partners and 'base' African practices were merely indicative of the amount of work that still needed to be done. Crummell and Blyden were cultural imperialists and, although Eddy Harris stops short of treading squarely in their footsteps, others before, and since, have done just this.

Richard Wright's *Black Power* was published in 1954. In it Wright presents his readers with reflections and insights gleaned from a trip to pre-independence Ghana as a result of an invitation from the soon-to-be president, Kwame Nkrumah. The first epigraph to the book is a stanza from Countee Cullen's poem 'What Is Africa to Me?'

> What is Africa to me?
> Copper sun or scarlet sea
> Jungle star or jungle track,
> Strong bronzed men, or regal black
> Women from whose loins I sprang
> When the birds of Eden sang?
> *One three centuries removed*
> *From the scenes his fathers loved*
> *Spicy grove, cinnamon tree*
> *What is Africa to me?*

Indeed, Cullen's central question informs the whole of Wright's book: 'What is Africa to me?' Sadly, it soon becomes clear that Wright's Africa is not too dissimilar to the Africa of Crummell and Blyden. Wright had thought about calling his book 'Stranger in a Strange Land', which betrays the degree of anxiety with which Wright entered Africa. At each turn the author meets individuals of whom he is suspicious, whom he distrusts, and who engender panic, or more properly, paranoia in his soul. He is disappointed with Africa and with Africans:

> there is too much cloudiness in the African mentality, a kind of sodden vagueness that makes for a lack of confidence, an absence of focus that renders that mentality incapable of grasping the workaday world. And until confidence is established at the center of the African personality, until there is an inner reorganization of that personality, there can be no question of marching from the tribal order to the twentieth century . . .

Wright is harsh, but his response to the continent is fuelled by a desire to take part in the unfolding drama of Africa. He had already 'rejected' the United States and the initial glamour of his entry into French society was beginning to fade. At this stage of his life and career, the last thing he needed to be reminded of was the extent to which he was an American. Wright knew that the troubling quality of his Americanness was there to be solved if he could make a connection with Africa that was based on race. Like Crummell and Blyden before him, the idea of racial solidarity was to be his salvation, but this strange, 'primitive' continent failed him. 'I was black and they were black, and my blackness did not help me.' Race did not help him in his quest to understand these Africans. A shared pigment unlocked nothing. 'I'm of African descent and I'm in the midst of Africans, yet I cannot tell what they are thinking and feeling.'

In 1997 Keith Richburg, an African-American *Washington Post* journalist, having served three years as an African correspondent based in Nairobi, published *Out of America: A Black Man Confronts Africa*. Richburg arrives in Africa predisposed to ascribe some of the continent's ills to the legacy of the colonial period, but he quickly changes tack and is soon sounding almost hysterical. 'Talk to me about Africa and my black roots and my kinship with my African-American brothers, and I'll turn it back in your face, and then I'll rub your nose in the images of the rotting flesh.' The author's disappointment is so deep that he claims he will never again refer to himself as an African-American. The very term 'African' offends him. 'Thank God', he writes, 'my ancestor got out, because, now, I am not one of them . . . In short, thank God I am an American.'

Richburg travelled to Africa as a bureau chief for one of America's foremost newspapers. He did not travel as 'an African-American', although his racial heritage was clearly a part of his carry-on luggage. Naturally enough, the nature of his African reportage differs from that of his predecessors. However, what he does share with those who went before him is a profound sense of disappointment with Africa. And this is, unquestionably, the legacy of his racial heritage. Africa faces a unique set of problems as it tries to orientate itself through the postcolonial nightmare of corrupt leaders, and beyond the resounding clash of the new world entering as its people are still trying to pick over the remnants of the old world which was destroyed by European incursion. All is not well in Africa, but the continent is no more guilty than Europe or Asia in the atrocity department. Richburg and his predecessors appear to be uncommonly eager to condemn. What Africa needs is critical self-analysis, and intellectually rigorous minds and impassioned voices to dissect the past and suggest a future. And it possesses such minds and voices. What Africa does not need is a continual flow of disaffected African-Americans, wounded by race, acting out their fantasies of belonging and alienation with a presumed authenticity which is underscored by the figment of the pigment.

The Fortunes of Wangrin by Amadou Hampaté Bâ

Amadou Hampaté Bâ liked to describe himself as 'one of the eldest sons of the century'. Born in what is now Mali in 1900, he died at Abidjan in the Ivory Coast in 1991. At the time of his death he was widely recognised as one of the great humanists of his time, a man who had pioneered ground-breaking ethnological, historical and linguistic research into the oral traditions of West Africa. He was fond of quoting his mentor, the Sufi mystic Tierno Bokar: 'Writing is one thing and knowledge is another. Writing is the photographing of knowledge, but it is not knowledge itself. Knowledge is a light which is within man. It is the heritage of all the ancestors knew and have transmitted to us as seed, just as the mature baobab is contained in its seed.'

Hampaté Bâ may have regarded writing as a form of photography, but he understood both its intrinsic value as a means of preserving the past and its aesthetic appeal as literature. He played a central role in the development of an Arabic script which enabled the Fulani language to move from the oral mode to the written, and he adapted and translated many tales of religious and social significance from the transliterated Fulani into the French language. Hampaté Bâ's major works include *L'Empire peul du Macina* (1962), which traces the development of Islamic religious authority before and during the period of French colonisation in the early nineteenth century; *Vie et enseignement de Tierno Bokar* (1957), in which he celebrates his mentor and spiritual guide, and *Aspects de la civilisation africaine* (1972), in which he relates Fulani culture to other West African traditions.

But it is the novel *L'Etrange Destin de Wangrin* (now skilfully translated by Aina Pavolini Taylor as *The Fortunes of Wangrin*), first published in 1973, which is widely considered to be Hampaté Bâ's masterpiece. Although he uses the novel to examine a familiar subject, the vexed relationship between the colonised and the coloniser, he also goes far beyond this theme. Implicitly and explicitly, *The Fortunes of Wangrin* addresses the moment when the world dominated by oral traditions begins to teeter in the face of written authority. It also adroitly captures the farcical duplicity that ensnares the lives not only of the French colonial authorities but of the people over whom they rule, all of whom must engage in a vigorous sort of performance art so that they may fully inhabit the roles bequeathed to them by history.

The novel's hero Wangrin is an interpreter in the service of the French; thus his job is to assist those who despise him. This is a situation from which many an author might spin tragedy, but instead Hampaté Bâ's novel becomes an often comic romp. Framed by accounts of Wangrin's birth and death, the central narrative takes us on the roller-coaster of his adult life, part picaresque adventure story, and part proverbial lesson in the dangers of existing in the twilight zone between two peoples.

In his Foreword Hampaté Bâ announces that the novel is based on stories that were related to him by a man who really lived, an older man who wanted the author to take down the story of his life and 'compose it into a book'. His only request was that his true identity be hidden behind the borrowed name Wangrin. The 'real' Wangrin hoped, according to Hampaté Bâ, that the book might 'not only amuse but also instruct those who read it'.

The novel's questioning, rhetorical and intrusive narrative voice is established from the beginning: 'Little Wangrin let out the cry that announces the arrival of all babies in this baffling world where everyone must endure a thousand and one discomforts and which no one ever leaves alive.' Young Wangrin grows up and proves to be an excellent pupil, but in this colonial world the highest level to which he can aspire is to be of service to a white man. After a short stint as a primary-school teacher Wangrin is 'called' to be an interpreter, 'which in those days was equivalent to slipping one's foot into a gold stirrup'. And he soon learns that the only way to survive in the service of the colonial administration is to embrace corruption with more guile and vigour than those all around him. This being the case, he sets out to exploit both the whites and the blacks, although he is careful to take only from the rich, and equally careful to distribute some of his ill-gotten gains to the poor.

Wangrin's contempt for the whites grows as he learns more about the hypocrisy of their 'system'. District officers would never, for example, ask their wives to accompany them to Africa, so it was understood that these Frenchmen might make a 'colonial marriage' with a local woman:

> French law, which as a rule takes such a serious view of bigamy, turned a blind eye on these colonial marriages. The real victims were the children born of these unions. They were officially registered as children of 'unknown fathers' and forgotten when the civil servants responsible for their birth left the country.

Predictably, Wangrin's 'working' of the system, his growing wealth and his own ruthless duplicity earn him enemies in both camps who seek to destroy him. He is transferred, investigated, briefly jailed, attacked and publicly vilified, but somehow he always survives. He also gains the admiration of ordinary people, who regularly come to this rogue's defence because they recognise a man who is true to his word and who is generous with his wealth. They also recognise that Wangrin is a man who respects the cultures that have shaped him. A product of the fusion of Islamic and traditional African beliefs, Wangrin has not forsaken his past in an attempt to mimic the 'white-whites'. In his pursuit of wealth and influence he remains true to his language, his dress, his customs and his beliefs.

Colonial and postcolonial literature are littered with the evidence of those who have 'crossed over' and the various tragedies that have befallen them. At first Wangrin is vigilant, but when he begins to tire of this life of ceaseless negotiation between 'them' and 'us', and he decides to 'retire' and establish himself in business, his behaviour begins to change. Freed from the restrictive boundaries of colonial service, Wangrin is able to indulge himself. He forms a trading company, establishes himself as 'Director-General', buys a sports car and begins to behave in a way which is surprisingly disrespectful to his own traditions. A strict Muslim who had sworn off drink, Wangrin develops a taste for alcohol; he also takes a white mistress. Worse still, he loses the pebble which symbolises his link with the spirit of his traditional god; not surprisingly, he eventually falls into a state of mental and physical disrepair. His mistress and her European 'husband' succeed in exploiting Wangrin so that he has no choice but to declare bankruptcy.

Before his lonely and miserable death, Wangrin re-establishes himself in the community as a 'public entertainer . . . who neither gloried in the past splendors nor reproached anyone for his dire fate'. At his funeral, even his sworn enemies pay tribute to his greatness, for, although he dies in poverty, everybody respects the spirit of the 'man of the people', recognising the lessons that they are able to draw from his life.

Hampaté Bâ narrates his novel with the cadences of a village elder who is steeped in proverbial knowledge. When, for example, Wangrin triumphs over an enemy, a rhetorical flourish suggests the nature of his victory: 'When a hyena falls into a well, may God and Death rejoice!' Occasionally the imagery feels somewhat forced and draws unnecessary attention to itself: 'As he was doing this, he oozed sweat like an earthenware pot full of water. Finally he looked up and noisily let out a deep breath, much like a diver when he returns to the surface.'

Hampaté Bâ's narrative tone is declarative and often didactic in a manner that will be unfamiliar to those steeped in a Western tradition of literary composition. But this is partly the author's point. *The Fortunes of Wangrin* is not a novel in the Western tradition. It is a remarkable work of fiction 'rescued' from a dying oral tradition, a work that, if we meet it on its own terms, will help us to understand better not only the colonial adventure, but the extensive roots of African belief systems. More importantly, it will lead us to recognise our common humanity as we laugh at, suffer with and eventually give thanks for the instructive life of Wangrin. His 'oral' tale is our tale and we should listen to it carefully. After all, it was Amadou Hampaté Bâ who observed that in Africa, 'When an old man dies, it's a library burning down.'

2000

Nadine Gordimer: The Beat of History

None to Accompany Me is Nadine Gordimer's first book since the changes in South Africa, and one is left with the feeling that history may have overtaken her swift and often perceptive pen. Change is occurring at breakneck speed, and in her struggle to keep pace Gordimer has produced a 'broken-backed' novel which has the feel of two books. One is an analysis of the 'new' South Africa, with special attention being paid to the return to their homeland of a particular black family, but with the focus fixed on continued violence and perhaps intractable socio-political difficulties. The other is a study of Vera Stark, a white South African lawyer in her sixties, who is 'a fixture at the Legal Foundation', an organisation which 'came into existence in response to the plight of black communities'. As her country moves uneasily from white minority to black majority rule, Vera finds herself faced with the physical evidence of her past in the form of her son, Ivan, and her grandson, Adam, both returned from England. At this time of great political and familial change, Gordimer's heroine casts her mind back across an unsatisfactory emotional life, which has included husbands, lovers and many betrayals of one form or another. Both of the books in *None to Accompany Me* are interesting in themselves, but they do not sit well together.

The difficulty, perhaps the impossibility, of living a 'normal' life in a racially divided country, and the problem of how one copes with the indignities and the contradictions of a government-sponsored system of oppression, are concerns that have been near the heart of Gordimer's fiction. She has explored these iniquities from both sides of the fence and occasionally, as in *My Son's Story* (1990), she has even adopted a third perspective, that of a 'coloured' South African. Her desire to face up to social responsibility as a writer has been explored in her many essays, the most important of which were collected in 1988 in *The Essential Gesture,* in which she revealed her personal repugnance towards the system of apartheid. But the essays also went further in their attempts to formulate a means by which an artist operating in such a socio-political climate might balance his or her primary responsibility as an artist with the moral obligation to speak out against perceived injustice. In the title essay, 'The Essential Gesture', one senses an indignant Gordimer, fatigued by the burden of synthesising her artistic vision with her political beliefs, and impatient with the carping of the cultural commissars of the West.

> When interviewed abroad, there is often disappointment that you are there, and not in jail in your own country. And since you are not – why are you not? Aha ... does this mean that you have not written the book you should have written? Can you imagine this kind of self-righteous inquisition being directed against a John Updike for not having made the trauma of America's Vietnam war the theme of his work?

In a footnote to this statement, Gordimer concedes that Western societies 'do not demand this "orthodoxy" of their writers because arguably their values are not in a crisis of survival constructed on a single moral issue'. This is almost certainly the case; but her concession by no means weakens the fundamental truth at the heart of her original statement. She proceeds to quote Camus, who once stated that 'it is from the moment when I shall no longer be more than a writer that I shall cease to write'. Writers such as Gordimer, and countless others like her, of different national, ethnic and political backgrounds, have always had no choice but to be 'more than a writer'. Gordimer is not only acutely aware of the problems involved in being 'more than a writer', she is also alert to the manner in which others, in South Africa and elsewhere, view a white female who chooses wilfully to abandon fealty to race in her public life and in the narrative strategies that she employs.

Nadine Gordimer was born in 1923 in Springs, a small gold-mining town in the Transvaal. In an autobiographical essay called 'A Bolter and the Invincible Summer' (1963) she recalled the state of torpor in which she existed in this somnolent part of South Africa.

> I played golf, learnt to drink gin with the R.A.F. pupil pilots from the nearby air station, and took part in amateur theatricals to show recognisable signs of life to the people around me. I even went to first aid and nursing classes because this was suggested as an 'interest' for me: it did not matter to me what I did, since I could not admit that there was nothing, in the occupations and diversions offered to me, that really did interest me, and I was not sure – the only evidence was in books – that anything else was possible.

Eventually Gordimer entered the world of books and started to write. She wrote her first short story at the age of fifteen, which was published in a liberal South African weekly, *Forum*. Twelve years later she published her first collection of fiction, *The Soft Voice of the Serpent* (1951), and for the forty years thereafter she has published a steady stream of short-story collections and novels. *None to Accompany Me* is her twenty-third book.

Gordimer emerged as a literary voice in the 1950s, at the same time as Dennis Brutus, Lewis Nkosi, Es'kia Mphahlele, Bessie Head and other South African writers who were using the English language as a literary medium were being forced into exile, or jail, or both. Gordimer managed to stay out of jail and avoid exile in part because she was not black, in part because she did not employ the political rhetoric of her contemporaries, and in part because she was blessed with some luck. While this politically driven diaspora weakened the heart of English-language writing in the 1950s and 1960s, Afrikaans writing was becoming both stronger and more adventurous. In both form and subject-matter writers such as Etienne Leroux, Breyten Breytenbach and André Brink were consistently breaking taboos and conventions in their work, with reference to religion, morality, sex and the narrative tradition. These 'writers of the Sixties', or 'sestigers' as they came to be known, flourished. It fell to English-speaking writers such as Nadine Gordimer to keep pace with her Afrikaner countrymen, and although her literary community was being depleted constantly, Gordimer rose to the task with discipline and dedication.

In the forty years that she has been writing and publishing, Gordimer's output has been evenly divided between the short story and the novel. Many critics have pointed out what they perceive to be her superior work in the short story and to an extent this would seem to be the case. Gordimer herself has spoken about the difference between the two forms, not in terms of personal preference but with reference to the structural and technical distinctions that, to her mind, mark out one form as separate from the other.

> But for me certainly there is a clue, there, to the choice of the short story by writers, as a form: whether or not it has a narrative in the external or internal sense, whether it sprawls or neatly bites its own tail, a short story is a concept that the writer can 'hold', fully realized, in his imagination, at one time. A novel is, by comparison, staked out, and must be taken possession of stage by stage; it is impossible to contain, all at once, the proliferation of concepts it ultimately may use ... A short story occurs, in the imaginative sense. To write one is to express from a situation in the exterior or interior world the life-giving drop – sweat, tear, semen, saliva – that will speed an intensity on the page; burn a hole in it.

Gordimer's short stories concern themselves with the various forms of repression, self-deception and humiliation, themes which occur naturally in the socio-political environment of South Africa, but which are at their most potent when they emerge out of a concern with the individual. In 'Rain Queen' (1972) an anguished young woman remembers her first lover and her unfulfilled dreams of happiness with him. The harsh predictability of his present-day life with his wife Eleanora appears to be his punishment for having failed to commit to her. However, her own life and her sense of her own worth have been damaged permanently.

> Poor Marco, sitting in Milan or Genoa at Sunday lunch, toothpick in his fingers, Eleanora's children crawling about, Eleanora's brothers and sisters and uncles and aunts around him. But I have never woken up from that dream. In the seven years I've been married I've had – how many lovers? A lot – if you count the very brief holiday episodes as well.

Gordimer is least successful, in the short story and the novel, when she attempts to comment directly on the South African situation, creating characters, black or white, who are forever in danger of becoming little more than vessels to convey their creator's thoughts and observations. *None to Accompany Me* becomes problematic at precisely those moments when it attempts to describe the events that are taking place in a changing South Africa, and departs from the revelatory nuances of Vera Stark's interior life. We are only two pages into the novel when presented with the image of Nelson Mandela outside his old Soweto cottage, with schoolchildren 'queueing to embrace him, while foreign diplomats presented themselves to be filmed clasping his hand'.

This 'snapshot' occurs as Gordimer is trying to introduce us to the marital landscape of Vera's life, a landscape that is central to any understanding of her as a character. The

Mandela reference catches our eye, albeit momentarily, yet it takes our attention away from Vera and in an entirely different direction. A few pages later, when Vera speaks of her husband, our attention is once more seized by socio-cultural 'information'. He is introduced as an ex-university teacher, and departs as a 'failed sculptor', but in between we learn nothing of him, the man.

> If Bennet had stayed on as Our Male Lead at the university, he would have been teaching a curriculum devised for the level of general education and Western cultural background of white students, difficult to attain for the black students who satisfied entrance standards nominally but came from township schools where boycotts were their history thesis, running battles with the police their epic poetry, and economic theory that of a home where there wasn't enough money for bus fare, let alone books. So what was the difference, whichever way a failed sculptor might make a living?

Throughout the novel, the demands of fiction become submerged beneath the author's desire to act as reporter from the front line of change. It is frustrating enough to be unable to focus clearly on character because of these 'interventions', but it is a much more serious problem when we feel that consistency of characterisation is being sacrificed to a political point. Vera remembers her former lover Otto, a German who works for an Austrian television network, a man she imagines to be a Jew whose parents were killed in the camps. Having listened to Otto voicing his growing horror at the daily violence being directed by the police towards young black schoolchildren, Vera comments, 'You haven't lived here long enough to know. The Nazis didn't end in the war where your parents died, they were reborn here.' Such a statement makes Vera appear at best insensitive and at worst stupid, for the analogy is crude. In fact, the Vera we have encountered so far, and the Vera we get to know, is neither insensitive nor stupid. Which leaves us wondering why a writer would risk making such a clumsy point knowing full well that its banality rocks the fictional construct to its foundations.

Gordimer's desire to keep abreast of changes in the bosom of South African society has damaged her writing in the past, even in her short stories. In 'Africa Emergent' (1975), a story that is both strong in characterisation and politically astute, the writing occasionally descends to reportage. The last lines of the story have a resonance clearly intended as ironic commentary on the hypocrisies to which the system introduces people, but the lines lack the subtlety and insight which the piece has possessed up until then. They are a graceless and clumsy conclusion to an otherwise fine story: 'And so we white friends can purge ourselves of the shame of rumours. We can be pure again. We are satisfied at last. He's in prison. He's proved himself, hasn't he?'

In 'Living in the Interregnum', an essay published in 1982, Gordimer asserted, 'I remain a writer, not a public speaker: nothing I say here will be as true as my fiction.' Precisely. It is only when, as a writer of fiction, she adopts the voice of a 'public speaker' that her tone becomes false. *None to Accompany Me* works best when it deals with the kind of life that politically active black South Africans, who were exiled during the later stages of white rule, have to face when returning to their country. Didymus, his wife Sibongile, and their daughter, Mpho, all recent returnees, have come to terms rapidly with both personal and political change.

This family's responses to the 'new' South Africa seem urgent and important because, unlike Vera and her family, they have been denied so vigorously the luxury of choice. For them questions of independence and self-determination are not abstract ideas to be juggled like husbands and lovers. The reality of enforced exile and perpetual vigilance in the face of physical danger have shaped their lives and continue to impinge upon them. Their homecoming, after years of sacrifice, can in no way be described as triumphant. When faced with the grim realities of their vermin-infested temporary accommodation, Sibongile's patience breaks:

> 'Accommodation.' How long can we be expected to carry on in this filthy dump, this whore-house for Hillbrow drunks, this wonderful concession to desegregation, what an honour to sleep under the white man's spunk. – What about all the others living here . . . it's no better for them – He was confronting her with herself, as she was every time she entered the foyer of the hotel or walked through the room smelling of cockroach repellent that was the restaurant, embracing unknown women, men and children in the intimacy of shared exile and return.

When Vera's son Ivan returns home to the 'new' South Africa, his observations and the difficulties of his adjustment, though no doubt important to him, appear emotionally flaccid when set against those of Sibongile and her family. We register the minutiae of social change as seen by Ivan, but there is little narrative verve to his story, nor is there any real insight into his predicament.

> The waiter arrived with plates ranged along his arm. Another hovered with the censer of a giant pepper-mill. The wine was uncorked, Ivan lifted his glass and mouthed a kiss blown to his mother across the table; – Where are the Indian waiters there used to be when I was a kid? They're all African now. –
>
> – Moved up a rung on the ladder. They've taken the place of whites who used to serve in shops – men's outfitters and so on. You're like an old man, reminiscing! That's what happens when you exile yourself. –

Gordimer's new novel comments freely upon the lives of both black and white South Africans, their lives apart and their lives together. Indeed, she always has been combative in defence of her right to comment on black lives, as she made clear in her essay 'The Essential Gesture'.

> White writers who are 'only writers' are open to related reproach for 'stealing the lives of blacks' as good material. Their claim to this material is the same as the black writers' at an important existential remove nobody could discount. Their essential gesture can be fulfilled only in the integrity Chekov demanded: 'to describe a situation so truthfully ... that the reader can no longer evade it'.

In *None to Accompany Me,* far from 'stealing the lives of blacks' – something of which Gordimer has never been guilty – she tries to show us how the lives of black people have been changed by transformations in South Africa, and in this she is largely successful. However, even here, Gordimer has a tendency to overstate her case, and we all too often find her drifting aimlessly in the shallow pool of cultural speculation. Rather than describe Mpho as she might any young girl, Gordimer becomes carried away with ethnocentric imagery which is irksome and, more perniciously, suggests a racial obsessiveness that does not appear to preoccupy young Mpho.

> This schoolgirl combined the style of *Vogue* with the assertion of Africa. She was a mutation achieving happy appropriation of the aesthetics of opposing species. She exposed the exaggeratedly long legs that seem to have been created not by natural endowment but to the specification of Western standards of luxury, along with the elongated chassis of custom-built cars. The oyster-shell pink palms of her slender hands completed the striking colour contrast of matt black skin with purple-red fingernails. Her hair, drawn back straightened and oiled to the gloss of European hair, was gathered on the crown and twisted into stiff dreadlocks, Congolese style, that fringed her shoulders.

Towards the end of the novel the worlds of Vera and Didymus and Sibongile come together. Mpho becomes involved with Oupa, a young black colleague of Vera's who has served time on Robben Island. Subsequently Oupa is killed in an ambush which Vera survives. The bullet passes through her. When Ivan's son, Adam – Vera's grandson – comes to South Africa from England, much to Vera's consternation he begins to show an interest in Mpho. Vera's objections are not racially motivated, it is simply that she feels that such a liaison might undermine her relationship with Mpho's parents. When the novel throws off its shackles of adherence to temporal commentary, and concentrates on family, with all the concomitant individual hurts, grievances and confusion, it is at its strongest. There is, in the final pages, a wonderfully ironic twist to Vera's life when her lesbian daughter adopts a black child. Despite all her years of political activism, Vera suddenly finds herself a part of the black community in a more intimate fashion than she ever could have imagined.

In 1974 Nadine Gordimer responded testily when asked by a journalist if she was a liberal. 'I am a white South African radical. Please don't call me a liberal.' Now, in her autumn years, her attachment to the word 'radical' has atrophied; and she may be more of a liberal than she thinks. In the context of present-day South Africa, certainly there is nothing radical about the political or literary mind that produced *None to Accompany Me*. For extended stretches of this novel one longs for Gordimer to find some other, more oblique way to be political, in the way that J.M. Coetzee has done, for all too often her narrative capitulates to the lure of rhetoric. And the fuller humanity of her characters is obscured as the prose scampers to the superficial beat of history. One hopes that in the 'new' South Africa, we will witness the emergence of a generation of writers who might be willing, despite continued troubles, to allow their prose to march to the beat of the human heart.

1994

J.M. Coetzee: Life and Times of John C.

J.M. Coetzee's seven works of fiction, and three collections of essays, have been produced in the long shadow cast by the last days of the apartheid regime and the emergence of what has become known as 'the new South Africa'. Unlike many of his South African literary colleagues, black and white, Coetzee has always maintained a wary vigilance over his creative imagination. He has been keen that it should not collapse into such clumsy antinomies as black/white, left/right, revolutionary/reactionary, or any of the other oppositions that threaten to reduce the complexity of life to easily adhesive slogans. To this end he has fought most vigorously against being labelled a political writer. 'Why should one automatically try to interpret my thinking in political terms?' he asked, in 1985. 'It is not necessary to know my ideas to understand my novels.'

John Michael Coetzee was born in 1940 in Cape Town, the son of a failed attorney and a mother who was a schoolteacher. He attended the University of Cape Town, where he received degrees in Mathematics and English, and thereafter he moved to London, where he worked as a computer programmer. In 1965 he left London for the United States, where he studied for a PhD in linguistics at the University of Texas at Austin. Between 1968 and 1971 he taught at the State University of New York in Buffalo, before returning to South Africa to pursue his academic career and to begin his literary one.

For most of the turbulent 1960s, then, Coetzee was exposed to the travails of the world beyond his native South Africa, in particular to the Civil Rights and anti-war struggles in the

United States. It is not by accident that his first published work, *Dusklands* (1974), contains two novellas which reflect the peripatetic nature of Coetzee's literary apprenticeship. The first, entitled 'The Vietnam Project', deals with an American specialist in psychological warfare who is working 'in the spirit of absoluteness' on a propaganda project to destroy the country of Vietnam. The second novella, 'The Narrative of Jacobus Coetzee', takes the author back to his homeland. It concerns a fictionalised relative of Coetzee who, in the 1760s, destroys an entire South African tribe because he assumes that they have humiliated him by their indifference to his authority.

It was in the 1960s that South Africa became the world's whipping boy as it edged closer towards social and political catastrophe. In 1960 the Sharpeville massacre took place and in 1966 the Prime Minister of South Africa, H.F. Verwoerd, was assassinated. A temporarily expatriated Coetzee was being reminded, at a distance, that he must step warily through the minefield that was his country's projected sense of itself and its history. Coetzee's memoir *Boyhood* makes it clear that he had practised this careful high-stepping already as a child. He grew up in a country which sought to make its history conveniently explicable not only to those living abroad, but more importantly to those white boys who would one day become white men and rule the country. In the case of young Coetzee, however, the litany of falsehoods that passed for history failed to take root.

In the fictions that follow *Dusklands* Coetzee began to locate his novels in a geographical and political setting that implied South Africa, but he did so without binding himself to the specifics which would preoccupy a social realist. In this way he accomplished two things: he freed himself from being viewed as a mere commentator on the political situation in South Africa; and this geographical anonymity enabled him to isolate and to scrutinise the psychological traumas of his 'exposed' characters, such as the magistrate in *Waiting for the Barbarians* (1980), who attempts to placate the nomadic people of his territory, but is eventually imprisoned and tortured. Or, most successfully, the eponymous hero of *Life and Times of Michael K* (1983), an apparently slow-witted and friendless young gardener who, after his mother dies, is left to fend for himself in a country at war. The vulnerable character in an unspecified landscape is a central component of Coetzee's fictional technique.

Coetzee's characters exist in imaginary 'societies' in which there is no shared culture and no shared understanding of what constitutes history. His characters struggle to survive alone; they do not make history, they merely endure it. The magistrate and Michael K (the allusion to Kafka is characteristically oblique) live in worlds which they are powerless to change, and in which the state abuses its power in an attempt to identify friends from enemies. Magda in *In the Heart of the Country* (1977) is similarly vulnerable. Repulsed by her father's relationship with his African workman's wife, she murders her father and then begins a relationship with the workman. Her world eventually collapses into insanity, and the reader learns to distrust the ravings and inventions of her unhinged and lonely mind. Coetzee's symbolic and at times allegorical fiction differs greatly from the realism of an older generation of South African writers, best represented by Alan Paton. Yet the self-conscious postmodernism of his narratives also sets Coetzee apart from his contemporaries such as André Brink and Nadine Gordimer. His best writing manages to achieve acute psychological insight, while never falling victim to what Cynthia Ozick (in a review of *Life and Times of Michael K*) calls 'the vice of abstraction'.

In 1990 Coetzee published his sixth novel, *Age of Iron*, and four years later his seventh novel, *The Master of Petersburg*. These two novels signalled a clear change of literary direction. *Age of Iron* is concerned with Mrs Elizabeth Curren, a retired professor of classics who is dying of cancer and writes to her daughter in the United States about a clearly named and labelled South Africa in the terminal stages of apartheid, just as she is in the terminal stages of her own disease. It is a documentary novel, curiously detailed by most standards, astonishingly so for Coetzee. Yet, it is unconvincing and lacks drama. The narrator's tone is flat, and the staunchly urban setting seems unsuited to Coetzee's lyrical pen. At one point the elderly Mrs Curren, who is waking up to the effects of apartheid on the black citizens of her country, announces somewhat melodramatically, 'now my eyes are open and I can never close them again'. Her interior narrative is rhetorical and clumsy:

> I say to myself that I am watching not the lie but the space behind the lie where the truth ought to be. But is it true? I dozed (it is still yesterday I am writing about), read, dozed again. I made tea, put on a record. Bar by bar the Goldberg Variations erected themselves in the air. I crossed to the window. It was nearly dark. Against the garage wall the man was squatting, smoking, the point of his cigarette glowing. Perhaps he saw me, perhaps not. Together we listened.
>
> At this moment, I thought, I know how he feels as surely as if he and I were making love.

The Master of Petersburg is even more troubling. The novel is set in 1869 and concerns Dostoevsky's journey to St Petersburg from Germany, and his subsequent sojourn in the city as he struggles to come to terms with the sudden death of his stepson. Dostoevsky follows the 'ghost' of his stepson, trying to determine whether the boy committed suicide or whether he was murdered by the local police. Again we are in a recognisable landscape, one that is even peopled with figures from history, but as with *Age of Iron* the plot seems contrived and uninspired, and the language patently fails to achieve the poetic intensity of Coetzee's novels of the 1980s.

Some have argued that there has been a falling off in the quality of Coetzee's work which is somehow connected to the collapse of the apartheid regime, but Coetzee was never a writer who used apartheid to hitch a literary ride. He left that to others. The engine that drives Coetzee is not political, indeed it is not even, in the strictest sense of the word, literary.

Coetzee is a trained linguist and theorist, a man who revels in what we might term 'deconstruction'. His later novels find him more interested in examining theoretical notions of authority – narrative and linguistic – than in drawing another non-specific landscape and peopling it with individuals who are powerless in the face of history's malignity.

A concern with authority and authorship is clearly discernible in Coetzee's early novels, but the theoretical aspects of these novels are properly married to acute characterisation and a dazzling use of language. Consider, for instance, the striking opening lines of *Waiting for the Barbarians*:

> I have never seen anything like it: two little discs of glass suspended in front of his eyes in loops of wire. Is he blind? I could understand it if he wanted to hide blind eyes. But he is not blind. The discs are dark, they look opaque from the outside, but he can see through them. He tells me they are a new invention.

It is the leaden, yet precise, language of the later novels that so disappoints; they lack passion and, more damagingly, they fail to obscure the theoretical scaffolding upon which the fiction has been raised. In *The Master of Petersburg* Dostoevsky talks with an acquaintance of his stepson, but behind the words of the character we can hear the bluff and bluster of a university lecturer.

> We are talking about a pamphlet, Fyodor Mikhailovich. Who cares who actually writes a pamphlet? Words are like the wind, here today, gone tomorrow. No one owns words. We are talking about crowds. Surely you have been in a crowd. A crowd isn't interested in fine points of authorship. A crowd has no intellect, only passions. Or do you mean something else?

Do we care about Dostoevsky searching for his son? Do we

ever really care about Mrs Curren in *Age of Iron*? The truth is we cannot get close to their hearts because the author does not seem interested in taking us there. And we cannot get close to the landscape of their world because, although this world actually does exist, the writer appears to be indifferent to its topography. In one passage Dostoevsky and his mistress are walking through the streets of St Petersburg: 'They have reached the embankment. Crossing the street, he takes her arm. Side by side they lean against the rail by the waterside.' But there is no description of the city, street, or river. Not now, not ever, which is remarkable for a city as visually arresting as St Petersburg.

If one examines Coetzee's nonfiction one will detect a similar movement away from the intuitions of a writer responding to the world and towards an almost scientific analysis of the subjects under scrutiny. *White Writing: On the Culture of Letters in South Africa,* which appeared in 1988, contains seven thought-provoking essays that discuss writing from the late seventeenth century to the present day by a people 'no longer European, yet not African'. Eight years later, however, *Giving Offence: Essays on Censorship* is a troubling, heavy-footed book that lumbers towards a highly questionable conclusion: that the censor is like the writer, and the writer is like the censor, and that all struggle against tyranny is to some extent futile because it will eventually result in our making tyrants of ourselves. Mercifully, we have the evidence of Coetzee's best fiction to remind us that this is not necessarily so.

Boyhood is a memoir by a writer whose literary output has successfully resisted an autobiographical reading. His personal life has been shrouded in privacy, so writing a memoir would seem to be an unlikely act; but Coetzee is cunning. *Boyhood* is written in the third person, which suggests construction rather than confession. Even in memoir, then, Coetzee is guarded. Our first glimpse of him is as a tormented, vulnerable boy. Very much like one of his own characters.

> There are ants in Worcester, flies, plagues of fleas. Worcester is only ninety miles from Cape Town, yet everything is worse here. He has a ring of fleabites above his socks, and scabs where he has scratched. Some nights he cannot sleep for the itching. He does not see why they ever had to leave Cape Town.

We soon learn that the world of young John Coetzee is a world riven with disturbing divisions. Between masters and servants:

> He burns with curiosity about the lives they live. Do they wear vests and underpants like white people? Do they each have a bed? Do they sleep naked or in their work-clothes or do they have pyjamas? Do they eat proper meals, sitting at a table with knives and forks?
>
> He has no way of answering these questions, for he is discouraged from visiting their houses. It would be rude, he is told – rude because Ros and Freek would find it embarrassing.
>
> If it is not embarrassing to have Ros's wife and daughter work in the house, he wants to ask, cooking meals, washing clothes, making beds, why is it embarrassing to visit them in their house?

Between English and Afrikaner:

> In Worcester the English are a minority, in Reunion Park a tiny minority. Aside from himself and his brother, who are English only in a way, there are only two English boys: Rob Hart and a small, wiry boy named Billy Smith whose father works on the railways and who has a sickness that makes his skin flake off (his mother forbids him to touch any of the Smith children). When he lets it slip that Rob Hart is being flogged by Miss Oosthuizen, his parents seem at once to know why. Miss Oosthuizen is one of the Oosthuizen clan, who are Nationalists; Rob Hart's father, who owns a

hardware store, was a United Party town councillor until the elections of 1948.

Between Coloureds and Natives:

> One can dismiss the Natives, perhaps, but one cannot dismiss the Coloured people. The Natives can be argued away because they are latecomers, invaders from the north, and have no right to be here. The Natives one sees in Worcester are, for the most part, men dressed in old army coats, smoking hooked pipes, who live in tiny tent-shaped corrugated-iron kennels along the railway lines, men whose strength and patience are legendary. They have been brought here because they do not drink, as Coloured men do, because they can do heavy labour under a blazing sun where lighter, more volatile Coloured men would collapse. They are men without women, without children, who arrive from nowhere and can be made to disappear into nowhere.

These divisions in society are given credence by the testimony of the adults who surround the young boy. Coetzee remembers his childhood friend Eddie, a native boy with whom he would wrestle.

> The smell of Eddie's body stays with him from these bouts, and the feel of his head, the high bullet-shaped skull and the close, coarse hair. They have harder heads than white people, his father says. That is why they are so good at boxing. For the same reason, his father says, they will never be good at rugby. In rugby you have to think fast, you can't be a bonehead.

Casual racism envelops the life of the young boy, but it never threatens to overwhelm him. He is aware of the myths and inconsistencies in his father's opinions, and he begins to wonder about the irrationality of the whole South African world picture. A boxing match between the South African Vic Toweel and the foreigner Manuel Ortiz forces the young Coetzee to once again question the authority of the opinions which govern the world in which he lives.

> For days the newspapers are full of pictures of the fight. Viccie Toweel is a national hero. As for him, his elation soon dwindles. He is still happy that Toweel has beaten Ortiz, but has begun to wonder why. Who is Toweel to him? Why should he not be free to choose between Toweel and Ortiz in boxing as he is free to choose between Hamiltons and Villagers in rugby? Is he bound to support Toweel, this ugly little man with hunched shoulders and a big nose and tiny blank, black eyes, because Toweel (despite his funny name) is a South African? Do South Africans have to support other South Africans even if they don't know them?

Coetzee has consistently sought to challenge the authority of master-narrators; and his most successful analysis of this condition of master-narrator as supposedly authoritative witness, and to some extent unquestioned creator of history, is accomplished in *Foe* (1987). This novel marks a transition between the unidentifiable landscapes of *Waiting for the Barbarians* and *Life and Times of Michael K*, and the clearly identifiable locales of Coetzee's last two novels. It opens on the desert island of Robinson Crusoe, a place in the 'real' world, but a place without society. Susan Barton, an English woman, is washed up on to the island, where she encounters Cruso (Coetzee's spelling) and Friday, a slave whose tongue has been cut out, thus rendering him speechless. Eventually all three are rescued, but Cruso dies on the return journey to England. Once Susan Barton and Friday reach England, the author Daniel Foe is engaged to write Susan's story. Yet the more Susan Barton learns about Foe's process of creation, the more she recognises fabrication, distortion and invention as the central pillars of 'truth' upon which the story is being constructed. There is also the additional problem of both Foe and Coetzee, 'author' and author, wondering who, if anyone, has the right to speak on Friday's behalf. Friday's provocative silence represents the tongueless mute condition of millions of people whose history is liable to be distorted and lost in the clumsy process of interpretation and master-narration.

As *Boyhood* progresses the young Coetzee becomes increasingly anxious about the contradictions and the silences in the South African world around him. He begins to write, but only after he has won the battle for language. In a country as deeply divided as South Africa, it comes as no surprise to learn that one's choice of language is as powerfully charged with meaning as all the other choices that society foists upon you. Typically and stubbornly though, Coetzee refuses to yield to either one camp or the other. An English speaker, he finds himself unwilling to yield up the Afrikaans language:

> One thing about the English that disappoints him, that he will not imitate, is their contempt for Afrikaans. When they lift their eyebrows and superciliously mispronounce Afrikaans words, as if veld spoken with a v were the sign of a gentleman, he draws back from them: they are wrong, and, worse than wrong, comical. For his part, he makes no concessions, even among the English: he brings out the Afrikaans words as they ought to be brought out, with all their hard consonants and difficult vowels.

Boyhood is unexpectedly revealing about the sources of the thematic anxieties that populate Coetzee's writing. Yet, the memoir becomes really surprising, and really moving, when it pushes beyond these concerns and tackles the writer's difficult relationship with his parents. He grew up in a country town not far from Cape Town, on a farm which had been in his father's family for some years. At school he was a gifted pupil, but at home he was a troubled, lonely child who sought refuge from an unhappy family life by playing on his beloved veld. He had little respect for his father, but he loved his mother deeply. From an early age the young Coetzee sought to escape the dull restrictions of his home and to please with his writing.

> For Mr Whelan he writes essays on The Character of Mark Antony, on The Character of Brutus, on Road Safety, on Sport, on Nature. Most of his essays are dull, mechanical performances; but occasionally he feels a spurt of excitement as he writes, and the pen begins to fly over the page. In one of his essays a highwayman waits under cover at the roadside. His horse snorts softly, its breath turns to vapour in the cold night air. A ray of moonlight falls like a slash across his face; he holds his pistol under the flap of his coat to keep the powder dry.
>
> The highwayman makes no impression on Mr Whelan. Mr Whelan's pale eyes flicker across the page, his pencil comes down: 6½. 6½ is the mark he almost always gets for his essays; never more than 7. Boys with English names get 7½ or 8.

Eventually Coetzee's father collapses with illness, and he endures a painful deterioration that fills the young boy with contempt. His father embarrasses him, for his limited vision of the world can never match that of his brilliant son. The young John Coetzee is anxious to expose weakness and hypocrisy in his headlong rush to maturity, and against his will the father finds himself swept up in the son's whirlwind acquisition of adolescent 'knowledge' and then summarily dumped when the son decides that the father is doing little more than impairing his youthful vision.

> He steps closer. His eyes are growing accustomed to the light. His father is wearing pyjama pants and a cotton singlet. He has not shaved. There is a red V at his throat where sunburn gives way to the pallor of his chest. Beside

the bed is a chamber-pot in which cigarette-stubs float in brownish urine. He has not seen anything uglier in his life. There are no pills. The man is not dying, merely sleeping. He does not have the courage to take sleeping-pills, just as he does not have the courage to go out and look for a job.

As a boy Coetzee feels compelled to learn how to negotiate the falsehoods that white South Africa offers up to those who wish to belong. In short, he develops the mentality of the writer. He fills his world with doubt, he rejects authority in all its forms – political, social, personal – and he cultivates the ability to resign himself to the overwhelming insecurity of the heart. He writes of his mother:

> This woman was not brought into the world for the sole purpose of loving him and protecting him and taking care of his wants. On the contrary, she had a life before he came into being, a life in which there was no requirement upon her to give him the slightest thought. At a certain time in her life she bore him; she bore him and she decided to love him; perhaps she chose to love him even before she bore him; nevertheless, she chose to love him, and therefore she can choose to stop loving him.

Coetzee's eventual rejection of his father's authority mirrors his rejection of the larger world of easy connections and lazy judgements that is South Africa. What he puts in its place is his love for 'weak' people; white, Afrikaner, coloured, native, it matters little to Coetzee. These same people will eventually inhabit his fictional worlds, their lives being acted out in the face of an unreliable and clearly paternal 'master-narrative'.

The memoir ends with death; not the death of his father, but the death of his Aunt Annie, who was a schoolteacher. A grim and beautiful scene marks the beginning of Coetzee's passage out of boyhood towards the adult calling of writing.

As Aunt Annie lies in the rain waiting for somebody to bury her, the young boy finds himself wondering about her books.

> He is left alone to do the thinking. How will he keep them all in his head, all the books, all the people, all the stories? And if he does not remember them, who will?

But he remembers.

1998

The Burden of Memory, the Muse of Forgiveness by Wole Soyinka

In Wole Soyinka's last volume, *The Open Sore of a Continent: A Personal Narrative of the Nigerian Crisis* (1996), the Nobel laureate lamented the fact that the democratically elected leader of his country, Moshood Abiola, was languishing in jail, while General Sani Abacha, the dictator who had placed Abiola in jail (and also confiscated Soyinka's passport), continued to rule unopposed. Three years on, both Abiola and Abacha are dead, and Soyinka has returned to Nigeria. But he is still addressing issues related not only to Africa but to the diaspora as well. In *The Burden of Memory, the Muse of Forgiveness*, his new volume of three essays, Soyinka squares up to the vexing question of whether the West owes those of African origin reparations for centuries of ill-usage.

The first essay, 'Reparations, Truth, and Reconciliation', states its case boldly. While observing the hearings of the South African Truth and Reconciliation Commission, it occurs to Soyinka that the problem with the method being employed is that it allows the 'defendants' to be questioned as though they were not criminals, relieving them of any onus to take responsibility for their past actions. Soyinka is adamant that justice is not 'served by discharging the guilty without evidence of mitigation – or remorse'. The author's indignation at having detected a lack of a moral ingredient in this process leads him to speculate about the concomitant lack of a material ingredient.

Soyinka builds his case for reparations by arguing that, without a material 'payment' for the crimes committed against

African people, the resentment and hatred engendered by the original actions will simply continue to simmer.

> Where there has been inequity, especially of a singularly brutalizing kind, of a kind that robs one side of its most fundamental attribute – its humanity – it seems only appropriate that some form of atonement be made, in order to exorcise that past. Reparations, we repeat, serve as a cogent critique of history and thus a potent restraint on its repetition.

While Soyinka offers no real evidence that cash or other forms of payment can seriously disrupt the often cyclical patterns of history, he does admit that there are grave problems which surround the question of how much, and whom, to pay. He once addressed executives from the World Bank and suggested to them that the slaving nations simply annul the debts of the African world and the African nations would, in turn, wipe clean the slate of injustice from the wounds of the past. The executives were not impressed and Soyinka quickly realised the impractical nature of his own suggestion. However, his present-day plea for reparations is equally flawed.

Soyinka points to recent evidence of the practice of reparations and wonders why the African world is being left out of this 'fever of atonement'. He identifies the rehabilitation of the victims of the 1692 Salem witch-hunt; the Japanese apology and compensation fund for Korean women forced into prostitution during the Second World War; the Spanish government's acknowledgement that the 1492 edict of Ferdinand and Isabella evicting the Jews from Spain was wrong. However, these seem to be particularly unconvincing examples when set against the huge and complicated problem of how to compensate a continent and its diaspora abroad for centuries of exploitation, some of which they contributed to themselves. In the end, it is clear that the task of formulating a strategy for reparations lies beyond the scope of this single essay and, for all his political acumen, beyond the brief of Wole Soyinka, writer.

'L.S. Senghor and Negritude', and 'Negritude and the Gods of Equity', the two essays that make up the remainder of the volume, find Soyinka exploring the philosophical impulse which he feels impels those of the African world to seek a premature closure to their travails by freely forgiving their victimisers. In the life and work of the well-known poet of 'negritude', former President Leopold Senghor of Senegal, Soyinka locates the literary equivalent of the Truth and Reconciliation Commission.

The term 'negritude' was first coined by the Martiniquan poet Aimé Césaire, and it was very much a Francophone response to such American black consciousness poets as Langston Hughes, Countee Cullen and James Weldon Johnson. The negritude movement assumed that culture was racially specific and that the culture of African peoples, rather than being something to be ashamed of, should be celebrated. However, this did not mean that French culture was to be rejected; far from it. Senghor, who became the first African member of the French Academy, replaced his affection for negritude eventually with a vigorously expressed affiliation to what he termed 'métissage', or cultural cross-fertilisation, in which French culture symbolised the apotheosis of human civilisation.

These 'assimilationist' Francophone writers fascinate Soyinka because he sees them as the progenitors of this desire to lay down the burden of memory and embrace the muse of forgiveness which, in his view, 'taints' Africa and Africans. The reasons for Soyinka's frustration with much of their writing is clear when he quotes Senghor who, among many other flights of poetic fantasy in praise of France, makes a special plea that on Judgement Day,

> Lord, among the white lands, set France
> upon the Father's right hand

Soyinka admits to finding Senghor's position a 'little taxing' to comprehend.

When Soyinka begins to yoke the literary to the political and explores the reasons why negritude never took hold in the English-speaking world, he is both inspiring and original. He reflects upon the manner in which Africa has been viewed from the diaspora as either 'past continuous' or 'past nostalgic', depending upon whether one is observing the continent from the United States or from the Caribbean, and as he does so it becomes clear that the free-ranging form of the essay is perfectly suited to Soyinka's restless mode of thought and his incantatory style of delivery.

The essay form, however, also brings out the worst in Soyinka, for it encourages him to wallow in excessive imagery, which draws attention to the language employed rather than the point that he is trying to make. For instance, when talking about the collusion of the traditional tribal chiefs in the ruination of Nigeria, he describes them as 'emissaries of this midget slavemaster, Sani Abacha' and as 'crawling' along 'sycophantic trails of slime'. At such moments the author's characteristic poise seems to be overpowered by the urge to indulge in personal invective.

Soyinka's analysis of the twentieth-century problem of memory and forgiveness in the African world is both timely and important. Africa cannot afford to endure another century of accommodating the West and at the same time failing to discipline its own so-called leaders. It cannot afford another century in which it slips easily from acknowledged 'truth' to convenient 'reconciliation' without adopting a more rigorous form of self-examination and a more confrontational attitude towards its former colonial masters. Soyinka's analysis of the problem is an initial volley in what will surely become a twenty-first-century debate, but already there is change afoot. In French Caribbean literature we are currently witnessing a tremendous backlash against 'negritude', in the work of Patrick Chamoiseau and Raphaël Confiant and others, which may prove to be a forerunner to changes in the political reality of France's relationship with her dependent territories. Unlike Senghor and others of the 'negritude' movement, the new writers of the Francophone Caribbean and the people they represent walk tall under the burden of memory. And unlike the South African Truth and Reconciliation Commission, there is nothing in their work or manner that suggests that they are interested in indulging the Muse of Forgiveness.

1999

The Caribbean

Introduction: The Gift of Displacement

Immediately upon leaving university I went to live in Edinburgh. I had graduated with a degree in English literature and language, but the first part of my degree was in experimental psychology and neurophysiology. Although I now wished to be a writer, I had not altogether abandoned my interest in the subject that I had originally intended to study. However, my mind was focused and my pockets shallow, and therefore the books I bought and read were almost invariably literary texts, mainly novels, written by African-American authors. These books best reflected the black and white divide that, to my mind, characterised Britain at that time. The Caribbean novels I attempted to engage with seemed foreign, exotic even, and so I spent little time with them. However, the work of one Caribbean-born author proved to be an exception to this rule. One Edinburgh afternoon I wandered into my local bookshop and picked up two books. On the cover of one was a photograph of a black man whose eyes were covered with a white mask. On the cover of the other book was a slogan inscribed as though it were a subtitle: 'The handbook for the black revolution that is changing the shape of the world'. Frantz Fanon's *Black Skin, White Masks* and *The Wretched of the Earth* became my Old Testament and my New Testament.

Frantz Fanon was born in Martinique on 20 July 1925. He fought and was decorated in the Second World War, and although initially he wanted to write plays, he chose instead to study medicine in Lyon, where he qualified as a psychiatrist. During the French-Algerian war he was assigned to a psychiatric hospital in Algeria, but his sympathies were with the Algerians.

He soon resigned his post and defected to the side of the rebels. Thereafter he became one of the chief advocates for the use of violence in overthrowing colonial regimes, claiming that the future of socialism now lay in the hands of the dispossessed as opposed to being in the control of those in the industrialised world. He recognised that the 'wind of change' was blowing through the Third World, but his analysis of this situation was not just political, it was also psychological. He understood the psychic damage that injustice and prejudice heaped upon the heads of the victims of colonisation, and his books not only utilised the broad strokes of history, he also took time to illustrate them with finer, more delicately drawn case-studies. Fanon's writings perfectly reflected my own anxieties, both personal and literary, but at this stage it had not occurred to me to connect his Caribbean heritage to his writing.

Back then I knew very little about my own Caribbean heritage. Some years later I saw a photograph of my father's mother and was shocked to discern traces of East India in her face. Soon after I was sitting in a bar in St Kitts with my brother and a friend told us that our grandfather had just walked in and taken a seat in the corner. My brother and I looked quizzically at each other, for we 'knew' that our grandfather, our mother's father, was dead. We had grown up in England with this 'knowledge'. But, sure enough, seated in the corner was Emmanuel de Fraites, a Jewish trader with Portuguese roots that reached back to the island of Madeira. I now understood that the cultural hybridity that is the quintessential Caribbean condition had certainly marked my person, and the quality of the blood that flowed through my veins was doggedly 'impure'.

Of course, I eventually began to read Caribbean literature and I soon recognised the techniques and rhythmic patterns that marked it out as being distinct from the literature of other parts of the world. Its restlessness of form, its polyphonic structures, its yoking together of man and nature, of past and present, its linguistic dualities and its unwillingness to collapse into easy narrative closure appeared to me to be characteristics that had grown out of something specific to the Caribbean region. And, then again, there was the evidence of the lives of the artists themselves. Why this seemingly compulsive desire to migrate, to move, to contribute to other people's literature and culture? Their blood seemed to be stirred by, and their craft fired in, the crucible of the Caribbean, and then they would depart, however temporarily, to another place.

But the migration of the Caribbean artist is a special kind of migration. Politically, culturally and linguistically, the Caribbean artist is better prepared for migration than most. Wherever one happens to be in the Caribbean, at least two or more continents and cultures have already provided the bedrock upon which one's identity has been forged. It is a birthright that embraces Europe, Africa and Asia. The journey from Jamaica to Lagos, or from Aruba to Amsterdam, or from Port of Spain to Bombay, can be surprisingly short, both historically and culturally. Migration is not a word to be feared, for Caribbean people are forever moving between versions of 'home', spurred on by the restless confluence of blood in their veins, an impure mixture that suggests transcendence and connectivity. This migratory condition, and the subsequent sense of displacement, can be a gift to a creative mind, and it marks the work of Aimé Césaire, V.S. Naipaul, Edouard Glissant, Derek Walcott, C.L.R. James, Samuel Selvon and countless others. It affords Caribbean writers and thinkers the opportunity to generate narrative energy out of these tensions and oppositions, and it also enables Caribbean writers and thinkers to easily slip the restrictive noose of race, to which those of the African-American tradition seem so firmly wedded.

Caribbean people are born into a region where European nations traditionally exchanged their verdant islands like chess pieces: culture and language were first imported, then imposed and 'real' history occurred elsewhere. The fact that the region is presumed to stand outside the grand procession of European history may occasion some to mourn, but this fact also means that many of the viruses of European culture have not taken hold. A self-determining history is still there to be created. The truth is, it could be argued that the synthesising new world vision of the Caribbean provides the perfect model for the age in which we live. An age in which migrations across boundaries are an increasingly familiar part of our individual lives as national borders collapse and are redrawn. An age in which nations bind together in regional clusters and eliminate old immigration laws, and in which illegal movements from one country to another become increasingly desperate as economies fail and wars continue to rage. How do we explain our new hybrid selves without recourse to the simplistic discourse of race? Perhaps the answer is to be found in the culture and literature of the Caribbean archipelago.

Frantz Fanon occupies a special place in this culture and literature. I first read him as the man who had written 'the handbook for the black revolution'. Jean-Paul Sartre's self-flagellating introduction to *The Wretched of the Earth* did not help: '. . . the European has only been able to become a man through creating slaves and monsters'. If, at that stage, I had known more about the Caribbean, I would have been more suspicious of the publisher's 'positioning' of Fanon. It is easier to market a 'black revolutionary' than it is a 'Martiniquan psychiatrist'. Fanon was certainly a man with a deep consciousness of race. When he realised that he was seriously ill, and in need of treatment for the leukemia which eventually killed him, he hesitated to be flown to the land of lynchings and racism and preferred to be treated in Moscow. However, his condition deteriorated and eventually he had little choice but to be flown to Washington DC. But it was too late. He died in the United States on 6 December 1961 at the age of thirty-six. Shortly after his death his body was flown back to Tunis, and then transported over the border into Algeria, where he is buried.

The fact that his publishers encouraged his writings to be appropriated as canonical texts during the black power struggle in the 1960s would probably have irritated Fanon. This complex, sensitive Martiniquan doctor understood that the revolution was not confined to tackling issues to do with race. Fanon was arguing for human dignity and racial origins were a subsidiary issue. In the conclusion to *The Wretched of the Earth* he makes it clear that he is anti-Europe: 'Europe now lives at such a mad, reckless pace that she has shaken off all guidance and all reason, and she is running headlong into the abyss; we would do well to avoid it with all possible speed.' He is also anti the United States. 'Two centuries ago, a former European colony decided to catch up with Europe. It succeeded so well that the United States of America became a monster, in which the taints, the sickness, and the inhumanity of Europe have grown to appalling dimensions.' However, he is clearly for people, as we see in *Black Skin, White Masks*.

> There is no Negro mission; there is no white burden ... I have no wish to be the victim of the *Fraud* of a black world. My life should not be devoted to drawing up the balance sheet of Negro values. There is no white world, there is no white ethic, any more than there is a white intelligence.

In fact, as his comments on anti-Semitism make clear, Fanon is a humanist whose sympathies traverse all boundaries, imaginary or otherwise: 'Colonial racism is no different from any other racism. Anti-Semitism hits me head-on: I am enraged, I am bled white by an appalling battle, I am deprived of the possibility of being a man.'

The shadow of purity does not extend far south beyond the Florida Keys. When a Caribbean voice attempts to extend its dark penumbra into the region, he or she soon becomes the object of controversy and possibly scorn. Attempts to 'deconstruct' this phenomenon of cross-cultural fluidity have largely been the provenance of those of the Francophone world; however, with or without theory, a creolising Caribbean consciousness has created a culture that is distinct from that of the United States, and certainly light years removed from that of Europe. Fanon's latest biographer, a 'white redhead' of an Englishman, describes, at the conclusion of his biography, his most emotionally charged memory of the whole enterprise. It was a conversation with an elderly Martiniquan who had played football with Fanon as a child and fought alongside him in the Second World War. 'He gently brushed his black fingers across my white wrist, looked at me and said, "Fanon ... race ... racism: it's nothing to do with *that*."'

St Kitts: 19 September 1983

It is only in the hour-long wait in Antigua, having left the British Airways 747 and watched it soar dramatically away towards Barbados, that I realise I am once again in the Caribbean. In England an hour could never last so long. The heat, and the noise, and the lethargy-inducing humidity, seduce from my body the equivalent of a whole London summer's sweat. And then mercifully the small Avro plane makes its scheduled appearance, and the forty-eight passengers rush (the plane is over-booked) headlong through the gate and on to the tarmac. As if participating in a second, a voluntary and more comfortable middle passage, the voyagers are all in a hurry to witness what has become for Britain a regular part of her year's foreign diplomacy. However, for these passengers this will be a unique and emotional moment in their lifetime. This will be something to relate to their children and to their grandchildren thereafter: independence. St Kitts, the mother colony of the British Empire, together with her sister island, Nevis, will soon become the last of Britain's associated states to achieve full political independence. St Kitts–Nevis, with a combined population of 45,000, will soon take her place as both the newest, and the smallest, country in the world.

Once on board the smaller plane (there are as yet no direct flights from London to St Kitts) the passengers look around anxiously, wondering if they might have overlooked a long-lost friend, or even a relative. But then they settle down and they stare out of the window with an uncharacteristic Caribbean reserve. Most of the people on board the flight are, like my own parents back in England, West Indian emigrants. People who many years ago had left St Kitts and migrated to England in the 1950s and 1960s. For most of them this passage would be their first acquaintance with 'home' for twenty-five or thirty years. Behind their unblinking eyes, their minds were troubled with considerations beyond those of flags and anthems, seats in the United Nations and bunting in the streets. Most of them were in danger of being undone by the troubling complexity of the word 'home'.

From the air the Caribbean sea is a beautiful medley of different shades of green, which are lighter or darker according to the presence or absence of coral reef or the shallowness of the water. After twenty minutes the more thirsty, parched green of land slides underneath the plane as we fly over the southernmost edge of St Kitts. People wrench themselves around into a position where they can get a better view of the island's cane fields, and the straggly chains of houses that meander along the hillsides. The same houses that they left? The same island? Nobody dares say anything. As the plane comes to a halt in front of the newly extended terminal building, the customary rituals of air-travel disobedience, principally the undoing of seat belts, lighting up of cigarettes, standing up and retrieving of luggage, are cast aside. We all remain seated and await instructions as if unsure of what to do next.

It was in 1493 that Christopher Columbus first came upon a Caribbean island known as 'Liamuiga' (fertile isle) supposedly inhabited by hostile Carib Indians. He named the island after himself, St Christopher. In 1623 Thomas Warner, an English merchant, landed on the Carib island, and subsequently persuaded James I that it was worth raising the English standard on this soil. Thomas Warner inaugurated British West Indian colonialisation. In the following year the French arrived and the Caribs gave their land freely to both the English and the French until the new settlers decided that the natives were expendable. In the wake of the genocidal slaughter of the Caribs, the number of Africans being imported quickly increased. On this small island, 23 miles by 6¼, the English and the French began to squabble and there followed a long struggle for control. In 1783 the Treaty of Versailles assigned St Kitts and Nevis to Britain, and the island's economy became increasingly dependent upon sugar produced by African labour. In 1967 St Kitts (as St Christopher is 'vulgarly' known) became a three-island associated state with Nevis and Anguilla, but the people of Anguilla rebelled and the associated state of St Kitts–Nevis came into being. Now, on the verge of independence after sixteen years of statehood, St Kitts was about to welcome yet another planeload of exiled sons and daughters.

In the hot and dusty capital of Basseterre (its name a hangover from the days of the French) the schoolchildren walk proudly clutching their new exercise books, the covers of which are adorned with the heading 'Youth Development for Greater Productivity'. Beneath these words there is a large picture of the new state flag. The children already know that the green represents the island's fertile lands, the yellow the all-year-round sunshine, the black the people's African heritage, the red the struggle from slavery through colonialisation to independence, and the two stars, hope and liberty. The children also know the words of the new national anthem, 'O Land of Beauty', for their teachers are under strict instructions to make sure that even if the children forget everything else about their country's imminent independence, by 19 September they will definitely know the words to the new national anthem. Although independence is still some days away, the tiny streets of Basseterre are already jammed with traffic. People litter street corners drinking beer and the air is filled with the sound of music and loud, over-animated conversations. It does not seem possible that a sleepy town of 16,000 people could sound like Brooklyn's Eastern Parkway on Labor Day, but the pitch of independence fever has already been established and it shows no sign of letting up.

Wearing my journalist's hat I make my way across to the whitewashed three-storey government headquarters, where the press officer informs me that to arrange to see the Minister of Education will be 'quite straightforward'. If I see his car (a grey Datsun) I should flash him down and pull over to the side of the road, where an interview will not be too difficult to obtain. At first this seems unreasonable, but the logic is sound enough: a) the press officer is busy, b) the Minister is busy, c) on an island this small leaving such arrangements to fate means they stand at least as good a chance of coming to fruition as trying to design them. From the government headquarters I walk across to Warner Park, the main arena for the independence programme, just in time to catch up with the island's final military parade as a dependent territory; it brings together the Scouts, the Sea Scouts, the Boys' Brigade, the territorials, the police, the cadets and the white-suited, pith-helmeted military brass themselves. There is much presenting of arms and inspecting of the troops, but as the late afternoon sky deepens to early evening and the palm trees above darken to silhouettes, the applause that has greeted even the simplest of drilling movements dies away and is replaced by large, somewhat embarrassing, silences. A dog wanders across the field, weaving its way in and out of the soldiers, then a loose-limbed boy ambles after it. The ZIZ local radio reporter next to me panics and forgets to stand up for the national anthem, the new one as opposed to the old one, which marks the conclusion of affairs. Those who recognise the anthem are happy to join in, and those who do not recognise it either leave for home or for one of the drinking bars 'downtown'.

As I join the throng making their way down towards the town centre a Ford Granada dashes by, sirens blaring, red and blue lights flashing. People stop and look; this car (there are three of them in all) is a recent gift from Britain to the St Kitts–Nevis police force. An innocent gift? A pay-off? Nobody is prepared to commit themselves on this point, but the cars noisily circle the island with the plastic still on their seats, looking as though something ought to be happening.

'Maybe they're just practising,' comments a friend, 'for when the Cubans arrive.'

In the morning the St Kitts–Nevis Technical College patriotic programme for independence provides a clue as to what was actually meant by the Cuban comment. From an overall student body of some 200 only twenty-five had turned up for the morning of singing and prayer dedicated to the new nation. Most of the absenteeism is as a result of a boycott of the whole independence celebrations by the opposition Labour Party, who feel that the terms negotiated with the British government are unreasonable and that this is not real independence. Labour Party supporters are keeping their children back from the college celebrations, which leaves me speculating about the country areas, which are traditionally supporters of the Labour Party. If such a boycott can be so effective in town, then how is this independence being received in the country?

The island of St Kitts has one main road, Island Road, which is about thirty-two miles in circumference and which envelops the island in an almost perfectly neat circle. Along the way its dozen or so villages and small towns are scattered around the perimeter of the island like numerals on a clock face, while the centre of the island is dominated by sugar cane, which swims out flat until it brushes up against the steep slopes of the island's towering Mount Misery. Driving clockwise it soon becomes clear that the island looks prettier than it did when I last saw it a year or so earlier. It transpires that the government have introduced a best-kept village competition, in which all but one or two villages have made some effort to participate. Most villages have whitewashed the loose stones and the trunks of the trees that line the road which passes through them, and some have even placed large decorative shells in the grass. However, when I occasionally swing off Island Road and up the side streets, it is clear to me that most of the houses are still battered, their walls peeling in the sun, and the only paint that has been applied to them spells out in a shaky hand something chillingly reminiscent of the slogans from V.S. Naipaul's novel *Guerrillas*, the new island motto, 'Country Above Self'.

All around the island, behind the gleaming kerbstones and

shells and the tree trunks and the ribbons, it is easy to observe a swollen-bellied, gap-toothed, despair in the bodies and faces of the country children, which betrays the true nature of the struggle in St Kitts at the moment. The superficiality of paint cannot hide the poverty of the young and unemployed population, who are not starving but who are evidently suffering from a poverty-related malnutrition. Independence for their parents means receiving their holiday bonuses for cane-cutting three days early so they have some money to spend on celebratory drinks, although they seem unclear as to what they should be celebrating. However, there appears to be no boycott of the independence celebrations. This is the point of the holiday bonus. The country people will spend their money, and drink, and therefore be seen to be 'celebrating'. Meanwhile, the Opposition will continue to maintain that this is not a real independence, arguing that it cannot be of any real significance, for the Queen is not coming. Instead she is sending her younger sister. This is part of their 'evidence'. One lady I speak with in Dieppe Bay, a village at the northernmost tip of St Kitts, is not aware of either the boycott or the Queen's sister. She still thinks that Harold Wilson is Prime Minister of Britain, for he had presided over the Anguilla affair in 1967. Cuban troops? Her dead husband had once worked in Cuba, she says. She points away across the sea in the general direction of Cuba. This is all Cuba means to her. She looks almost hurt that I think it might mean something more.

Back in Basseterre I begin to recognise some of the people from the plane wandering about in the street. Some appear to be managing to relate to the island they had left during the 1950s when England looked to them like the 'Promised Land'. Others are quite clearly having difficulty and are unsure whether to drop the Midlands accent or the Yorkshire accent, not knowing if people are laughing at them. Only one man whom I speak to, a van driver from Leeds, positively states his intention of selling up to come back 'home', but even he tempers his enthusiasm by admitting that he might need to come back out one more time just to make sure. The others, basking in 90°F sunshine, drinking rum and coke, or beer from the neck of a bottle, are all clear that they need to go back to England and work some more and save till they are ready, but nobody can actually say when they will be ready. Five years, maybe ten? It all sounded so familiar. The highlight of the day was the arrival of Princess Margaret (according to ZIZ radio, 'the Countess of Sundown') at Golden Rock airport. She sped quickly, with motorcycle escort, through the half-deserted streets of Basseterre waving at the few who had bothered to turn out to greet her. Most of the island were sleeping off the previous day's community programme, which had involved selling beer at fifty cents a bottle and all shorts at ten cents a shot. This throwback to the prices of a previous time seemed to have captured the imagination of the nation, for on the previous evening the fever-pitch noise of Basseterre had momentarily explored a new octave. Now the people slept and waited.

Nevis, the smaller island, which broods two miles away on the horizon, had already played host to approximately half of the independence events, including a disastrous calypso competition that was washed out, and an elocution contest in which the virtues of patois were not actively encouraged. The true extent of the inter-island rivalry between St Kitts and Nevis became apparent at the Miss Independence competition (a show held in St Kitts) when a girl from Nevis's victory was greeted with a resounding silence. As one would expect, supporters of the opposition Labour Party have little time for Nevis, feeling that the smaller island has the better deal in the constitution negotiated by Prime Minister Dr Kennedy Simmonds. The headline of the *Labour Spokesman* just two days before independence left nothing to the imagination: 'Independence for Nevis but a new form of colonialism for St Kitts'. Even the supporters of Kennedy Simmonds's government, a coalition of the only Nevis party and the smaller of the two St Kitts parties, dislike Nevisians. Naturally, the Nevisians have little time for their 'partners' on the larger island. A popular joke during the celebrations refers to the 'boat people' problem St Kitts will have if Nevis should ever secede, for her people will flock to St Kitts for work and pleasure. Other jokes begin with, 'Did you hear about the man who had to spend a night on Nevis . . .' C.L.R. James's much-hoped-for Caribbean unity seemed a long way away.

At Warner Park the state service for independence begins slowly. The park is large, like the Oval cricket ground, although the stands are much smaller. However, when floodlit (with under-powered lights) the whole park looks vast and eerie, like Hardy's Egdon Heath removed to the tropics. Before the Union Jack actually slithers down the pole the Royal Marines band insists on torturing the 5,000 or so people with their version of 'Sailing'. Then their drill team causes a moment's consternation, for one of their ten members is black, a sort of military Roland Butcher. However, the minutes soon begin to quicken towards midnight and the atmosphere suddenly becomes more solemn, and I begin to think of the 35,000 people who died in Zimbabwe struggling for a different kind of independence: the kind that has to be fought for. I also think of my co-passengers from the small plane and I wonder what they must be thinking to themselves. Princess Margaret appears on stage and stares at what must look to her like a cackle of vultures with long Japanese beaks. The press photography corps gives her not a moment's peace, despite the fact that they are all under 'heavy' instructions from the police not to let off any flashes while she reads her sister's message. Do they listen? Together they create more light than the floodlights in Warner Park. In the pages of the local newspapers and on the streets, the people of St Kitts–Nevis have already complained about not being catered for. As I look around I can see that most of the space in Warner Park has been turned over to the dignitaries from around the world and their bodyguards. Local people have arrived in their droves, found that they could not achieve any kind of vantage point, and they have simply gone home. Prime Minister Simmonds's impassioned independence speech falls flat; a cursory glance at his audience makes it clear why.

And overnight the bunting disappears. The return to daily life is astonishingly fast. The streets become unclogged and overhead planes are taking off at an alarmingly regular rate. At the airport official delegates jostle with foreign prime ministers, who jostle with expatriates leaving once more for London. And the Opposition calls the boycott of the celebrations a great victory, while the newly appointed government ministers fly off to the United Nations in New York to celebrate their country becoming the 158th member and the smallest independent federation in the world. British passports can now be exchanged for St Kitts–Nevis passports, Mount Misery now becomes Mount Liamuiga, and one can now pay in US dollars in the Royal St Kitts Hotel casino; local currency is not permissible. Clearly a new age is dawning for St Kitts–Nevis, but nobody seems to be able to define the nature of this 'new age'.

My abiding memory of the week is of the Chinese journalist who wandered for days through the streets of Basseterre smiling at everybody from beneath his black umbrella. He was hot and sticky, but studiously observant. After all, despite China being a nation of one billion people it has no more power in the United Nations than St Kitts. One nation, one vote. We all need friends. Before my departure I travelled to the village of Middle Island and stood in silence by the 'founder's' resting place. Some 350 years after he first set foot on the island, Thomas Warner can rest happy in his grave and watch Britain close the book at the end of another chapter in her history. And he can also watch as many hands scramble to write a new one. Cuban, American, Chinese, Canadian hands are all poised. Maybe the van driver from Leeds was right: he had better wait a while and then come back and take a second look.

1983

A Small Place by Jamaica Kincaid

In her two autobiographical novels *Down by the River* and *Annie John* Jamaica Kincaid succeeds where few contemporary Caribbean novelists, and certainly no women from this part of the world, have succeeded in capturing the languid rhythms of tropical life in a rich and evocative prose that is also both urgent and poetic. *A Small Place* is a departure, not so much of style but of content. Kincaid has chosen to write a powerful nonfiction essay which, like her novels, centres on her native Antigua, but unlike her novels spills over into an assault of great *saeva indignatio* not only towards the English, who colonised Antigua, but also towards the local natives, who 'liberated' and now rule the small independent country.

The essay begins with an account of how it feels to arrive as a tourist in a country such as Antigua.

> You disembark from your plane. You go through customs. Since you are a tourist, a North American or European – to be frank, white – and not an Antiguan black returning to Antigua from Europe or North America with cardboard boxes of much needed cheap clothes and food for relatives, you move through customs with ease.

The author is aware of the physical and psychological discomfort of being a tourist, and she moves from the familiar guilt induced by hassle-free immigration channels and luxury hotels to more particular, but nonetheless important, problems.

> You have bad manners (it is their custom to eat their food

with their hands; you try eating that way, you look silly); they do not like the way you speak (you have an accent); they collapse helpless from laughter, mimicking the way they imagine you must look as you carry out some everyday bodily function.

The power-play between those who gawk and those who suffer the stares is captured by a writer who, having divided her life between Antigua and the United States, possesses enough understanding of both worlds to be able to draw a convincing picture of their coming together. It is a tension that is felt in many parts of the world, from Africa to India to Latin America, places where the affluent use the 'underdeveloped' world as a beach on which to lie. It is only when the author steps beyond her preoccupation with the 'tourist' that the essay begins to develop a flavour which marks it out as not only original but historically important as a document that throws light on Caribbean history past and present.

Kincaid reminisces about her childhood in 'English' (colonised) Antigua. As she castigates the English for their behaviour and attitudes in the 'old' Antigua, we are led to assume that the newly independent Antigua will be for her a place of spiritual rebirth. But when she returns to her island, she finds the place darker. Her disappointment fuels the essay and it soars with the passion of Baldwin's *The Fire Next Time* as she exposes the corruption and double-dealing which exists in all areas of modern Antiguan life. The St Lucian Derek Walcott and the Trinidadian V.S. Naipaul have launched similar attacks against the parochialism of their home countries and it is into this tradition of West Indian literary exiles, looking back with a sense of loss compounded by disappointment, that this book falls.

The essay begs one question. Why does somebody who lives so comfortably outside think she has the right to criticise those who have to live inside? After all, it is easy to arrive with a return air ticket, make sweeping judgements and depart. Baldwin, a longtime French resident, was often accused by his peers of a lack of 'commitment' to the United States, but his answer is to be found in the same place we find Kincaid's riposte to those who might castigate: in the passion of the writing. Kincaid may reside in the United States but only somebody with her heart in Antigua could have written with such ferocity of purpose and self-revelatory hurt. Quite simply, she has a right to criticise because, irrespective of residence or nationality, she belongs.

Once or twice, the author allows her chastisement of England to become a little cynical: 'But the English have become such a pitiful lot these days, with hardly any idea what to do with themselves now that they no longer have one quarter of the Earth's human population bowing and scraping before them.' At other times, her anti-English line is historically questionable. Was Nelson a 'criminal'? If so, the onus is upon the author to explain to us, however briefly, the nature of his criminality. But these are small points.

A generation ago, the Martiniquan poet Aimé Césaire wrote *Return to My Native Land*, an epic poem on the same theme, in which he found much more cause for optimism on his return to Martinique from metropolitan France. Kincaid's pessimism reflects the changing Caribbean, a small but increasingly complex part of the world, burdened with cable television, Japanese cars, the evils of American materialistic splendour and now veterans of an actual American invasion. This new Caribbean stands at a political and moral crossroads, and Kincaid is a witness to what is happening in our West Indian backyards. And I trust her.

1988

The Arkansas Testament by Derek Walcott

Last year Derek Walcott's *Collected Poems* appeared in a 500-page volume. It seemed to me then, and his new collection of verse confirms my feelings, that it may have been a premature assembling of the poet's work. *The Arkansas Testament* not only finds Walcott examining some of his old themes, but doing so with youthful invention.

Born in 1930 on the small Caribbean island of St Lucia, Walcott now divides his time between Boston and Trinidad. He is part of the poetic gang of four (Joseph Brodsky, Czeslaw Milosz and Seamus Heaney being the other three), the internationally displaced poets who teach in the United States.

Walcott's poetry draws on an awareness of the lack of any viable West Indian literary tradition or consensus of culture. He emerged from an often intellectually restricted environment and he has mastered the vocabulary of the English language, and gone on to explore the rhythms of syntax, the power of metaphor and the intellectual game-playing of allusion. But the problems of a West Indian writer working in a tradition tied to British imperialism have always been present in Walcott's mind.

> The riot police and the skinheads exchanged quips
> You could trace to the Sonnets or the Moor's eclipse
>
> 'Midsummer'

Walcott's seven previous collections have been steeped in an ambivalence towards the outside world and its relationship to his own native land of St Lucia. The clash of Europe and colony, language and landscape, the 'old world' and the 'new world' of the Americas: these have been his themes. That there are always choices to be made implies a rejection of something and an inevitable sense of loss. In *Midsummer* (1984), one felt a growing awareness of mortality, which bestowed upon his poetic journey the qualities of a pilgrimage. The volume ended shrouded in overwhelming forfeiture.

> . . . though no man ever dies in his own country
> the grateful grass will grow thick from his heart

The Arkansas Testament is a collection of thirty-nine poems divided into two parts – 'Here', referring to the author's native Caribbean, and 'Elsewhere'. The voice of the Caribbean part of the volume moves easily between the received European tradition and the local oral one. The author is able to employ both when necessary. This accounts in part for Walcott's distinctive tone, pitched somewhere between the rhetorical and the vernacular.

> as I watch a low seagull race
> its own cry, like a squeaking pin
> from the postcard canoes of La Place,
> where the dots I finished begin,
>
> and a vendor smiles: 'Fifty? Then
> you love home harder than youth!'
> Like the full moon in daylight, her thin,
> uncontradictable truth.

The high point of 'Here' is the poem 'The Light of the World', a sensitive and heart-rending account of a Saturday-night bus journey from the town marketplace back to a small house on a country beach where the speaker is staying. On this serene, moonlit evening the speaker, having walked about the town he was born and grew up in, now 'lusts' peacefully after two girls on the bus and falls in 'love' with a third. Here is a perfect opportunity to feel in tune with his past. But no, thoughts of discord disturb the tranquillity of his communion with his people. The truth is painful, ever-present, and reduces the speaker to tears.

> I, who could never solidify my shadow
> to be one of their shadows, had left them their earth,
> their white rum quarrels, and their coal bags,
> their hatred of corporals, of all authority.

The moment when he should belong is the very moment he is acutely aware of the fact that he no longer does.

In 'Elsewhere', Walcott the poet who did not want to leave home but at the same time needed to aspirate his mind, addresses the West. He pays homage to a past master, in a eulogy addressed to W.H. Auden.

> It was such dispossession
> that made possession joy,
> when, strict as Psalm or Lesson,
> I learnt your poetry.

He dedicates the title poem 'Elsewhere' to another 'master', Stephen Spender. But with each poem, the degree to which Walcott remains a West Indian becomes increasingly clear, with Europe or America claiming attention only inasmuch as they cast light back upon his central dilemma. He is able to write:

> I remember the cities I have never seen
> exactly. Silver-veined Venice, Leningrad
> with its toffee-twisted minarets. Paris . . .

A man of Walcott's classical education and intellect is sensitive to these centres of international culture, but one senses that he has come to understand that (as Seamus Heaney, to whom this volume is dedicated, once wrote) the provincial state of mind, which needs the affirmation and approval of the metropolis, is not as important as the parochial imagination, which has no doubt about 'the artistic validity of its own parish'.

Therefore as we quarry on through 'Elsewhere', with its formal invention, its classical allusions, its references to Cambodia, Chernobyl and Gorbachev, there is a suspicion that although Walcott may be embracing cosmopolitan ideas and subjects, he does so with less emotional assurance than when he is barefoot and feeling sand trickling uneasily between his toes, and in the grip of the obsession that compels him to address the more essential questions of his origins and identity.

This is not to suggest that Walcott should confine himself to the Caribbean; far from it. 'The Young Wife' is as painful and universal a poem about cancer as one is ever likely to read, and 'God Rest Ye Merry Gentlemen: Part II' depicts the urban squalor of Newark, New Jersey with at least as much passion as the writing of its most famous literary inhabitant, Amiri Baraka.

> Johannesburg is full of starlit shebeens.
> It is anti-American to make such connections.

The title poem of the volume, 'The Arkansas Testament', picks up where 'God Rest Ye Merry Gentlemen: Part II' leaves off. It handles 'the stripes and scars' of modern American racism with dignity and urgency. Walcott checks into a $17.50-a-night motel in Arkansas. He wakes early, needing a five a.m. caffeine 'fix', and drives into the nearest town, Fayetteville.

> I bagged the hot Styrofoam coffee
> to the recently repealed law
> that any black out after curfew
> could be shot dead in Arkansas.

This is no protest poem. True, it concerns the history of the South; it concerns racism and the feelings of contempt that white ignorance often engenders in black people's souls. But it is a poem about writing, about a man's struggle to bear his soul and talent in an environment other than that which nurtured it. It is a poem about a particular type of black man: a West Indian writer, in America.

As another outstanding West Indian writer, C.L.R. James, once said, 'it is when you are outside, but can take part as a member, that you see differently from the ways they see, and you are able to write independently'. Walcott 'the outsider' is the supreme poet of the Caribbean because he has rejected the easy labelling that might have enabled him to make a peace with himself. *The Arkansas Testament* is witness to his ongoing struggle. Having held at bay the anger brought forth by his treatment in Fayetteville, Walcott knows that

> There are things that my craft cannot
> wield, and one is power;

He refers here to the Southern power of 'Lee's slowly reversing sword', not the moral power of which his work contains an abundance.

1987

C.L.R. James: Mariner, Renegade and Castaway

The difficulty with C.L.R. James has always been location, both in the literal sense (his life being a testament to compulsive itinerancy), and in terms of the many categories under which he is acknowledged to have achieved. He broke ground in the fields of literature, literary criticism, cultural studies, political theory, history and philosophy, and in more than one of these areas he can be looked upon as a pioneer. He was born in Trinidad in 1901 and was laid to rest there in 1989, and between these two certain locations there sprawl a remarkable life and a formidable body of achievement. In a century that has produced talents as diverse as the economist Arthur Lewis, the poets Derek Walcott and Aimé Césaire, and the novelist Alejo Carpentier, there is little doubt that James will eventually come to be regarded as the outstanding Caribbean mind of the twentieth century. The whole edifice of his work was constructed on two guiding principles. First, he believed in the power of reason, which was a clear legacy of his classical British education in early twentieth-century colonial Trinidad. James's appeal to reason was always accompanied by reference to, and a scrupulous regard for, history. Second, he believed in the inventive potential of the masses when engaged in social movement. While he acknowledged the necessity for charismatic leadership (and he was certainly blessed with a charismatic personality of his own), James believed that beneficial political change could only ever emerge when the masses democratically stated their desires.

Cyril Lionel Robert James was born in the village of Caroni, Trinidad on 4 January 1901. He was the eldest child of Robert

James, a schoolteacher, and Ida Elizabeth (Bessie) James, a devout Anglican who read widely in books and magazines. Bessie would read anything that she could lay her hands upon, and as soon as she had finished with a book her eldest son picked it up and read it for himself. She developed a particular fondness for Kipling, Austen, Trollope, the Brontës and Dickens, a fondness inherited by her son. In 1910 James won a scholarship, or 'exhibition', to Trinidad's first secondary school, the august Queen's Royal College. Opened in 1870, the college's 'expatriate' masters were generally Oxford- and Cambridge-educated men who taught a staple diet of classics which centred on Latin, Greek and ancient history. James was an assiduous student, to whom good grades and high praise came easily. But by the age of fourteen the quirky, idiosyncratic nature of his personality had begun to display itself. He found solace reading in class rather than listening to his schoolmasters, and after school he preferred to play cricket (a sport at which he was only proficient) rather than attending to his schoolwork. By this stage of his life he could claim to have read Thackeray's *Vanity Fair* at least a dozen times. It became his 'key text'. He took particular delight in the satirical manner in which Thackeray exposed the pretensions of middle-class British society; and he must have recognised the self-aggrandisements and the frustrations of middle-class Trinidadian life in the British writer's work. He would delight friends by having them open the book at any page and start to read, at which point he would take over, quoting from memory.

The Trinidad of the early part of the century was essentially British, politically and culturally. Like the rest of the Caribbean, it lay at that peculiar crossroads, where Europe, the Western hemisphere, Africa, and the indigenous world of the Carib and Arawak Indians all came together in a chaotic rush. It was a world which, compared to Britain, and certainly to the United States, was free of the cruder forms of racial prejudice. Many years later, in *Beyond a Boundary* (1963), James commented on his schooldays by observing that 'In our little

Eden' racial discrimination 'never troubled us'. In a later passage he reflects upon being denied admission on racial grounds to the local English regiment, but claims that this incident left him unscarred. James's lifelong lack of interest in addressing questions of race in a one-dimensional manner was owed to his Caribbean upbringing. Growing up in a British environment, albeit in a colony, the 'child' of empire soon comes to understand the relationship between race and class, and to see how, in certain situations, a failure to grapple with class makes it impossible to tackle questions of race. James's self-confident 'colonial' bearing was always a challenge to those outside the Caribbean who, by virtue of his dark complexion, wished to reduce him to the status of a mere commentator on race. When, some years later, he spoke in the United States, his future wife Constance Webb was in the audience and she noted how James's 'deracinated' presence seemed to confuse some of those present.

> Very few, if any comrades in Los Angeles, in 1939, had met anyone from the West Indies. C.L.R. was a man beyond their understanding – a middle-class Englishman, straight out of Thackeray. And they had never heard a black man speak with such authority and grace . . . some of the comrades told him: 'You don't act like a black man.'

James's academic career was a disappointment to his parents, who had hoped it might lead to one of the professions open to black men such as the church or medicine. James, however, left school and followed in his father's footsteps, taking the first tentative steps along the path of becoming a schoolteacher. For a while he earned his living at his alma mater, Queen's Royal College, but teaching was not a vocation about which he felt deeply. It simply provided him with a living and the ability to indulge his twin passions, cricket and literature. For James it was not only the competitiveness of cricket that interested him, but the aesthetic and social 'rules' of the game held him spellbound, and he began to write passionately on the subject. His one extant poem, 'Pascall Bowled', a tribute to a legendary Trinidadian cricketer, Victor Pascall, dates from this period. The poem imagines how Pascall might have performed if matched against the best that England could send out to bat.

> And when to England back they reach
> And tread the sands of Dover's beach,
> And people crowd around to know
> The reason for their wretched show,
> A tear will shine in Hendren's eye,
> Jack Hearne will heave a bitter sigh,
> And Hobbs will shake his head and cry,
> 'Well, friends, we made a decent try,
> Armstrong, and Bardsley, Hearne and I,'
> But – Pascall bowled.

Yet it was as a writer and not as a cricketer that James first came to public attention. He co-founded and edited two of the Caribbean's pioneering literary journals, *Trinidad* (1929–30) and *The Beacon* (1931–3). As a young man in his twenties, he wrote and published short stories, and a number of essays on history and philosophy, as well as practically completing the novel called *Minty Alley* that would eventually be published in 1936. James's early short stories are characterised by an unsentimental concern with the life of the working-class poor of Trinidad. These stories do not resort to rhetorical flourishes in form or narrative technique. *Minty Alley* marked a forward development. In this novel James explored the relationship between the educated black Trinidadians (such as himself) and the uneducated; and he did so by embracing the Trinidadian vernacular as the language of his novel, as opposed to the usual imitations of metropolitan English. James's dialogue in this book provided his successors, most notably V.S. Naipaul, with a model for a true treatment of this material:

'You have cigarettes?'

'No,' said Haynes, feeling his pocket. Benoit asked him to get some.

'Let's have another beer.'

'Yes, man. Liquor is helpful.'

When, in 1932, it became possible for James to leave Trinidad and travel to England and meet up with his old friend, the cricketer Learie Constantine, he effectively ended his career as a writer of fiction. He might well have written more, and finer novels, but James was still developing as an intellectual and he fully understood the centrality of the British and European high culture which underscored his colonial education. As he observed in *Beyond a Boundary*, 'In March 1932 I boarded the boat for Plymouth. I was about to enter the arena where I was to play the role for which I had prepared myself. The British intellectual was going to Britain.' It would be twenty-six years before James returned to the country of his birth, but the next six years brought a remarkable transformation as he forced himself beyond the world of Thackeray and into the world of Marx.

James settled in Nelson, Lancashire, a town in which Constantine was playing cricket and which was known as 'Little Moscow' owing to the left-wing sympathies of its inhabitants. He soon gained a reputation as a man prepared to grapple with the intricacies of Marxism. He read and was greatly impressed by Trotsky's *The History of the Russian Revolution*, and in 1934 he joined the Trotskyist Marxist Group within the Independent Labour Party and promptly denounced Stalin. At the same time he was busy with research, in French and English, on the life of Toussaint L'Ouverture and the origins of the San Domingo slave revolution. These labours resulted in *The Black Jacobins*, a Marxist analysis of the Haitian slave rebellion. The book was immediately recognised as a masterpiece and has had a profound effect upon the way in which scholars and politicians have viewed colonial struggles in Africa and in the diaspora. Among its more radical challenges was James's invitation to view issues relating to race in their proper perspective: 'The race question is subsidiary to the class question in politics, and to think of imperialism in terms of race is disastrous. But to neglect the racial factor as merely incidental is an error only less grave than to make it fundamental.'

The Black Jacobins painted an unforgettably vivid portrait of its extraordinary subject. It was also the book which put forward the idea that the abolition of slavery in the British Empire was not motivated by strictly philanthropic reasons. The increasing financial strain of trying to control the slaves meant that inevitably the British would have to stanch the loss of money and lives being expended to maintain a moribund system. As James pointed out, slave owners could often not even afford to feed their 'property'. 'The ration was so small and given to them so irregularly that often the last half of the week found them with nothing.' In 1949, a little over a decade after James's book appeared, Eric Williams, formerly a student of James's at Queen's Royal College and soon to be Prime Minister of Trinidad, published *Capitalism and Slavery,* which was originally his doctoral dissertation at Oxford, and which dealt the death blow to any idea that there was not a strictly commercial rationale behind this act of decency; but Williams freely admitted that the chapter in James's book entitled 'The Owners', in which James makes a full-frontal attack on what he terms that 'venal race of scholars, profiteering panderers to national vanity, [who] have conspired to obscure the truth about abolition', provided him with the blueprint for his work.

It was not only in this area of historical reinterpretation that *The Black Jacobins* startled its readership. James's analysis of the nature of servile revolt had far-reaching consequences in the struggles for independence that soon erupted in both Africa and the Caribbean, for James had made it clear that black emancipation was always to be viewed as an integral part of wider historical changes. An extremely favourable review of *The Black Jacobins* in 1938 in the *New York Times* recognised the originality of James's approach. '"It is impossible to understand the San Domingo revolution unless it is studied in close relationship with the revolution in France," Mr James remarks almost casually in the course of his six-page bibliography.' By viewing the San Domingo rebellion in the context of the French Revolution, James forced his readers to rethink not only the past, but also the present.

Indeed, the work which *The Black Jacobins* most clearly complements is W.E.B. Du Bois's *Black Reconstruction* (1935), which also looked to rescue independent black radical thought from being divorced from, or buried beneath, the prevailing historical forces. The unforgettable conclusion of *The Black Jacobins* suggests how important the book was for the African world, which could glimpse, at last, the distant prospect of self-determination.

> Finally those black Haitian labourers and the Mulattos have given us an example to study. Despite the temporary reaction of Fascism, the prevailing standards of human liberty and equality are infinitely more advanced and more profound than those current in 1789. Judged relatively by these standards, the millions of blacks in Africa are as much pariahs in that vast prison as the blacks and Mulattos of San Domingo in the eighteenth century. The imperialists envisage an eternity of African exploitation: the African is backward, ignorant ... They dream dreams ... The Blacks of Africa are more advanced, nearer ready than were the slaves of San Domingo.

In an interview many years later, James reflected upon his departure from Trinidad in 1932: 'I arrived in England intending to make my way in the world as a writer of fiction, but the world went political and I went with it.' Inter-war England was at the hub of pan-African thought and activity, and James was refining his theoretical understanding of Marxism at the same time as he was becoming involved in the nascent movement for decolonisation. He fell in with Jomo Kenyatta and T. Ras Makonnen (the latter was the alias of the British Guianan pan-African leader George Griffity), and together with others, including his fellow Trinidadian George Padmore, they formed pressure groups and intellectual bureaus which they defined as 'clearing houses[s] of information', which could supply 'speakers to organisations [and] convene meetings and discussions' to organise in a militant fashion against the colonial fascism that they saw all around them. But it was James's increasing sympathy for Trotskyism that was the most important aspect of his intellectual growth in this period, and his fascination with the Trotskyite school of thought resulted in his eventual departure from England. He set sail for New York in 1938 with every intention of returning to London in the spring of 1939 for the cricket season.

He was leaving England with a quite staggering list of achievements. In 1932 he had published *The Life of Captain Cipriani: An Account of British Government in the West Indies,* and in the following year Leonard Woolf, of Bloomsbury fame, had published an abridged version of the same book under the title *The Case for West Indian Self-Government.* In 1932 there also appeared Learie Constantine's autobiography *Cricket and I,* which James was largely responsible for writing. Soon afterwards James found himself employed as a cricket correspondent for the *Manchester Guardian,* travelling the length and breadth of England. In 1936 his novel *Minty Alley* was finally published and in the same year his play *Toussaint L'Ouverture* opened on the stage of London's West End with Paul Robeson in the lead role. In 1937 he published *World Revolution: 1917–1936* and in the following year he began to edit the journal *International African Opinion.* In 1938 he also published both his translation from the French of Boris Souvarine's huge biography, *Stalin,* as well as *The Black Jacobins,* and 1939 saw the appearance of *A History of Negro Revolt.*

He had left Trinidad a man of letters, but he was leaving England six years later as one of the foremost political thinkers and historians of his age. His reason for moving on was Trotsky who had become interested in having James supervise the 'negro' work of the Socialist Workers' Party in the United States, the idea being that James might help to recruit black people from all strata of society. Trotsky had read James's 'orthodox' *World Revolution: 1917–1936* and, while not in agreement with every aspect of the book, he recognised in James a uniquely gifted individual. The thesis of James's book was that Stalin had chosen to rely upon the party bureaucracy to carry out the 'interests' of the Russian state, while Lenin had largely relied upon the powers of the mobilised masses. The formation of a new power base in the state bureaucracy itself was not viewed by James as a 'logical' development of Soviet Communism. Exposure to America, and the opportunity to meet Trotsky, would further 'radicalise' his thinking.

Almost immediately upon his arrival in the United States, James was seduced by what he perceived to be the vast and untapped revolutionary potential of this dynamic young nation. He completed a coast-to-coast speaking tour on behalf of the American Socialist Workers' Party, then travelled south to Mexico, where he spent some weeks with Trotsky discussing the desirability of developing a separate black movement within the party. James saw no need for this. He staunchly defended the rights of black people to struggle for equality independently outside the party; and he reminded Trotsky and others that it was the responsibility of the party to respect the unique nature of the black struggle. Despite their differences, James left Mexico with a profound respect for Trotsky and a year later, shortly after Trotsky's assassination, he remembered his friend:

> To appreciate his powers and his past, the enormous force of this many-sided and yet perfectly integrated personality, and to see him listening patiently to some inexperienced comrade putting forward his inexperienced ideas, to read letters in which he took up some apparently minor point and elaborated it meeting all possible objections one by one, was to have a great lesson in the difference between the superficial arrogance which often characterizes essentially sensitive men, and the ocean of strength, patience and resiliency which can come from complete devotion to a cause.

On his return to the United States, James was recognised by the leaders of the various Trotskyite organisations as an intellectual who could inject new life into a movement that was bogged down in sectarian disputes around the vexing 'Russian question'. War had just been declared in Europe, and a return to England was unlikely, so James threw himself into his work for the SWP, becoming a prolific pamphleteer and speaker. James's contact with black America, and his pronouncements upon it, forced a new debate on 'the negro question' within Marxist circles. Even as James became increasingly interested in the radical promise of black America, he guarded against black nationalism. Against the Marxists, James insisted on the autonomy of the black struggle and its compatibility with their own, but against the black nationalists he insisted that they see their struggle in the context of other like-minded struggles. The fact that Marcus Garvey could not, or would not, do so, resulted in a series of pronouncements on Garvey that could be shockingly hostile, such as this one: 'Garvey, however, was a race fanatic. His appeal was to black against white. He wanted purity of race. A great part of his propaganda was based on the past achievements of blacks . . . With that disregard of facts which characterizes the born demagogue, he proclaimed that there were 400 million Negroes in the world, when there are certainly not half as many. What does this remind us of? Who but Adolf Hitler?'

James fell deeply in love with the United States. His fifteen-year sojourn in the country, between 1938 and 1953, was characterised by his zealous attempts to match his own politics to the unique nature of the political culture that he discovered. He became the leader of a Trotskyite sect, the 'Johnson–Forest Tendency' (J.R. Johnson was his pseudonym as a pamphleteer), and with this small group of like-minded theorists he tried to develop a form of Marxism that was applicable to the United States. By the late 1940s his political and intellectual evolution had reached the stage where he had decided to reject his earlier conception of building a 'small mass party' and to emphasise instead the capacity of the masses for independent mobilisation.

Notes on Dialectics: Hegel, Marx, Lenin (1948), a volume based upon letters from James to other members of the Johnson–Forest Tendency, and distributed among them, argued that Trotsky and his followers had underestimated the importance of the Hegelian dialectic in favour of the construction of more pragmatic methods by which they might 'Bolshevise' America. Hegel's writings provided the Johnson–Forest Tendency with its language and its philosophical direction, which insisted upon a study of historical patterns and a more structured approach to dealing with the realities of modern capitalism. Thinking his way beyond Trotsky, James began to develop a strategy for building a revolutionary political party in an advanced capitalist society. He envisioned socialists working together with other social movements, as opposed to forming monolithic vanguard parties. In some ways, he anticipated the social unrest that came later with the Civil Rights movement and the campus protests of the 1960s.

James's brand of Marxism was shrewd in its appreciation of the conservative nature of American political culture, but it was also wildly optimistic in its analysis of the revolutionary zeal of the American people. One suspects that the increasingly theory-soaked Johnson–Forest Tendency would have fallen into political disrepair much sooner than it did, in the 1950s, had it not been for James's attachment to popular culture. This managed to keep the faction grounded in something approximating to reality. During his fifteen years in the United States James produced, along with countless articles and papers on politics, a sizeable body of cultural criticism. In his cultural writing he was often brilliantly accurate, as in his observation of Richard Wright's work and talent. It was James who first praised his younger friend's abilities, then warned him that his fiction would be 'blighted' if he continued to participate in the activities of the Communist Party. As James put it, 'the artist in uniform soon ceases to be an artist'.

While continuing to proclaim his faith in the revolutionary potential of the American masses, James always believed wholeheartedly in the individuality of the artist, and justified his belief in the importance of the artist by insisting that art offered an avenue of access to the minds of the people. Yet his belief in the political utility of art – his notion that art reflected the inner desires of the American masses, and would ultimately help to lead them to the barricades – resulted in some less than trenchant observations. To wit:

> To put it more harshly still, it is in the serious study of, above all, Charles Chaplin, Dick Tracy, Gasoline Alley, James Cagney, Edward G. Robinson, Rita Hayworth, Humphrey Bogart, genuinely popular novels like those of Frank Yerby (*Foxes of Harrow, The Golden Hawk, The Vixen, Pride's Castle*), men like David Selznick, Cecil De Mille, and Henry Luce, that you find the clearest ideological expression of the sentiments and deepest feelings of the American people and a great window into the future of America and the modern world.

In truth, a 'serious study' of Hollywood was likely to teach more about the cultural expressions of capitalism than about the 'deepest feeling of the American people'.

As brilliant as James could be in the field of cultural criticism, the driving force behind his work in this period was his concern for reconstructing Marxism in the United States, and this passion was always likely to distort his judgement in other fields. At one point in the 1940s, Richard Wright suggested to Ralph Ellison and James that together they produce a book called *The Negro Speaks*. Such a book would have had an important influence on American thinking about race, but James preferred to write for the SWP paper *Labor Action*, which was distributed free at factory gates.

As the 1940s gave way to the 1950s, James found himself in a quandary. He continued to believe in his political creed, but he had to acknowledge that he was toiling in the political somnolence of Eisenhower's America. Meanwhile, his political 'tendency' was beginning to divide along ideological lines, his health was beginning to fail him and then in 1952 he was arrested for 'passport violations' and interned for six months on Ellis Island. While waiting to see if his application for American citizenship would be accepted, James wrote *Mariners, Renegades and Castaways* (1953), a study of Melville. This short work of literary criticism offers a particular focus on *Moby Dick*, seeing Ahab as the embodiment of the totalitarian impulse behind capitalism's hunger for conquest and exploitation. In James's essentially political and moral reading, the 'renegade' Ahab loses his soul as he seeks to dominate man and nature. In its engagement with, and profound respect for, American literature this book was intended to bolster his case for citizenship, but in the autumn of 1953 James was ordered to leave the country and he set sail for England.

In later years James was to look back upon this period of his political life with disappointment. Despite his abiding affection for the United States, the country had defeated him in its refusal to rally behind his cry for 'World Revolution'. Much of his energy had been expended upon developing as fine a command of theoretical Marxism as any political thinker in the world, yet in doing so he had found himself addressing a severely limited section of the population, and in a vocabulary that was technical and exclusive. A decade later, in December 1962, James wrote to Martin Glaberman, one of his American political allies, and reminisced about his fifteen-year sojourn in the United States. 'It is perhaps the only thing in my life which I look back [on] not so much with bitterness, but with regret, with recognition of the fact that I wasted my strength, my time and my physical health on something that was absolutely useless.'

Between 1953 and 1958 he was based in London. From that vantage-point he was able to follow the decline and then the collapse of his political work in the United States, as his former colleagues squabbled among themselves and split into even smaller factions. But he was finding satisfaction elsewhere.

Some of his pan-Africanist work in the 1930s was now beginning to pay off, as the Gold Coast became the newly independent country of Ghana in 1957, and back 'home' in the Caribbean there was talk of independence and of a federation among the English-speaking islands. In 1958, at the invitation of Eric Williams, James returned to his native Trinidad to edit the political weekly of Williams's People's National Movement Party. James changed the title of the paper to *The Nation* and opened it up to national debate. But he had been away from his country for a quarter of a century, and after his long intellectual and political journey he found it difficult to deal with the insularity of Trinidad. He was insisting that the Caribbean region should identify with pan-African and Third World struggles for emancipation, but the newly formed West Indian Federation was already collapsing.

He had arrived in Trinidad fully aware that the Caribbean society of the 1950s was not revolutionary and that nationalism was clearly the most urgent issue on the agenda. Although he had no intention of abandoning his Marxism, he was also keen to take part in a regional struggle to identify a specifically Caribbean culture and sense of self. *Modern Politics* (1960) and *Party Politics in the West Indies* (1962) addressed the difficult issues facing the young nation states of the Caribbean, urging them to rally to the sides of their emerging artists such as V.S. Naipaul and George Lamming, and honour them as providers of a mirror in which Caribbean people could clearly view their lives being played out on the world stage. James felt that the peoples of the Caribbean might be stirred to action only if they could first identify and then be proud of their culture, high and low. In a lecture delivered as early as 1959 he got to the heart of the problem:

> In the Caribbean there are many things that are denied to us and will be denied to us for a long time to come. But the production of a supreme artist and all that he or she can give to us (including what lesser artists will gain), that we

> need not despair of . . . Let us create the conditions under which the artist can flourish. But to do that, we must have the consciousness that the nation which we are hoping to build, as much as it needs the pooling of resources and the industrialization and a higher productivity of labour, needs also the supreme artist.

But James underestimated the reactionary lassitude that permeated the Caribbean middle classes. Though he was scornful of a purely working-class and Afrocentric conception of West Indian identity, preferring to stress the classical Greek and modern European influence in art, politics, culture and morality, James was still perceived by large elements of the middle class as a firebrand. His view of the modern Caribbean as an outgrowth of the international capitalist economy, its cultural and historical uniqueness notwithstanding, disturbed many middle-class Caribbean people who, on the threshold of political independence, were fearful of the mass mobilisation of the poor and the working class.

Some ten years later, in 1973, James reflected on the intellectual bankruptcy of the West Indian middle class:

> I do not know any social class which lives so completely without ideas of any kind. They live entirely on the material plane. In a published address, Sir Robert Kirkwood quotes Vidia Naipaul, who has said of them that they seem to aim at nothing more than being second-rate American citizens. It is much more than that. They aim at nothing. Government jobs and the opportunities which association with the government gives allow them the possibility of accumulating material goods. That is all.

Inevitably James's 'radicalism' soon brought him into conflict with his old friend and pupil, Eric Williams, and so James, now in his sixties, again left Trinidad, only a few days before the country's independence.

That James went unheeded at this critical moment in twentieth-century Caribbean history may prove to be one of the region's most momentous mistakes. Soon after his departure the islands were swiftly exchanging the colonial yoke of British imperialism for the neo-colonial yoke of mass tourism and the more fully developed colonial yoke of trading 'agreements' and political 'assistance' from North America. There has been no sustained Caribbean effort to create an independent world in literature, politics or music, despite the fact that the Caribbean has produced extraordinary artists and writers.

James understood, as he said in a speech at the University of the West Indies in the 1960s, that it was only by the assiduous development of a 'national consciousness' that Caribbean people would be able to transcend 'this matter of shallow roots'. He also understood – and cited the Greek city-state and Ibsen's Norway as precedents – that size was no impediment to significance. To him it was essential that the Caribbean should embrace its great artists such as Wilson Harris, the calypsonian 'Mighty Sparrow', and of course Frank Worrell, Gary Sobers and countless other cricketers, and celebrate the uniqueness of their talent. But while James was busily providing the intellectual platform upon which a genuinely 'independent' Caribbean future might be built, politicians were already festooning themselves with titles, looking askance at their neighbours, and emptying their national treasuries in a pantomime of reactionary stupidity that eventually resulted in the unsavoury sight of Caribbean politicians urging Ronald Reagan to invade one of their neighbours.

James returned to England in 1962 and was now ready to complete and publish the book that would become his epitaph. *Beyond a Boundary* (1963) is part memoir, and partly a very personal book about cricket, but it is really an attempt by James to define the world of politics and the world of art. The great triumph of *Beyond a Boundary* is its ability to rise above genre and in its form explore the complex nature of colonial West Indian society. It accomplishes this by placing at its allegorical heart the most quintessentially English of games. James admired cricket because it was a great team sport and a great individual sport; the game allowed for sudden savage onslaughts of batting or bowling and suddenly it could turn and demand that the individual subordinate himself to the collective. This 'moral' game, he maintained, mirrored the unpredictability of life, in that it was both personal and social, highly formal yet open to abuse. As Derek Walcott pointed out in 1984, 'he [James] loves cricket above everything else, not because it is a sport, but because he has found in it all the decencies required for a culture'.

James had an extraordinary ability to write about sport in a way that linked it to other avenues of life concretely and provocatively. In this way he promoted not only our understanding of the game but also our understanding of the culture. When speaking of George Headley, the great West Indian batsman, he is as likely to compare him to Napoleon as to other practitioners of the cricketer's 'art'. Or, as in this example, James might remember something from his reading in American literature that will help his readers to grasp the nature of Headley's achievement:

> Mark Twain was once a pilot on the Mississippi. The bed of that river is always changing and a man is sounding all the time and calling out the changes. Mark Twain says that a pilot, whether on duty or not, is always hearing these soundings. Even when playing poker his mind registers them automatically and days after uses the latest results when piloting. Great batsmen are the same, they are not like you or me. An experience is automatically registered and henceforth functions as a permanent part of the organism.

In 1965 James returned to Trinidad as a journalist for the London *Times* to report on an England cricket team's tour of the West Indies. Upon his arrival in Trinidad, Eric Williams placed him under house arrest. After an international outcry James was released and allowed to continue his reporting, but the following year he chose once more to return to his native Trinidad and fight an election against Williams. James's party, the Workers' and Farmers' Party, captured a mere 2.8 per cent of the vote. Having suffered this electoral indignity James abandoned Trinidadian politics for good and returned to England.

After 1966 James continued to travel widely between Africa, the Caribbean and Europe, lecturing on politics, cricket, art and popular culture. He was now a truly diasporan man, at home in a Tanzanian village, on British television, or in a lecture hall at the University of the West Indies. In many ways his final two decades represent the richest period of his life as he was consulted by writers, politicians and scholars from all over the world, and extensively republished on both sides of the Atlantic. He was also able to renew his association with the United States, and in the late 1960s and 1970s he taught for a short while as a professor of humanities at Federal City College (now the University of the District of Columbia). This was a turbulent time in the history of the United States and James's 'colonial' notion of the interdependence of the African diaspora with Western civilisation brought him into conflict with those who advocated black nationalism and black separatism. When, in 1969, he found himself lecturing to a group of black students and teachers in Washington DC, he took it upon himself to remind them of exactly where he stood in the contemporary debate. 'I am not boasting about black is beautiful . . . Please, I don't go in for that. If other people want to, that's their affair, if they say "Black is beautiful", "Black is ugly", black is whatever they like. I am concerned with historical facts.' As always, he appealed to history and to reason. He would have made short work of the politically correct of our day.

The interconnectedness of historical events, and their dependence upon each other, was a principle most fully expressed in *The Black Jacobins,* and by adhering to this principle James was always able to place 'the whole' in some order without ever losing sight of 'the individual'. In an interview in London in 1967 he remarked,

'What you need in studying any historical subject is you must get some idea of the economic circumstances, you must also get some idea of the political circumstances, and you must get to know the literary circumstances. Only when you know these three, [do] you have some idea of the historical development of the period.' When he concluded that one element of a dearly held theory seemed either ahistorical or flawed, James never lacked the courage to tear down the whole structure and begin anew. Thus, in *Facing Reality* (1958), James is clear about his 'new' response to Leninism. 'It was a particular theory designed to suit a specific stage of working-class development. That stage of society is now past. The theory and the practice that went with it are now an anachronism, and, if persisted in, lead to one form or another of the counter-revolution. The first thing we must do is to purge ourselves of it.'

A few years ago V.S. Naipaul published his strangely compelling 'novel', *A Way in the World*, in which there is a character whose biographical details bear an unmistakable similarity to those of James. Naipaul, who like James was a product of Queen's Royal College in Trinidad, had reviewed *Beyond a Boundary* when it first appeared. He concluded his review by stating that the book 'gives base and solidity to West Indian literary achievement'. In subsequent years Naipaul would seldom be so generous towards either James or the Caribbean. James too had his quarrels with the Caribbean but, unlike Naipaul, he believed in the possibility that its people may achieve at the highest level. Wherever he went, he was always proud of himself as a product of the Caribbean. Naipaul's Caribbean, by contrast, is often intellectually moribund and backward-looking – not the sort of place that could have produced, say, himself. James is buried in Trinidad, and inscribed upon his tomb is a quotation from *Beyond a Boundary* which nicely epitomises the tenor of his life.

> Times would pass, old empires would fall and new ones take their place, the relations of countries and the relations of classes had to change, before I discovered that it is not the quality of

goods and utility which matter, but movement; not where you are or what you have, but where you are going and the rate at which you are getting there.

James's view of the world was fundamentally generous. While he wished to impress his opinions upon his readers and his listeners, he respected individuals whom he disagreed with, and saw virtue in work that ran counter to his political beliefs. (Paul Robeson remained loyal to Stalin in the 1930s, but James maintained a friendship with him and described him as the most remarkable man he had ever met.) He never lost sight of the autonomy of art and literature, and never sought to use either for crassly political purposes. 'Thackeray, not Marx, bears the heaviest responsibility for me,' he wrote in *Beyond a Boundary*. He believed in ideas, but he had an even greater faith in people, and this faith in people may have placed a humanising noose around his political neck.

As we are assaulted by our culture of the soundbite, the discursive, restless, curious and ultimately annealing intellect of this man is a measure of what we have lost. James knew where he came from and he knew where he was going, as he restlessly quarried his way towards knowledge. In the 1980s, in Thatcher's Britain, he found himself sought out by a new generation of admirers. I was among them. It was to his small room above the offices of *Race Today* in Brixton that I went to see him, not long before he died. I recall climbing a couple of flights of stairs and being ushered into his presence by the Jamaican-born poet Linton Kwesi Johnson. The frail James was watching cricket on television the way others ponder a chessboard. I talked idly, searching for a subject that would claim his attention. Finally, I mentioned the possibility of my going to teach in the United States. He turned from the television and looked at me. I asked him, should I go? He looked puzzled. Of course I should go. 'A young man must always go to where he can learn.'

1996

Edouard Glissant: Promiscuities

Edouard Glissant was born in 1928 in the hilly commune of Sainte-Marie in Martinique. He received a French colonial education at the Lycée Schoelcher in the capital, Fort-de-France. The school was generally acknowledged to be the best on the island; Frantz Fanon, who was three years older than Glissant, was a pupil there, and Aimé Césaire, who had recently returned to the island, was the professor of classical and modern languages. After finishing at the Lycée, Glissant travelled to Paris, where he studied ethnology and completed a doctorate in philosophy at the Sorbonne. Glissant was politically active in Paris, particularly in the Front Antillo-Guyanais pour l'Indépendance, a party which agitated futilely for the political independence of the Francophone regions of the Caribbean. In Paris he also published three volumes of verse, foremost among them being *Les Indes: Poèmes de l'une et l'autre terre,* which appeared in 1955. This epic poem about Columbus's voyage of discovery to the New World lays bare the rapacity and greed of that 'civilising' mission and locates Columbus's Atlantic crossing at the beginning of a tradition which continues to this day: the tradition in which Europeans distort the history of the Antillean world to legitimise their killing of the native peoples and their enslavement of the blacks. The poem begins with Columbus's first act of misrepresentation as he declares, 'And if the Indies are not where you are, I do not care! Indies you will be. West Indies, so that my dream will be fulfilled.'

The first of Glissant's six novels, *La Lézarde*, appeared in 1958. It is a tale of political intrigue set against the backdrop of the elections in Martinique in 1945 and tells the story of a group of idealistic political activists, who plot the assassination of a government official in order to ensure electoral victory. The novel is full of existential musings about the emphatically anti-linear notions of Martiniquan space and time, the twin concepts which, even at this early stage in his career, Glissant believed underscored Antillean consciousness. Although the novel won the prestigious Prix Renaudot, its discursive form and meandering narrative structure baffled many readers and critics. The events in Glissant's second novel, *Le Quatrième Siècle* (*The Fourth Century*) (1964), prefigure those in *La Lézarde*, and some of the individuals in Glissant's fourth novel, *La Case du commandeur* (*The Overseer's Horse*) (1981), are characters who first saw the light of day in *La Lézarde*. In *Le Quatrième Siècle* Papa Longoue, the wise old medicine man of *La Lézarde*, who is a last Caribbean link with Africa, encounters a young intellectual named Mathieu, who tries to encourage the older man to interpret his history in terms of Western dates and motives, a reading that the old man resists. In *La Case du commandeur* Glissant traces the historical roots of Marie Celat, one of the young radicals from *La Lézarde*, to the arrival of an indeterminate slave-ancestor who probably arrived in the Caribbean around 1715. Glissant's fictional remapping of the Antilles involves not only the continuity of character across the boundaries of individual novels but also something that distinguishes such fiction from its European counterpart: his affirmation of his belief in the dialectical relationship between hill and plain, forest and ocean, so that nature becomes a central part of his vision.

Malemort, Glissant's third novel, which appeared in 1975, has no chronologically sequential plot line and ranges back and forth as it contrasts the plight of the newly arrived slave with that of the Martiniquan bourgeoisie. During the course of this dense and complex novel, many characters are referred to and examined as though they are just one person. This innovative approach to the details of space and time is repeated in the novel *Mahagony* (1987), in which the history of the maroons is linked to the history of the mahogany trees and, by extension, to the history of the island as a whole. Once again characters from Glissant's earlier works make an appearance, including the narrator of *La Lézarde,* who deigns to comment on his 'creator', one Edouard Glissant. Events and relationships are self-consciously blurred in this novel and, true to form, Glissant encourages his readers to dig the tunnels and build the bridges that link his disparate narratives. Glissant's latest novel, *Tout-Monde* (*One and All*), appeared six years ago and further develops his formally complex historical and literary vision, but, in common with those that preceded it, the novel was regarded by many critics as being somewhat wilfully oblique. It is the obliqueness of Glissant's vision, surely, that has led him to pursue his interest in William Faulkner and to produce a book about him.

Faulkner's universe was defined by the plantation, the twilight zone where black and white met and danced a strange, often highly artificial, dance around the inconvenient fact of the other's presence. Ultimately it was a paradoxical world of strained co-existence; a world of cruelty and injustice, but a world in which both black and white had little choice but to recognise each other. At times, the validity of their very existence could only be properly authenticated by the grating presence of the 'other'. This 'fact' led Faulkner to the structural strategy that provided the greater part of his finest writing. In such a world of vigorously and uncomfortably close relations, there can never be just one story, a master-narrative to which the storyteller (or, if truth be told, the historian) can claim fealty. There is always the disruptive 'truth' of the other person's presence, the other person's story. Glissant properly recognises Faulkner's fiction as a type of writing in which 'linearity gets lost' and he admires Faulkner for it. He understood that the quest for purity, for legitimacy, was bound to fail in Faulkner's New World: in *Absalom! Absalom!* an inseparable tangle of relationships throws a dark shadow across family, in this case the Sutpens. Try as hard as they may, Faulkner's people can never view their history as simply encounter and transcendence. Southern space and Southern time deny the Sutpens and other Faulknerian families access to such reductive strategies.

When he was a visiting professor in Baton Rouge, Louisiana in 1988, Glissant decided to take the opportunity to travel to Oxford, Mississippi to seek out Faulkner the man and Faulkner the writer. 'The Road to Rowan Oak', the first of seven chapters, begins conventionally enough with the writer and his family preparing for, and then undertaking, the journey across the state line into Mississippi. Only a few pages into the book, however, the travel narrative suddenly stumbles and Glissant begins to digress. One moment Glissant is visiting a Southern plantation and being shown a clump of trees where slaves were probably buried; the next moment the author's mind appears to have drifted off into an entirely different world:

> In our countries victimized by History where the histories of many peoples are intertwined, works of nature are the true historical monuments: Goree Island, where all those Africans were hurled into the abyss of slave ships; Mount Pelée, and the disappearance of the city of Saint-Pierre; the underground dungeons of Dubruc Castle at Caravalle Point, again in Martinique, where those same Africans arrived (at least those who survived the voyage); the Sierra Maestra and the adventures of the Bearded Revolutionaries; and the Caiman woods, where the first oath of the Haitian Revolution was taken, a wood whose trees are scarred by erosion and where the wind yawns no longer.

Suddenly we seem to find ourselves in a lecture hall trying hard to follow the complicated thoughts of a lecturer who appears oblivious to the fact that he has lost his audience.

Eventually Glissant arrives at Rowan Oak, the house in which Faulkner lived and worked for most of his productive life. Once again there is a noticeable tonal shift. Indeed, the prose swells in such a grandiose manner that it serves to obscure Glissant's actual response to the place.

> It was as though the aura of his works had elevated the building and its surroundings to a state of splendid indifference, so that they transcended their origins. Can literature make one forget grief and injustice? Or, rather, is literature, and particularly the work of Faulkner, inextricably tied to grief and injustice so as to be able to point them out or fight against them?

Is the house bigger or smaller than Glissant imagined? Is it dark or light? Is it overrun with tourists, or is it abandoned? With Glissant, there seems to be an almost indecent rush to the discourse of abstract theoretical speculation. When we return to *terra firma,* it soon becomes clear that Glissant is now more concerned with Faulkner the writer than with Faulkner the man. In fact, he is stubborn in his refusal to drift too far beyond the 'professional' Faulkner.

> We sit down on the narrow staircase that leads up to the bedrooms. I have no desire to go upstairs, an utter lack of interest in the personal. Faulkner was above all a man who would sit at his desk or conscientiously laze on his veranda. I choose to wander in the garden. He and I are alike in the way we focus on huge ants employed in a task we cannot define or really place, ants like the characters in our works.

The greater part of *Faulkner, Mississippi* is taken up with Glissant's reflections on the writings of his hero.

Those reflections are generally sound, but they hardly add up to a redrawing of the Faulknerian map. It is difficult to disagree, for example, with this typical rumination:

> When Faulkner was writing, what he put at risk was

> the supreme institution of this Southern community. He questioned its very legitimacy, its original establishment, its Genesis, its irrefutable source. All his works are shaped by an unsurpassable *a priori*, a question putting everything in vertigo: How to explain the 'beginnings' of the South – this monopoly of the land by Whites from Europe, actually from nowhere, all of them (in the writing) prone to violence? They clearly had no right to buy these 'Big Woods' from the hands of the last Indians, guardians of the earth, who themselves clearly had no right to sell it.

No controversy there; but at the conclusion of such a passage one is left wondering where this is leading. Certainly not towards a deeper understanding of Faulkner, or an original reassessment of his work.

The truth is the subject of Glissant's enquiry into Faulkner is Glissant. The further one reads in this book, the clearer it becomes that Glissant's fascination with Faulkner is an unapologetic attempt to understand his own concerns, thematic and structural. Being a writer from the 'impure' world of the Caribbean, where miscegenation has necessarily contributed to the identity of the society, Glissant cannot hope to make literature without bumping up against the enormity of this topic. And this was also Faulkner's predicament and opportunity.

> It is not fitting to assume that Faulkner (whom I see neither as an aristocrat nor as a commoner but as a man of the world) was brutally shocked by miscegenation or illegitimacy. Both loom as the torment to which individuals are subjected . . . If Faulkner was not offended by racial mixing, he nonetheless may have thought that it was a potential ordeal for those who bear it. He especially feared (the people in the county feared) the idea of miscegenation.

Glissant sees himself and Faulkner sharing a concern with the tangled world of the plantation, which means that they must both embrace the *idea* of miscegenation, and also reflect upon violence, genealogy, defeat, loss and a future which can only be understood by travelling into the past.

Faulkner's narrative technique fascinates Glissant, for he has employed a similar method in his own novels, so that he might convince his readers of the irreducibility of history to a single story. Glissant's Faulkner, like Glissant himself, rejects linearity and celebrates 'feeling'.

> The techniques of this literature, its prose and its architecture, also serve to defer. Faulkner suspends the rigorous narrative rules that have dominated Western literature. Through this gap, this suspension, for example, he gives depth to his characters' 'interior monologues' and explorations of conscience.

Ambiguity, evasion, speculation: these also are the devices he has utilised in his own fiction. Faulkner turns out to be a rather Glissantian writer: Glissant employs these Faulknerian methods also in his book on Faulkner. That's the trouble. Such complications and strategies of indirection may deliver riches in a novel, where the drama of events unfolding (however slowly) and the pleasures of discovering character (however obliquely) can compensate for the writer's peculiarities of narration, but in other forms of writing, such as history or literary reflection, in which there is more necessity for characters to be explained than discovered, we have a right to expect the writer not to obscure his focus. A little narrativity goes a long way, particularly if the writer intends to dispense with the linearity of time.

In order to understand Glissant's stubborn refusal to engage with the 'rules' of narration, we must turn in part to politics. Many left-wing French writers have long viewed political activism as an essential part of their task, and some have even reached the conclusion that their activism gives them certain epistemological privileges, in that it allows them to be as subjective as they wish in their written work. And Glissant has certainly been active on the political stage. Between 1959 and 1965 the French government, nervous about his commitment to anti-colonial political activity, forbade his return to Martinique and prevented him from leaving France for Algeria. However, it is possible that an explanation for the riot of subjectivity in Glissant's style may be found not in the left-wing politics of France, but in the left-wing politics of the Francophone Caribbean – specifically, in the political ideal of the literary imagination formulated by Aimé Césaire.

In the 1930s Césaire returned from Europe armed not only with his belief in 'negritude', but also with the much more alarming idea that utilising the poetic imagination was in itself a political instrument which might lead to revolution. Césaire believed that the colonial mind was essentially inert and fossilised, and that only a radical descent into subjectivity by the writer could break the atrophied psychology of the Antillean. Because a full engagement with the unconscious processes of memory and imagination had been deemed unacceptable by the colonial powers, Césaire insisted that those were precisely the regions of human thought that needed to be stimulated if there was to be any hope of liberating the Antillean mind. According to Césaire, a Francophone Caribbean writer had an overwhelming responsibility to be extremely intense in his experience; this heightening of subjectivity was itself a political commitment. The writer should be allowed to fly high and wild, for his political commitment would keep him anchored in the world. The dense, often impervious, nature of the writing mattered little as long as the writer continued to probe his own imagination and stimulate that of his imaginatively oppressed readers.

Francophone intellectuals – metropolitan or Antillean – have a habit of formulating their ideas at the level of generality, while those of the Anglophone world prefer something more empirical, pragmatic, accountable to reality. At the First Conference of Negro-African Writers and Artists in Paris in 1956, a conference reported on by James Baldwin in an essay called 'Princes and Powers', Edouard Glissant spoke at great length. Other speakers included Alioune Diop and Leopold Senghor from the Francophone world, and Richard Wright and George Lamming from the Anglophone. Baldwin remarked on the frustration and incomprehension of the morally demanding 'Bible-clutching black Anglo-Saxons' when faced with the abstractions of French philosophical thought.

Such intense subjectivity and rampant discursivity will seem even more baffling when they are used as the keys to Faulkner's kingdom. Nobody can accuse Faulkner of easy accessibility, but he certainly never confused impenetrable subjectivity with revolutionary action. Again, Glissant's account of Faulkner sheds more light on Glissant than on Faulkner. But then Glissant has been consistent across time and across genres: he flouts the old expectations of literary discourse in everything he writes. In 1961 when his play *Monsieur Toussaint* was published and performed, one exasperated critic was moved to comment:

> the development of the plot is not predicated on the chronological unfolding of events as a long chain of interlinking causes and effects. The play records an ever-expanding consciousness that tends to encompass the entire insular space and times. Hence, the text abounds in place names and events that have no significance in the story line.

Why should Faulkner have been spared the 'revolutionary' style?

Glissant's essays are no different. His first collection of essays, *Soleil de la conscience* (*The Sun of Consciousness*), appeared in 1956 and was written while he was still in Paris. It immediately established his concern with his own status as an Antillean man trapped within the framework of French culture. He declared his intent to search for a poetics capable of syncretistically joining Antillean time, space, language and nature into new artistic forms that might more properly reflect the disruptive lack of symmetry which, in Glissant's view, characterised the New World. *L'Intention poétique* (*The Poetic Purpose*) was published in 1969 and includes reflections on art, literary figures, cultural problems and history. At its centre is a long meditation on the essence of language and on its complex relationship to the poetry that is produced in the Caribbean. In this essay Glissant insisted on the introduction of new concepts of language to replace the concepts of old Europe. He wished to knock the bourgeois stuffing out of French, to test its limits, to imbue it with new meaning and style. Only in this manner, he argued, would the Antillean world arrive at an aesthetic that could be true to all the realities of the region.

Glissant broadened his canvas in *Le Discours antillais* (*Antillean Discourse*), which appeared in 1981, and added essays on sociology, anthropology and economics to his literary and linguistic discussions. His aim was essentially the same: to provide a model of how an Antillean person might think with independence and pride in a manner that is not Caribbean, but 'Creole'. To be 'Creole' involves accepting *métissage* or race mixing as the dynamic element in the creation of a uniquely 'impure' Antillean society. To grasp the import of Glissant's idea one needs first to understand the difference – as he would see it – between 'Creole' and 'Caribbean'. Caribbeanness is generally understood to be the process of Americanisation that is visited upon those of European, African and Asian origin in the Caribbean archipelago. In many ways this Americanisation can be seen as a form of New World colonisation, so that one can arrive from Spain or Portugal (as was the case with many who travelled to the Dominican Republic or Cuba), and become Americanised without ever becoming creolised. Creolisation involves the vigorous interaction of European, African and Asian elements to produce something new and unique, on the same shared soil and in the same crucible of history. And just as Faulkner's South was dying towards the end of his life, and being replaced by a new order of Civil Rights and integration, Glissant is similarly worried about the 'dying' of the Creole tradition, for, to this day, the French Antilles remain *départements* which must share their identity with metropolitan France. Moreover, there are no more Africans arriving in the region to replenish the process of creolisation, and those who do arrive are traditionally Europeans, who are generally very receptive to Americanisation as opposed to creolisation. It is against this background of an Americanisation, which is in danger of ousting the creolising Antillean society, that Glissant continues to produce his work, including his influential essays.

Poetics of Relation is Glissant's fourth collection of articles and talks, dating back to the 1980s. (The book originally appeared in French in 1990.) It is a ruminative volume, which attempts to map a future for the Caribbean region, a future that involves the region first discovering the courage to look the past in the face with neither shame nor fear. Unfortunately, the essays are shot through with the now familiar philosophical ponderings and theoretical digressions, which subvert any possibility of coherent argument. Discussing his notion of *échos-monde,* Glissant seems to stir together as many disparate examples as he can find. But, after the 'dazzle', one is left wondering about the relevance of the overall point that has been made.

> William Faulkner's work, Bob Marley's song, the theories of Benoit Mandelbrot, are all *échos-monde.* Wifredo Lam's painting (flowing together) or that of Roberto Matta (tearing apart); the architecture of Chicago and just as easily the shantytowns of Rio or Caracas; Ezra Pound's *Cantos* but also the marching of schoolchildren in Soweto are *échos-monde.*

Is there anything that isn't? And Glissant's attempts at further explanation – 'In Relation analytic thought is led to construct unities whose interdependent variances jointly piece together the interractive totality. These unities are not models but revealing *échos-monde*' – only make matters murkier.

What is clear is that Glissant's theory of Relation involves a restatement of his refusal to accept the Western logic of linear sequence as a mode within which he is prepared to trammel his thought. Time is to be regarded as mutable, and the true Creole aesthetic is one that accepts that neither time nor history – in the Western sense – is to be trusted: 'Memory in our works is not a calendar memory; our experience of time does not keep company with the rhythms of the month and year alone.' Glissant understands Relation to be a synthesising space in which opposites can live comfortably together and where, as in the works of Alejo Carpentier, there is little difference between the animate and the inanimate. Glissant detects a similar synthesis in the Guyanese landscapes of Wilson Harris, in which the notions of exterior and interior co-exist as one unity. According to Glissant, this vision of New World space and time first became clear after Columbus's 'discovery' that the world was not linear but circular. Therefore, in the consciousness of the Antillean world, time is to be read as cyclical. It is also to be understood that the Antillean world has the capacity to bestow culture upon nature, and the propensity to introduce the seasonal rhythms of nature into the very soul of man.

Not surprisingly, Glissant looks for evidence to back up his theory of Relation in the works of Faulkner, who (in this book, as in *Faulkner, Mississippi*) he claims as an essential man of the plantation. But it is among his own Caribbean contemporaries that Glissant is most successfully able to identify the 'irrelevance' of the Western construction of linear historical time as the writers go about their business of creating what Glissant understands to be a fully Antillean vision of self and society.

> Just how were our memory and our time buffeted by the Plantation? Within the space apart that it comprised, the always multilingual and frequently multiracial tangle created inextricable knots within the web of filiations, thereby breaking the clear, linear order to which Western thought had imparted such brilliance. So Alejo Carpentier and Faulkner

> are of the same mind, Edward Kamau Brathwaite and Lezama Lima go together; I recognize myself in Derek Walcott, we take delight in the coils of time in García Márquez's century of solitude. The ruins of the Plantation have affected American cultures all around.

Glissant uncovers ample evidence of the prevalence of associative, as opposed to linear, thought in the literature of the region, and he bestows upon the artists the responsibility of being in the vanguard of building a new and more relevant society, regarding them as the key architects of a confident, independent Caribbean.

By insisting on the essentially associative character of the Antillean mind, however, Glissant leaves himself open to the accusation that perhaps the people of the Antilles are not capable of logical or Western thought (as if logical thought is only a Western form of thought, and there is such a thing as 'the Antillean mind'), and therefore suffered from a need for rule from Europe. And that is not Glissant's only error. Even more damning is the suggestion that those who do think in a logical manner, in both literature and politics, are somehow betraying their own people's essence. Such romanticism, with its simple and sentimental notion of authenticity, does not serve the people about whom Glissant writes, nor does it illuminate their past, their present or their future. Too much of the 'revolutionary' rhetoric of the colonised world has involved the easy embrace of self-serving essentialisms (even as it thunders against other essentialisms) that reject the 'West' but offer only myths and abstractions in return. In the realm of literature, certainly, one is all too often left shaking one's head in bewilderment. And in the political arena such romanticism is generally the prelude to a new era of postmodern, postcolonial underdevelopment, which all too quickly segues into civil strife, poverty and worse.

There is little in *Poetics of Relation* to surprise readers who are familiar with Glissant's earlier work, or those who have read the essays of Wilson Harris or Antonio Benítez-Rojo. These writers have already, like Glissant, pointed to the existence of cracks and fissures in the narrative line of Caribbean thought and literature, and attempted to account for the subsequent emergence of what Benítez-Rojo has called 'ethnologically promiscuous texts'. All three writers would probably find themselves in agreement with V.S. Naipaul's observation in *The Middle Passage* (1962): 'Living in a borrowed culture, the West Indian, more than most, needs writers to tell him who he is and where he stands.' In their similar ways, and in three different languages, they have all embarked upon the literature of nation-building. As Wilson Harris states about his own work (and it remains applicable to them all), he is writing literature 'which reads back through the shock of place and time for omens of capacity, for thresholds of capacity that were latent'.

In the French Caribbean world, the younger writers, most notably Raphaël Confiant and Patrick Chamoiseau, have already taken up Glissant's thinking and developed it into their own theories of 'Créolite', according to which they view the entire world of the Francophone Caribbean, its language, its history and its literature, through a single theoretical lens. The avatars of Créolite seek to undermine French cultural influence by destabilising the language, which they accomplish by synthesising the grammar and the vocabulary of the Creole 'language' with those of 'standard' French. With this new diction, they claim to have created the instrument with which writers can now properly explore Antillean reality. While Glissant's notion of 'creolisation' strives to concentrate upon process, Créolite always seems to be in danger of establishing rules, approving texts and generally dictating a hierarchy of action and values, all of which appear to be antithetical to individual literary practice. Still, it has not impeded the literary practice of Confiant and Chamoiseau themselves. Like their distinguished elder, the younger writers have a radical theory, but they seem able to produce 'ethnologically promiscuous texts' which nonetheless rise to a sustained, legible and affecting dramatic mode. Indeed, the introduction of plot and character into their polyphonic worlds, brings to a welcome end the Francophone fondness for 'revolutionary' difficulty, the compulsive and programmatic discursiveness to which, on the evidence of both *Faulkner, Mississippi* and *Poetics of Relation*, Edouard Glissant remains firmly committed.

1999

V.S. Naipaul

I

That writers have a huge capacity to dwell, somewhat self-indulgently, upon the price paid for success in their vocation, will come as little surprise to most. From Rilke's assertion that one must look 'in the deepest places of your heart, [and] acknowledge to yourself whether you would have to die if it were denied you to write', by way of Faulkner's declaration that he would kill – a grandparent if necessary – in order to write, through to Mailer's unashamedly pugilistic metaphors for prosodic composition, one is left in no doubt that writing is not for the faint-hearted.

V.S. Naipaul has long been a proponent of this philosophy of the writer as vocational victim. Yet Naipaul has not been so much concerned with letting us know what he will do in order to write, it is what he has done to himself – what he has given up over the years – that he has seemed inordinately keen for us to acknowledge. He has long sponsored the myth of himself as a man who has spurned any sense of place or community in order to pursue his global peregrinations and deliver judgements in legendary, unforgiving prose. Moreover, the region of the heart is a place that Naipaul, more than any writer of his generation, has seemed determined to avoid. In fact, until he published *Finding the Centre* (1984) it was a place of which Naipaul – *A House for Mr Biswas* (1961) apart – seemed ignorant, the inference being that to submit to any emotion or passion might deflect him from his demanding, all-consuming career as a writer. Now, in his autumnal years,

Naipaul appears to be slowly undertaking his most difficult journey, as he travels across the landscape of his life towards this one elusive zone.

Naipaul's decade-long desire to locate the heart appears to have been born out of his growing sense of mortality. *A Way in the World,* his twelfth work of fiction (and twenty-second book), continues this process of 'revisionism' and inches him one step closer to a true 'confession' of his yearnings and his needs. In its moving climax the novel seems to suggest that even Naipaul now realises that to give up everything to be a writer, particularly the generosity of spirit which allows one to tolerate the foolishness often to be found in one's fellow man, is to commit an act of great folly. To adopt a heartless position – one that has little concern for people beyond ridiculing their sad manifestations of self-delusory grandeur, one that seemingly relishes the exposition of man's essential fragility, one that ceaselessly mocks man's capacity to dare and dream – is to pour scorn on oneself as son, brother, father, husband. Such a position undermines the elemental bonds that unite us one to the other and ultimately, if one is a writer, damages one's capacity to write fiction or nonfiction.

Vidiadhar Surajprasad Naipaul was born in the small market town of Chaguanas in central Trinidad on 13 August 1932. His family were Orthodox Hindus of East Indian origin and one of his grandparents had migrated to Trinidad as an indentured labourer at the turn of the century. The family were untypical of the average Indian migrants in that they were, on both sides, Brahmins, high-caste Indians who, by the very act of migration, defiled themselves and lost caste. Naipaul's family (the maternal side of which provided a model for the Tulsi family in *A House for Mr Biswas*) fought a vigorous, but inevitably losing, battle to maintain some form of 'purity' in the face of the creolising ways of the Caribbean. Sadly, the truth was they were lost. To return to India was economically impossible and, even if they found some way to do so, regaining caste status there would involve complex purification rituals. There was no choice but to make the best of it and remain in Trinidad, a 'no man's land', a colonial milieu of second-rate Europeans and former negro slaves.

As a child born into this world, Naipaul desired only to leave it and as soon as possible. In 1950, at the age of eighteen, he won a scholarship to study at Oxford University: he later described this departure as having been 'saved' from 'extinction'. No longer West Indian East Indian or East Indian West Indian, in England he could begin to remake himself as something new. Not, however, as an Englishman: as a 'double' migrant he knew better than to try to remodel himself as a man tainted with the transitory, unreliable connotations of nationality. There would be no fealty to place, to personal history, to family, to people. Vidiadhar Surajprasad, soon to become the more anonymous V.S., would remake himself as a writer, unburdened by responsibility to anything beyond the word and himself.

The literary career that Naipaul began, post-Oxford, has been outstanding, there being hardly a literary prize which he has not collected. His books are published in uniform editions, they are widely translated and he travels the world giving lectures and receiving awards and honorary degrees. Still, his has been a controversial career, not because of the quality of his output, but because of the nature of his commentary on the people of the developing or Third World – in other words, his own people. It has often appeared as though, in order to distinguish himself as separate and apart, Naipaul has decided to be hypercritical of and at times extraordinarily insensitive to the human condition as it appears in, what he would term, less civilised parts of the world than the West, including, of course, his native Trinidad. As long ago as August 1958, in the *Times Literary Supplement*, Naipaul contemptuously dismissed Trinidad: 'Superficially, because of the multitude of races, Trinidad may seem complex, but to anyone who knows it, it is a simple, colonial, philistine society.'

In July 1961, in *The Times*, he speaks again of Trinidad, this time as 'a very small, unimportant island, where no building was 150 years old, and where the weather never varied'. The sardonic, often bitter tone was established early in Naipaul's career. The subsequent years have been peppered with a litany of depressingly familiar transgressions in both his work and his public utterances. One of his most controversial interviews was with the *New York Times* in 1980. Referring to his Asian readers, Naipaul claimed that they 'do not read ... If they read at all, they read for magic.' Of the African, he said, 'I don't count the African readership and I don't think one should. Africa is a land of bush, again, not a very literary land.' He went on to speak of Trinidad:

> I can't be interested in people who don't like what I write, because if you don't like what I write, you're disliking me ... I can't see a Monkey – you can use a capital M, that's an affectionate word for the generality – reading my work. No, my books aren't read in Trinidad now – drum-beating is a higher activity, a more satisfying activity ... I do not have the tenderness more secure people can have towards bush people ... I feel threatened by them. My attitude and the attitude of people like me is quite different from people who live outside the bush or who just go camping in the bush on weekends ... These people [Trinidadians] live purely physical lives, which I find contemptible ... It makes them interesting only to chaps in universities who want to do compassionate studies about brutes.

Naipaul first came to literary attention in the late 1950s and early 1960s, as part of a group of writers from the Caribbean who relocated themselves in England. Alongside him were such novelists as George Lamming, Edgar Mittelholzer, Sam Selvon, Andrew Salkey and Jan Carew. Naipaul, however, differed from his colleagues in his unequivocally expressed desire to put his Caribbean past behind him, to escape from what he perceived to be colonial oblivion. Unlike other Caribbean writers, or African writers such as Chinua Achebe, Wole Soyinka and Ousmane

Sembène – writers who, at this historical stage, were inspired by the ambition to give a new voice to their people's history, to create a modern literature for their respective countries, to re-examine the whole legacy of a colonial past – Naipaul wanted nothing whatsoever to do with such 'political' writing. From the onset he consciously wrote in an oppositional tradition to these other Commonwealth or, as they later came to be known, postcolonial writers. For him neither Africa, nor the Caribbean, nor for that matter India, was a viable world in which to pursue a writing career. The only set of cultural values which possessed any validity was that of the West. In a radio interview in New Zealand in 1972 he explained his feelings as follows:

> Coming from a place like Trinidad which I always felt existed on the edge of the world, far away from everything else, not only physically but also in terms of culture, I felt I had to try very hard to rejoin the world. So I had this great drive to achievement.

Naipaul's early work, up until *A House for Mr Biswas,* can be seen as a critical exploration of Trinidad. After this novel Naipaul's misanthropy emerges as he builds a wall of self-regard between himself and the people who produced him. At this juncture the form of the novel seems to fail him as his vision becomes smaller and soured. People begin to irritate him with their foolishness and with their adherence to old and irrational beliefs. But novels are about people, and if the novelist believes in nothing else, if he has no political fealty, or national drum to beat, he must care for people. Naipaul's sense of his own Trinidadian history having marked him out as inferior, having failed him before he even had a chance to begin, caused him to spurn the Caribbean and to begin his global wanderings. But such alienation, such despair as he carried with him, never slipped gracefully from his shoulders as he discovered new worlds. His trudging became, over the years, more ponderous, his fictions more laboured, more caustic and impatient.

During the 1960s and 1970s Naipaul increasingly equated Western experience with universal experience, and when he examined Third World societies he rendered judgements which made it clear that he saw these societies only in terms of mimicry and barbarity. His became a dark vision, particulary in *Guerrillas* (1975) and *A Bend in the River* (1979), novels that stubbornly refused to engage with the complex issue of what created these societies in the first place. These 'Conradian' novels do not provide any sense of redemption, or just plain hope, beyond the colonial phase. We lurch from doom to despair as Naipaul denies the evidence of continued resistance and struggle against tyrannies, some of which grow like a cancer within the bellies of developing societies, some of which are imposed from outside.

This undisguised contempt for the people of the Third World has been the most problematic aspect of his career. He has fired off volley after volley of disaffected bulletins, in fictional and nonfictional forms, from what he terms 'half-made societies', places the West has abandoned or 'dark' regions of the globe it has simply chosen to ridicule or ignore. Naipaul the chronicler of 'primitive' societies is highly conscious of his role in the tradition of delivering 'truths' about heathens, a role which follows in the footsteps of Trollope, Conrad and Graham Greene. Naipaul's castigation of these 'barbaric' non-Western societies, where neo-colonial elites merely ape the West, where the 'resistance' of the masses is to be understood only as 'resentment', has gone unchallenged by the West, in large part due to his presentation of himself as a man with colonial connections of his own, despite his obvious distaste for, and impatience with any cultural value which is non-Western.

Through it all, Naipaul has appeared thoroughly oblivious to the disparaging response from Third World critics, who have come to view him as merely a Eurocentric foreign correspondent for the West. He has ignored their criticism and continued to emphasise anti-intellectualism among the 'other', deep-set primitivism, social malaise, filth, crime – all the inevitable conclusions of these people having had the temerity to reject the civilising presence of a colonial master. Naipaul's only concern seems to have been to plough his own path as a deliverer of veracities which he, in his unique position as a part of both worlds, is duty-bound to deliver. Such writings fly in the face of the tradition of the Empire writing back, a tradition that dates back to the 1950s. It is against this tradition of African, Caribbean and Indian writing that Naipaul so consciously works, for he has been reluctant to see any ills in the Third World which could be intimately connected with European 'barbarity'.

With *Guerrillas* and *A Bend in the River,* Naipaul left his Caribbean contemporaries far behind in terms of the critical praise that was heaped upon him. He had achieved his aim of making it clear that he was not one of 'these Commonwealth writers who specialize in stories of local colour'. His nonfictional works of this period, *India: A Wounded Civilization* (1971), *The Return of Eva Peron with the Killings in Trinidad* (1975) and *Among the Believers* (1981), are informed by Naipaul's growing intolerance for the 'bush'. By the time he is travelling for *Among the Believers* it is clear that he has undisguised contempt for worlds which do not accord with his own view of civilisation. He travels with a permanant scowl, for the world is no longer a mystery. To define himself is all that remains and he can do this without this tedious journeying. The most recent years of his writing career, beginning with *Finding the Centre* (1984), have been dominated by this preoccupation with self. He has continually explained and re-explained his colonial predicament, continually dwelt upon his 'lamentable condition', and while doing so he has shown less contempt for, or perhaps just less interest in, those poor deluded souls who continue to inhabit the uncivilised world. The truth is, he has come to the conclusion that he has no uncertainties about the world, only about himself.

In 1987 Naipaul published an autobiographical novel entitled, appropriately enough, *The Enigma of Arrival.* The place he had arrived in was a small Wiltshire village. Shortly after the publication of this novel, he was knighted. How far he had come since those early days with Lamming, Carew, Selvon and their like in the foggy London of the 1950s. The wound that Naipaul perceived the Caribbean to have inflicted upon him had been, to some extent, healed by a generous Britain. Still, the most enigmatic fact about his 'arrival' in 1987 was the form of the book. Novel or autobiography? Novel as autobiography? Autobiography as novel? In reviewing *The Enigma of Arrival* the late Anthony Burgess delivered a judgement that is equally appropriate for *A Way in the World.*

> This book, whatever we call it, is art of an exceptional order . . . if this is not autobiography, it is because it admits more poetry, more descriptive detail, indeed more soul-baring than we can expect in a mere bundle of memoirs . . . It has great dignity, compassion, and candour. It is written with the expected beauty of style.

The Enigma of Arrival presents itself as fiction, but it is properly to be seen as autobiography, much like Wordsworth's *The Prelude,* art which charts the anxious steps towards maturation of the artistic spirit. Devoid of sustained narrative energy, paying scant heed to the demands of characterisation and indulging in reflective meditation, the book moves tentatively, but with elegance. Derek Walcott, while recognising the beauty of the novel's 'periods' and commenting ironically upon Naipaul's positioning of himself as an 'English elegiac pastoralist', is finally unable to detect a change in Naipaul's tone and attitude. He observes no 'mellowing', preferring eventually to judge Naipaul according to the strictures of familiar criticisms. Walcott comments that 'Trinidad injured him. England saves him.' He infers that this is the thesis behind the novel.

> And if the cost to that [Naipaul's] spirit has meant virulent contempt toward the island of his origin, then rook, shaw,

> and hedgerow, tillage and tradition, will soothe him, because although he may reject his own soil, his own phantoms, the earth everywhere is forgiving, even in Trinidad, and rejects no one.

Walcott's graceful, but dismissive, characterisation of the novel as a 'melodious whine' fails to acknowledge Naipaul's attempt to continue the process of sitting in judgement on himself which he began with *Finding the Centre*, a process which, though still tainted with his familiar distemper, is nonetheless clearly visible in *The Enigma of Arrival*.

A Way in the World, like *The Enigma of Arrival*, advertises itself as a novel while paying scant attention to the imaginative demands of the novel form. This novel – or sequence, as it is subtitled – is a deceptively complex narrative in nine parts, comprised of autobiographical fragments which are set against reworkings of Naipaul's earlier writing. But, whichever way the narrative takes us, it is always intimately connected to the life and work of one V.S. Naipaul, with characters, ideas, events from his past being elegantly juggled, set down and picked up again with a technical brilliance that comes from a lifetime's experience. Eliot's tribute to Lancelot Andrewes best sums up the majesty of *A Way in the World*: 'In this extraordinary prose, which appears to repeat, to stand still, but is nevertheless proceeding in the most deliberate and orderly manner, there are often flashing phrases which never desert the memory.'

In his opening chapter, aptly titled 'An Inheritance', Naipaul takes us back to the Trinidad of his childhood and confesses to his current state of mind. 'We cannot understand all the traits we have inherited. Sometimes we can be strangers to ourselves.' This is an altogether different Naipaul from the man who wrote the stinging *Among the Believers*. Here we find a man not entirely sure of himself; it is, if truth were told, a more becoming Naipaul. As the novel unfolds we can clearly see the journey of his life fertilising the work, the work fertilising the life. His own pilgrimage from Trinidad to Oxford to writer, from old world to new, from obscurity to fame, is mirrored in the stories of Sir Walter Raleigh and the Venezuelan revolutionary Francisco Miranda. These narratives form the heart of the novel, the Raleigh section a reworking of material that Naipaul first made use of in his history of the Spanish conquest, *The Loss of El Dorado* (1969), the one-hundred-plus pages of Miranda an obsession which Naipaul admits has concerned him for twenty-seven years. This Miranda section – or sequence – has a broad cinematic sweep to it as Naipaul indulges in scene-setting, high dramatic wordplay, and anecdotal asides. He seems to be revelling in the sheer joy of prose writing.

But *A Way in the World* assumes a more familiar sobriety when Naipaul recalls the imaginary Englishman, Foster Morris, an author who 'helps' the narrator at the onset of his career, but who ultimately castigates him for 'pretending to write a kind of Jamesian novel where the writer does not intrude too much'. Morris seems to be a composite representative of the British literary establishment, trying to control, shape and ultimately patronise a young colonial author. The narrator, however, soon dispenses with Foster's 'services' and strikes out on his own as he comes to recognise that his own artistic development will necessarily take him beyond Foster and others like him. His rejection of Foster is fuelled neither by pride nor by ingratitude; it is a necessary rejection if the narrator is to find his own voice and learn to trust his individual talent, irrespective of how marginal a talent it might appear to those at the 'centre'.

Lebrun, a disaffected West Indian revolutionary, another 'ghost' of narrators past, like so many others in this novel, is probably C.L.R. James, an intellectual, revolutionary, ultimately 'shipwrecked' man, who lives on beyond his lifetime. But here, even while he affirms the correctness of his original judgement of 'Lebrun' and his politics, Naipaul betrays an affection for a man who is finally, like himself, a Trinidadian in 'exile' in England, who has made a mark in the West. If this were all Naipaul had to say about Lebrun, it would in itself be a remarkable enough 'confession' for Naipaul to be making. But in the most revealing passage in the entire novel Naipaul's narrator stops and asks himself, 'How could one enter the emotions of a black man as old as the century?' In any previous work by Naipaul this would have been the end of it. A question proffered rhetorically, to be forgotten. But not in *A Way in the World.* Some thirty pages later, he not only makes the effort to understand these 'emotions', but arrives at a brilliant and compassionate conclusion. When speaking of 'the profile-writers and television interviewers' who pestered Lebrun in his later years, he makes the following observation:

> They risked nothing at all. They had no means of understanding or assessing a man who had been born early in the century into a very hard world, whose intellectual growth had at every stage been accompanied by a growing rawness of sensibility, and whose political resolutions, expressing the wish not to go mad, had been in the nature of spiritual struggles, occurring in the depth of his being.

In light of this passage it seems remarkable that anybody could have ever charged Naipaul with possessing a dyspeptic attitude towards 'primitives', let alone point the stern, accusatory finger of negrophobia in his direction.

Perhaps the most disturbing, and memorable 'sequences' of the novel are those that retell the story of Blair. When the narrator was a seventeen-year-old clerk in the Registrar General's Department in Trinidad, waiting to go to England, busily copying out birth, marriage and death certificates, it was Blair, a twenty-seven-year-old senior clerk, who was responsible for checking Naipaul's work. Blair, whom everyone looked up to as an embodiment of industry, good manners and pride, sometime after the narrator's departure for England almost inevitably entered local politics. Many years later, when resident in Africa, the narrator receives word that Blair, like almost all the characters in this itinerant novel, is about to cross the water and take up a diplomatic posting close by. A poignant reunion between the narrator and Blair occurs, a reunion by turns awkward and tender, but as in the Lebrun 'sequence' there is a concerted, and moving, attempt by the narrator to somehow repair the past.

The early work of most writers has a tendency to be written in the shadow of their own lives, the narratives often tracing the emotional contours of the writer's own development towards maturity. Naipaul is no exception to this. His early novels, *The Mystic Masseur, The Suffrage of Elvira* and the hectic, wonderful *Miguel Street,* are replete with characters forged in the Trinidadian crucible that Naipaul remembers from his childhood. *A House for Mr Biswas,* his fourth, and finest, fictional work, is a beautifully crafted Dickensian novel which pays moving homage to the troubled life of his own father. Curiously enough, in his autumn years, Naipaul seems to have come full circle. No longer the imaginative leaps of the middle period, as demonstrated in such novels as *Guerrillas, In a Free State* and *A Bend in the River.* The 'autumnal' novels, *The Enigma of Arrival* and *A Way in the World,* are once more written in the shadow of his own life. And mercifully, if somewhat surprisingly, we now find ourselves wondering if Naipaul did not – as he would have once had us believe – give up everything for his art.

That he has never allowed himself to be absorbed fully into the English tradition is something many critics have misunderstood. Naipaul is best understood as an inquiline, as a man whom the English have tried to absorb, but a man who has clung to displacement like a floating buoy. Only two years ago, in an interview with the *Sunday Times,* he made clear his feelings about England. 'When I see the sun set – here at Stonehenge – there is a way that it is somebody else's sun, somebody else's history connected with it. I can't avoid that: that's the way I think.' His views on Britain, although less well publicised than his views on the developing world, are familiarly dismissive. In 1980, in an interview with *Newsweek,* he described Mrs Thatcher's country as one of 'bum politicians, scruffy writers and crooked aristocrats ... This is not the country that led the world in industry and law.' In his writings he has always distrusted the coloniser, whilst being unforgiving towards the colonised. But he has perhaps saved his sharpest words for those Westerners who visit 'revolutionary lands' with return air tickets in their back pockets. In short, Naipaul has never much liked anybody and he has never wanted to be a part of anybody's world.

In both *The Enigma of Arrival* and *A Way in the World* Naipaul challenges the notion of form, as well as trying to redefine and re-examine himself. Eight years ago, in a speech delivered in Chicago, Naipaul spoke of writers who have 'their gifts diluted or corrupted by the novel form as it existed in their time'. Naipaul has never been a formally inventive novelist, like Grass, Márquez or Kundera. In fact, he has often commented on his own loss of faith in the novel, and spoken of the novel 'as a form that no longer carries conviction'. Indeed, his wry Trinidadian social comedies of the early years have come to be recognised as his best fiction. The weighty fictions of the 1970s are outgrowths of his travel writing. Naipaul's discovery of, in his own words, 'a strange book – a strange and original and beautiful form, part autobiography, part literary criticism, part fiction – called *Against Sainte-Beuve,* where the criticism of the critic and his method, releasing the writer's love of letters, also releases the autobiographical and fictive elements of the work', provided him with a Proustian model for both *The Enigma of Arrival* and now *A Way in the World.*

His subject is himself. But his theme is a tender and delicate one: it is death. Naipaul is engaged in rumination of the most superior kind as he waits for the inevitable. This period of taking stock is being written out in brave, philosophical prose and Naipaul, whilst not apologising for his 'furrowed brow' and previous judgements, is clearly trying to explain his life to himself, and in turn himself to us. And this is fascinating to partake of. Why begrudge Naipaul the largesse to play with form, to debunk, to tease? Novel? Sequence? Who cares.

Naipaul is certainly no longer a novelist in the conventional sense. And he is too tired, his mind too set, to travel with the hawklike vigour of his middle years. Proustian reminiscence seems an appropriate way for him to celebrate himself and his achievement.

At the end of the novel, in the final section, 'Home Again', the narrator speaks of Blair, his old Trinidadian colleague who, shortly after their reunion in Africa, is tragically murdered. The narrator imagines the details of Blair's body being returned to Trinidad, and at this moment the heart quickens, for it becomes clear to the reader that Naipaul is speaking eloquently, and with a wistful passion, about himself.

> The body would have been embalmed in Africa; that meant the internal organs would have been removed. At the airport in Trinidad the flaps of the hold would have opened, and when the time came the box would have been transferred to a low trailer, and perhaps in some way hidden or covered. There would have been formalities. Would the embalmed body in its box then have been transferred to a hearse? The hearse didn't seem right. I made enquiries. I was told that the box would have been taken away in an ambulance to Port of Spain, and then the shell of the man would have been laid out in Parry's chapel of rest.

Naipaul's great achievement is now to be making art out of displacement and despair. He has found an appropriate form and with this novel he has cleared the way for a fuller reconciliation with his past and with himself.

2

Six years ago the less acerbic tone of V.S. Naipaul's *A Way in the World* (1994) suggested that the writer was beginning to make peace with his homeland of Trinidad, a place that he had often vilified as one of the many 'half-made societies' of the colonial world. The book was not quite 'affectionate', but it was certainly freighted with nostalgia. Suddenly Naipaul was displaying an interest in people other than himself – a most un-Naipaulean conceit.

Since the publication of that book, sadly, Naipaul appears to have rediscovered his antipathy towards people and ideas that are not in tune with his own. *Beyond Belief*, a report of his 'Islamic excursions among converted peoples', which appeared in 1998, is just a dyspeptic reworking of *Among the Believers* (1981), a book in which Naipaul seems incapable of restraining his loathing for the Islamic world and its people, and appears to regard a great number of Muslims as little more than 'half serf' and ahistorical 'fundos' who are wedded to a triple heritage of veiling, whipping and amputation. Like so many of Naipaul's travel narratives, *Beyond Belief* is a serious book that is undermined by the author's inability to hold his own prejudices in check. Whereas *A Way in the World* appears to have been written by a writer with his eyebrows arched, *Beyond Belief* is a retreat to the art of writing while curling one's lip.

The reappearance of Naipaul's tendency to belittle people and places is disappointing, as is his continued sponsorship of himself as a writer whose passage towards maturity was uniquely difficult. We are forever being encouraged to sympathise with poor Naipaul for having started so far back in the race. In an interview in an Indian publication in 1998, Naipaul quickly finds his stride:

> My life was very hard, in 1955 the world was very hard for people like me. Can you imagine writing a book like *Miguel Street?* People wouldn't even want to look at it. Today people are interested in writing from India or other former colonies. But at that time it was not considered writing. It was a very hard thing to have written this material, to have copies made, to wonder about it being lost, and have that book with me in loose manuscript for four years, before

> it was published. It really upset me and it is still a great shadow over me.

More than four decades later the entirely predictable problems of an ambitious young man hawking a manuscript around London in search of a publisher still cast a 'great shadow' over him. Why exactly was it 'a very hard thing' to have written *Miguel Street*? And are we really expected to believe that 'writing from India or other former colonies' was being ignored? Those were the years when George Lamming, C.L.R. James, Edgar Mittelholzer, Samuel Selvon, R.K. Narayan, Raja Rao and many others were being published and praised.

Having tried to convince us of the existence of vague difficulties, which plagued his early writing years ('the world was very hard for people like me'), Naipaul continues:

> It all seems very easy now. The books coming out one after another, but they were created by great anxiety, great suffering. I could have been given a much easier ride, but I wasn't, because of the time. It was very hard for me to get a job, very hard for me to find a place to live, very hard for me to find my own voice. It was very hard for me to have done all that. Having written those books, to get them published, and then it was very hard to get them adequately reviewed.

What makes Naipaul's whining so distasteful is the implicit suggestion that these difficulties were visited upon him because he was tainted by a colonial past that he was duty-bound to rise above. Not only are we expected to believe that he – and he alone – suffered the hardships of discovering a job and finding somewhere to live, and attracting the attention of a publisher, we are also to understand that he was miserably burdened by the unfortunate accident of the place and the date of his birth. He was cursed in not being born in Sloane Square or in Bloomsbury, but in a 'dark' region populated by individuals unfit to dignify real literature; and so he had little choice but heroically to escape. As he remarked in *Vanity Fair* in 1987, 'If you're from Trinidad you want to get away. You can't write if you're from the bush.'

Naipaul's new book is a collection of letters to and from his father, from the crucial years of 1950 to 1954, when Naipaul left Trinidad, undertook his studies at Oxford and attempted in earnest to make himself into a writer. Although *Between Father and Son* is being published under Naipaul's name, the volume was in fact assembled and scrupulously edited by Gillon Aitken, his long-time English agent. In characteristically blunt fashion, Naipaul has made it plain that he, the 'author' and the holder of the copyright, has no intention of reading his book. One sympathises with this decision: few of us would be keen to reread the letters of our youth.

Upon opening the volume, one discovers nine chronologically arranged bundles of letters that are principally between V.S. Naipaul (known affectionately as Vido) and his father, Seepersad Naipaul, a failed writer and struggling journalist. There is, in addition, a substantial body of correspondence between the younger Naipaul and his older sister, Kamla, who for the entire length of this book is studying at the Hindu University in Benares in India. In fact, the volume begins with three letters to Kamla, written during Naipaul's last year in Trinidad. Thereafter Naipaul writes a short letter to Sati, his younger sister, from New York, where he stops briefly en route for England. Eventually, in August 1950, he arrives in England, where he spends a few weeks in London before going up to Oxford in October. Thereafter the letters between Naipaul and his father, and between Naipaul and Kamla, continue unabated as Naipaul studies for his degree in English literature and language at University College.

The letters in *Between Father and Son,* letters written at the very start of his career, deal with Naipaulean 'issues' with which we are now thoroughly familiar: himself, his singular struggle and the necessity of his having to create a subject for himself where none (or so he claims) existed. In this sense they are a logical, if anachronistic, addition to Naipaul's writing of recent years; and reading them one begins to detect a large and somewhat unattractive continuity in his development as a writer. But a close reading of these letters allows us also to espy something else: the possibility of a subject, a subject that Naipaul wilfully spurned, a subject that, had Naipaul grasped it, would not have necessarily made him into a better writer, but would almost certainly have made him into a more likeable one.

From the beginning these letters express Naipaul's desire to be a writer. What appears to mark him out from other seventeen-year-old boys is the fact that he *can* actually write: 'At about 12 midnight we were over New York, acres of lights strung in asterisks mottled with red and green and blue.' Or, even more impressive, the youngster's first impression of snow, on 11 December the same year:

> Last week I had my first snow. It came down in little white fluffs; you felt that a gigantic hand had punched a gigantic cotton wool sack open, letting down flurries of cotton shreds. The camera doesn't lie in this respect. Snow is just as you see it in films and in photographs. It snowed for about two hours. The streets were not covered, but the tops of the naked branches of the trees were white with it – a white that showed more beautiful because the limbs of the trees were in comparison stark black.

The early letters also reveal ample evidence of Naipaul's precocious intelligence, which had earned him a highly competitive government scholarship. In a letter to Kamla, written before he had even left Trinidad, Naipaul displays no qualms about challenging the English canon.

> Jane Austen appears to be essentially a writer for women; if she had lived in our own age she would undoubtedly have been a leading contributor to the women's papers. Her

> work really bored me. It is mere gossip. It could appeal to a female audience. The diction is fine, of course. But the work, besides being mere gossip, is slick and unprofessional.

By the time Naipaul reaches England, his notion of himself as a literary man standing apart from all is clearly evident. What is equally evident is the determination of Naipaul's father that his eldest boy should succeed as a writer. He addresses his first letter to his young son in England to 'V.S. Naipaul, Esq.' Before his son has even reached Oxford, he is proffering encouragement and advice. 'I have no doubt whatever', he writes on 22 September 1950, 'that you will be a great writer; but do not spoil yourself: beware of undue dissipation of any kind . . . You keep your centre. You *are* on the way to being an intellectual.'

Seepersad Naipaul was possessed by an ambition to be a writer, an ambition that sputtered but never caught fire. In 1943, this avid reader of Dickens privately published a small and unsuccessful novella about Indian life in Trinidad called *The Adventures of Gurudeva*. The failure of the book did not deter him from pursuing what he believed to be his rightful course, and he continued to subscribe to periodicals and magazines in England and America. These journals gave him a tantalising glimpse into the world of letters, but ultimately he felt trapped by the demands of family and his deep sense of obligation to provide. Eventually the pressure led to a nervous breakdown; and the letters suggest that after the breakdown the father attempted to live his literary life through the increasingly prodigious achievements of his eldest son.

> I feel so damned cocksure that I *can* produce a novel within six months – if only I had nothing else to do. This is impossible. *But I want to give you just this chance*. When your university studies are over, if you get a good job, all well and good; if you do not, *you have not got to worry one little bit*. You will come home – and do what

> I am longing to do now; just write; and read and do the things you like to do. This is where I want to be of use to you. I want you to have that chance which I never had; somebody to support me and mine while I write.

While at Oxford the young Naipaul begins to write in earnest; and his father not only offers unstinting praise, he also begins to intervene and act as his son's editor: 'You will see two x's in the body of your article. I think if you would delete the matter between the two x's; and also put some "ands" in places of full stops, to make your sentences less telegraphic, it will be quite a good article.' Throughout the breadth of this correspondence we are presented with an anxious father who, were we to read his letters in isolation, would come across as an overbearing parent. But the hopes that are lodged in the father are more than matched by the ambitions lodged in the son.

Young Naipaul experiences some anxiety which, at the end of his first term at Oxford, he expresses pithily: 'I have got to show these people that I can beat them at their own language.' And beyond this competitive concern he is seriously focused on his literary ambition, having earlier in his first term written to Kamla in India. On 22 November 1950 he writes:

> I have been engaged on a novel. It is about 8 chapters gone – about 140 pages in any Penguin book; but it is only in a very rough form. I shall not touch it again until the end of next term. I am exhausted. I want new ideas to incubate a bit. I shall have it complete in a year's time. And think what will become of me if it is published! For I am sure of one thing – once it is published, it is bound to sell. It is a humorous novel.

Naipaul's first novels were indeed humorous and, soon after leaving Oxford, he found himself in print. But this did not bring him satisfaction, exactly: the deeply ingrained sense of expectation that was part of his paternal heritage, compounded by his own ambition and sense of entitlement, resulted in the young writer developing a hard – and decidedly unhumorous – attitude towards everything about him. During his first year at university he writes to the family ('Dear Everybody') about Oxford: 'There are asses in droves here ... Nearly everyone comes to Oxford on a state grant. The standard of the place naturally goes down. If you want to find superficial young men, and even more superficial young women, Oxford is the place.'

Naipaul's judgemental nature does not spare those West Indian writers publishing and gaining a reputation in England, whom he already identifies as 'rivals'. He continually praises his father's writing and he easily finds the yardstick by which he can measure his father's talent: 'You ought to know that I am perhaps more keen on your work than anyone else is. And, furthermore, as I have often told you, you have the necessary talent. [Edgar] Mittelholzer has no talent, neither has [Samuel] Selvon, who has just written what he calls a novel, but what I call a travelogue.'

When faced with displays of emotion, Naipaul responds as though he considers such behaviour to be despicable. In 1950, after quoting at length, to his sister, from 'the most beautiful letter I have ever had from a woman', a young woman who is evidently in great pain as she explains that she cannot be involved with him because she is 'in love with another', Naipaul pats himself on the back.

> Good! Not bad, eh? Imagine – your own brother, just turned 18 but lying to every girl that he is 22, drawing that letter from a girl after whom nearly everybody in the English class is rushing! ... Goodbye now, my dearest Kamla, and keep well and don't write letters like the one above, because, you see, I lied to that girl.

At so many points in these letters, one detects a fine

intelligence betraying itself as it collapses into smugness. While still a teenager he writes to Kamla about a cousin back in Trinidad: 'Just in case you haven't, you must hear now that Deo is chasing penniless men, Phoolo niggers, and Tara douglas.' ('Dougla' is a pejorative Trinidadian term for somebody who is half-Indian, half-African.) Already comfortable with his prejudices, sure of his judgement and determined to write, there is something alarming about young Naipaul's lack of self-knowledge. Again, he writes to Kamla: 'A friend told me the other day that people don't like me because I made them feel that I knew they were fools. What do you think of me? And don't tell me of your cousins. They are all asses, as you well know.' One begins to wonder where, in all this, is the compassion that is necessary if one is going to write with real understanding. Young Naipaul seems to have already adopted the exacting tone of a man mired in certainty, a man afraid of ambiguity, and incapable of stooping to the kind of doubt that fuels great imaginative writing.

Of all Naipaul's books, it is the thinly disguised autobiographical novel *A House for Mr Biswas,* which appeared in 1961, that suggests the existence of a compassionate Naipaul. It is his most personal novel and it was created out of material that Naipaul saw and experienced as a child. The novel tells the story of Mohun Biswas, a man who marries young, becomes somewhat dependent upon his in-laws, tries to make a living as a journalist, buys a semi-derelict dream house and dies unfulfilled at forty-six. A prose epic on a nineteenth-century scale, its comic warmth eventually gives way to tragedy as Anand, Biswas's intelligent son, is left by himself to succeed the father and take on the world.

Mohun Biswas is a frustrating and somewhat inert man who is forever in danger of sinking below his own dreams. Clearly Naipaul saw his own father in this way. At the end of his first year at Oxford, he drives home the point in a letter to his father, its block capitals the hectoring measure of the degree to which his admiration of his father was turning into desperation about his father:

> YOU HAVE ENOUGH MATERIAL FOR A HUNDRED STORIES. FOR HEAVEN'S SAKE START WRITING THEM. YOU CAN WRITE AND YOU KNOW IT. STOP MAKING EXCUSES. ONCE YOU START WRITING YOU WILL FIND IDEAS FLOODING UPON YOU . . . I HATE LECTURING YOU THIS WAY BUT I WANT TO HEAR THAT YOU ARE WRITING. I WANT TO HEAR THAT YOU ARE WRITING VERY VERY MUCH. YOU HAVE BEEN IDLE SUFFICIENTLY LONG . . . You are the best writer in the West Indies, but one can only judge writers by their work.

There certainly is passion here; and there is passion in *A House for Mr Biswas*, and in the three books that preceded it, *The Mystic Masseur* (1957), *The Suffrage of Elvira* (1958) and *Miguel Street* (1959). In the post-*Biswas* years, however, it is difficult to detect much passion, or compassion, in Naipaul's work. Its guiding principle became his so-called analysis of so-called inferior societies and inferior peoples. Then, in more recent years, the work has transformed itself once again and become an extended meditation upon himself. What appears to have been lost in this growth to maturity as a writer is any real expression of affection for his homeland or its people.

Having written about his father in *A House for Mr Biswas*, Naipaul had fulfilled an obligation. His primary task in life, to make himself into a writer, had already been accomplished. *A House for Mr Biswas* was his fourth book, after all, and it enhanced an already impressive reputation. But by placing his father at the centre of a novel which depicted his father's difficulties in the world of colonial Trinidad, Naipaul was both dignifying, and paying tribute to, the life of the man who had steered him towards the writing life. And having completed this book, and fulfilled this duty, Naipaul's hostility towards Trinidad began to gather steam.

He began now to claim publicly that he had yet to find a real subject. When Derek Walcott asked him, in an interview for the Trinidad *Guardian* in 1965, if he felt 'displaced' on returning home for a short visit, the aloof and dismissive Naipaul was clear: 'Oh yes. I find this place frightening. I think this is a very sinister place ... Also, manners are not very good.' Six years later, in 1971, Naipaul told the *Listener* in London that he no longer even imagined the West Indies to be a real place.

> I saw myself as leaving the rather empty, barren place where I was born and rejoining the old world. It was as simple as that. Joining the real world again. I used to spend so much time trying to analyse why the world I was born in was not real. I used to think it was perhaps the light ... The society was such a simple one that I don't think there would have been room for me.

Why this antipathy to Trinidad and the Caribbean? What was it about 'simple' Trinidad that rendered it incapable of further stimulating Naipaul's literary imagination? After all, Trinidad had provided him with the subject-matter for his first four books. In *Reading and Writing: A Personal Account*, a slim volume comprised of two short essays which appeared in 1999, Naipaul returns to his well-worn theme of how he began his uniquely difficult task, against all the odds, of heroically making himself into a writer; and here he suggests what it was about Trinidad that he found deficient.

> Unlike the metropolitan writer I had no knowledge of a past. The past of our community ended, for most of us, with our grandfathers; beyond that we could not see. And the plantation colony, as the humorous guidebooks said, was a place where almost nothing had happened ... As a child trying to read, I had felt that two worlds separated me from the books that were offered to me at school and

> in the libraries: the childhood world of our remembered India, and the more colonial world of our city ... What I didn't know, even after I had written my early books of fiction, concerned only with story and people and getting to the end and mounting the jokes well, was that these two spheres of darkness had become my subject.

According to Naipaul, colonial Indian Trinidad has to be understood as the heart of darkness; a Third World within a Third World, a dark place within a dark place.

As a young man Naipaul had already begun to cultivate hostility towards his homeland. On 27 January 1951 he wrote to his father from Oxford about his contempt for Trinidad and Trinidadians:

> Do you know? I got some Trinidad papers, read them, and found them hilariously absurd. I never realized before the *Guardian* was so badly written, that our Trinidad worthies were so absurd, that Trinidad is the most amusing island that ever dotted a sea.

One can only imagine how Seepersad Naipaul, who worked for the Trinidad *Guardian*, wrote stories about life in Trinidad and wished to make a reputation for himself as a West Indian writer, must have felt upon reading these words, and others like them.

In the 1960s Naipaul began to travel, first to the Caribbean region for *The Middle Passage* (1962), and then to India for *An Area of Darkness* (1964). Alongside his constructed sense of himself as a writer, he was now beginning to construct his subject-matter, his 'two spheres of darkness'. He 'investigated' this darkness, promoting his own vision as the only beacon of light that could penetrate these 'half-made societies', and he seemed incapable of confining his often clichéd and ill-informed commentary to the pages of his books; he revelled also in providing sharp copy for Western journalists, all the while insisting on how stupid non-white, non-Western people really are. In 1979, when Elizabeth Hardwick asked him, in the pages of the *New York Review of Books,* what the dot on the forehead of Indian women means, he replied, 'The dot means: My head is empty.' And when she asked about the future of Africa, he offered an even more idiotic response: 'Africa has no future.'

These days, Naipaul appears to have grown weary of 'the two spheres of darkness', and prefers to rehearse and re-rehearse his 'civilising' journey out of Trinidad and into the 'real' world. The examination of his 'solitary' journey is his principal subject, with himself as the central character. From *Finding the Centre* to *Reading and Writing: A Personal Account,* the story remains the same: in a journey unique to myself, I left my worthless home, with its small people, and I sailed against the tides of chance and history looking for a better place – the centre – where I suffered greatly and made myself into a writer.

The truth, of course, is that aside from the specific personal details, there is nothing at all unique about Naipaul's journey. Contemporary literature, in all regions of the world, is populated with writers who, for various reasons, felt compelled to leave home and remake themselves as writers in another place. Joseph Skvorecky, Wole Soyinka, Joseph Brodsky, Milan Kundera, Ngugi Wa'Thiongo, Charles Simic, Guillermo Cabrera Infante, the list is almost endless. But these writers have not promoted the myth of enduring a painful, solitary journey, understandable only against the awful backdrop of their barbarous 'homeland' and its foolish people, among whom their own individual intelligence stood out as superior. They understood that their journey makes sense only in the context of a people and a place about which they choose to write truthfully, and with sympathy. So why is it that V.S. Naipaul continues to attempt to inscribe his self-aggrandising, and frankly embarrassing, narrative into the literary conscience of the West?

In 1953 Naipaul's father died suddenly of an unspecified nervous disorder and cardiac arrest. We might well assume that he died of a broken heart. The younger Naipaul was just entering his final year at Oxford. Two years earlier he had written to his sister in India:

> As I grow older, I find myself doing things that remind me of Pa, more and more. The way I smoke; the way I sit; the way I stroke my unshaved chin; the way in which I sometimes sit bolt upright; the way in which I spend money romantically and foolishly.

The twenty-one-year-old Naipaul was understandably shaken by his father's death. The short telegram he sent to his family on 10 October 1953 is racked with the pain of loss, and replete with the anxieties of new responsibilities.

> = NAIPAUL 26 NEPAUL STREET PORT OF SPAIN TRINIDAD
> = HE WAS THE BEST MAN I KNEW STOP EVERYTHING
> I OWE TO HIM BE BRAVE MY LOVES TRUST ME =
> VIDO

This is one of the few moments in this revealing volume of letters when young Vido lowers his guard. A year earlier, during the winter of 1952, young Vido had lowered his guard even further. He wrote to his Pa from University College:

> I feel nostalgic for home. Do you know what I long for? I long for the nights that fall blackly, suddenly, without warning. I long for a violent shower of rain at night. I long to hear the tinny tattoo of heavy raindrops on a roof, or the drops of rain on the broad leaves of that wonderful plant, the wild tannia. But in short I long for home, or perhaps, the homely atmosphere. And I miss my bicycle rides, and the sea, and the pit at Rialto, and the sort of cigarettes I used to smoke, to everyone's scandal.

Such letters help us to see that however much Naipaul may

wish to protest that he had to find his subject-matter, and to write about his 'two spheres of darkness', and to reach the safety of the 'real' world (by which we are to understand London), the truth is that he already had his subject-matter. He merely elected to look away from it.

Naipaul's subject-matter was rooted in the same material that has served countless artists, including Aimé Césaire, Edouard Glissant, Alejo Carpentier and Derek Walcott. There is nothing contemptible about this subject-matter. It is called Caribbean life – the people, the music, the heat, the flora, the fauna, the sunrise, the sunset, the history. But Naipaul did not trust this material, for it appeared to have failed his father. He wished so desperately to succeed that he decided to go beyond what was in front of his face, and beneath his feet, and underneath his nails; beyond what was, in fact, in his soul.

Naipaul has justified his decision to turn away from the Caribbean by arguing that the Caribbean was not a fit and proper place to support his superior imagination. He attempts to account for the 'accident' of his early – and, in the end, probably most enduring – work by describing it as 'concerned only with story and people and getting to the end and mounting the jokes well'. As far back as 1971 he was disparaging this work. He told Ian Hamilton, in the *Times Literary Supplement*: 'At the back of my mind the thing that embarrasses me slightly about my very early work is that because of my assumptions about the nature of the world I really thought I was writing about a world that was fairly whole.' And ten years later, in *Newsweek*, Naipaul tried again to disown the early work, which looked upon Trinidad with some affection. We are to understand that he reached the civilised world by having written early work that was not of much consequence.

> Of course, when you're starting, you really have got to try to establish a world and it's much easier if you can even

> pretend that the tribal culture is a world, that the life of the street puts you in touch with the wider world. The early comedies made this pretense, I think, and they include *Biswas,* a book I think I remember, though I haven't read the book since I wrote it, you know.

'A book I think I remember'! But in 1983, in his foreword to the paperback edition of *A House for Mr Biswas,* Naipaul states that one evening in 1981, in Cyprus, he was surprised to hear an instalment of the novel being read on the BBC World Service: 'I listened. And in no time, though the instalment was comic, though the book had inevitably been much abridged, and the linking words were not always mine, I was in tears, swamped by the emotions I had tried to shield myself from for twenty years.' But inevitably, Naipaul's fear of weakness, and his contempt for feeling, kicks in, and he soon scampers back to his official narrative. Again we are to understand that *Biswas* and the other early books about 'tribal culture' were written at a time before he had found his true subject-matter. He once remarked that 'The life I wrote about in *Biswas* couldn't be the true nature of *my* life because I hadn't grown up in it feeling that it was mine.' He might have remarked more accurately: I had grown up *fearful* that this life, and this life alone, was mine, and as soon as I felt confident enough to ditch it, I did.

Despite the brickbats of many Third World critics and writers, Naipaul has enjoyed a much-acclaimed career. And despite his success and his reputation, Naipaul continues to peddle 'his story' with an almost pathological vigour. This suggests that something is amiss. And it clearly is. Naipaul's career makes sense only if one accepts the fact that he has known and subsequently escaped the 'darkness'. Here is a man who can visit the Ivory Coast, or Iran, or Pakistan, or his native Trinidad, and make the most outlandish, racist, unscholarly, inaccurate statements in books and in interviews, and still be taken seriously. Incredibly enough, in many quarters he is regarded as an authority. The luminosity of his prose no doubt lends him credibility in the opinion of some readers, but Naipaul's supreme qualification is that he has himself been a part of the unreal Conradian darkness which he is shedding light upon. He, too, has been moored in a place of no history, but by some supreme individual effort he has dragged himself to civilised higher ground – to a place of good manners. It causes him great anxiety and stress to continue to gaze upon such bestial places, but he will do so for our sake. It is his duty, his vocation. He has known no other. And we must trust him because he knows.

Well, he certainly does know. He knows that unless he can persuade editors and critics in the West to subscribe to the myth of his unique journey, he will just be an extremely gifted travel writer with a bee in his bonnet about filth, order and 'primitives'. The narrative of escape from a near encounter with tribal doom elevates Naipaul to a position of authority, and over the years countless interviewers have listened patiently to his prejudice and simply scratched away in their notepads. What was Elizabeth Hardwick's response to Naipaul's stupid comment about the dot on the forehead of Indian women? It was: 'In Naipaul's fiction the narrator is often a lonely, displaced Indian, far from home. Nothing is quite real to him, and yet he must summon a sort of hope, take on enterprises if he can find them.' It would have been bad form, presumably, to wonder about his bigotry.

I miss Vido, the one who misses his bicycle rides, and the sea, and the pit at the Rialto, and who longs for nights that fall blackly, and the tinny tattoo of heavy raindrops on a roof, and the drops of rain on the broad leaves of the wild tannia. Unfortunately, he makes only the briefest of appearances in the letters. This Vido trusted Trinidad to stir his heart, but eventually the Naipaul in Vido decided that Trinidad was best left to the inferior 'West Indian' writers. And so Naipaul stifled Vido and invented somebody else. In 1983, in an interview with Bernard Levin, it is clear that Naipaul also invented an entirely different Trinidad from that which Vido remembers. Levin says, 'You were born in Trinidad,' and Naipaul comments:

> I was born there, yes. I thought it was a great mistake ... I didn't like the climate. I didn't like the quality of the light. I didn't like the heat; I didn't like the asthma that [it] gave me. I didn't like a lot of the racial tensions around me ... I didn't like the music; I didn't like the loudness. I just felt I was in the wrong place ... I didn't like my family particularly either. To grow up in a large, extended family was to acquire a lasting distaste for family life. It was to give me the desire never to have any children of my own ... I developed a fantasy, I suppose, of civilization as something existing away from this area of barbarity. The barbarity was double: the barbarity of my family and the barbarity outside.

Would his father have approved of such sentiments? I doubt it. In the second essay in *Reading and Writing* ('The Writer in India') Naipaul remembers his father:

> ... the desire to be a writer came to my father in the late 1920s. He did become a writer, though not in the way he wanted. He did good work; his stories gave our community a past that would otherwise have been lost. But there was a mismatch between the ambition, coming from outside, from another culture, and our community, which had no living literary tradition; and my father's hard-won stories have found very few readers among the people they were about ... He passed on the writing ambition to me; and I, growing up in another age, have managed to see that ambition through almost to the end.

But the son had no desire to try to give his community a past. In fact the son could not run quickly enough to 'another culture', to a 'living literary tradition'.

The father did what all writers do when faced with an apparent absence or distortion of their history; he attempted to write that history. This is the story of Skvorecky, Soyinka, Kundera, Wa'Thiongo and the others; and it is also the story of Seepersad Naipaul. But it is not the story of V.S. Naipaul. Having fled to 'the outside', to England, where he 'discovered' his 'two spheres of darkness', Naipaul then proceeded to people these 'spheres' with ungenerous, unsympathetic portraits of 'primitive' people, all the while sponsoring the myth of himself as an exhausted truth-teller whose dispatches can only be fully understood in the context of his own remarkable journey. Of course a writer does not have a duty to stay at home and to write about home. A writer is not only a son and literature is not primarily an expression of loyalty. But surely a writer cannot conclude from his own unhappiness at home that home is in some essential way unworthy. Surely it is not necessary, or even interesting, for a writer to distort or to destroy whatever it is that he wishes to – and is free to – leave.

The real hero of these letters, in the end, is the father, Seepersad Naipaul. By turns naïve, desperate and irresponsible, he believed both in literature *and* in people. He was determined *and* generous. He was ambitious *and* sympathetic. Unlike his son, he did not confuse the lack of a tradition with the lack of a subject-matter. It was true that Trinidad had a short and underdeveloped literary tradition, but the tradition was there to be built, as is the case in many postcolonial societies. And whatever else it may have lacked, Trinidad certainly had subject-matter. Unless, of course, one really does believe that the island, as Naipaul told the *New York Times* in 1980, is populated by 'Monkeys' who 'live purely physical lives which I find contemptible'. Seepersad Naipaul once had occasion to chastise young Vido, who had, incredibly enough, suggested to his father that a man is only writing well when people start to hate him. The father knew better.

And as to a writer being hated or liked – I think it's the

other way to what you think: a man is doing his work well when people begin liking him. I have never forgotten what Gault MacGowan [editor of the *Trinidad Guardian*] told me years ago; 'Write sympathetically'; and this, I suppose, in no way prevents us from writing truthfully, even brightly.

If only the son had listened.

1994, 2000

Patrick Chamoiseau: Unmarooned

In an essay called 'Beyond Despair', the writer Aharon Appelfeld reminds us that 'by its very nature, art constantly challenges the process by which the individual person is reduced to anonymity'. For the people of the African diaspora, art, particularly the art of the story, has been of primary importance. The physical and psychological horrors of the middle passage, and the subsequent descent into slavery, were compounded by the attempt on the part of the colonial masters to strip those of African origin of any connection to a remembered past. This accounts for the importance of the theme of memory and remembering in the storytelling tradition of the African diaspora.

All such attempts to remember are subject, however, to the scrutiny of the 'European' man of the Americas, who can think of nothing more pitiable than a man without a past. After all, his knowledge of his past is the thing he most cherishes in his New World sojourn, whether he is a man of the Dominican Republic who celebrates his connection to Spain, or a Dutchman in Surinam who professes to know The Hague better than his own country, or indeed a whole range of citizens of the United States who are anxious to hyphenate their identity (Irish-American, Italian-American, Swedish-American) so that they don't fall off the continental shelf into the void of anonymity. When the people of the African diaspora attempt to reclaim their past they risk being viewed by the formerly European as either foolish, as in the case of Marcus Garvey, or wilfully nostalgic, as in the case of Alex Haley, or as unnecessarily fussy, as in the case of those who now insist upon describing themselves as African-Americans as opposed to black Americans, coloured Americans or negroes.

The African people of the Caribbean face problems of identity which are different from those that trouble their northern cousins in the United States. Owing to the unique nature of the colonising process in the region, the African people who populate the mainland and islands of the Caribbean have had to learn to view themselves in a variety of what Milan Kundera describes as 'mediating contexts'. There is, for a start, the European context, irrespective of whether the colonising country is Britain, France, Spain or Holland. Then there is the context of the amputated past of Africa, which is tainted with loss, misunderstanding and a certain shame. And finally there is the context of the new world of the Americas, which includes not only the neighbouring islands and territories, but during the course of this century has come to include the ever-widening shadow of the United States.

In the formerly British possessions the mediating context of Britain is fast disappearing, as political independence has been granted to these once-lucrative sugar islands. As they attempt now to steer a course of their own, the islands are coming to understand that their close relationship to Britain is truly a thing of the past and that geographical proximity to, and cable television from, the United States has made it the new dominant political and cultural influence. This is not the case with the French Caribbean islands of Martinique and Guadeloupe. A flight to Paris from either of these territories is a domestic flight, for these *départements* are essentially France. A visitor to the French islands from any of the neighbouring English-speaking territories cannot help but be struck by the modern facilities, the fine roads and bridges, the essentially 'first world' ambience. Martinique and Guadeloupe do not need to see themselves *in* the context of Europe, for there is already the ready-made illusion that they are Europe.

The writer Edouard Glissant has suggested that there is no cultural or psychological hinterland (*arrière-pays*) into which the African people of the small islands of Martinique and Guadeloupe can flee from the overbearing French influence. Yet on the larger, less claustrophobic islands such as Jamaica, or the 'French' island of Haiti, this psychological hinterland was not only spiritually possible, it was also physically represented by the ability to retreat into the hills and establish an African alternative to the European cultures. The people of Martinique and Guadeloupe have no such luxury of identity. They are forced continually to develop something new and different out of their 'European' circumstances so that they may keep reaffirming and replenishing the connection with their African past. To simply do nothing would be to submit to the colonial-assimilationist system that disempowers African people culturally even as it materially rewards them as French citizens. In 1962 V.S. Naipaul referred to this as 'the French colonial monkey-game'.

The French Caribbean literary movement of the late 1930s and 1940s, the one which came to be known as 'negritude', was born out of the desire of those of African origin to avoid the fate of being reduced to the 'anonymity' of Frenchmen. The man who coined the term 'negritude' and who became the undisputed leader of both Martiniquan literature and politics was the poet Aimé Césaire. According to André Breton, Césaire's narrative poem *Cahier d'un retour au pays natal* (1939) was 'the greatest lyrical monument of our age'. Césaire was also one of the editors of the journal *Tropiques*, which brought out nine issues between 1941 and 1945. A hugely influential review, it established the foundations of the Martiniquan cultural renaissance that flourished in the years during and immediately following the Second World War. The importance of storytelling, particularly in the form of folk tales, was not lost on Césaire and his followers, for they recognised that much of their African history was contained in this oral material.

Naturally enough the folk tales had survived in French 'Creole', which even today remains the spoken language for a large number of people on both Martinique and Guadeloupe. Creole 'languages' – a fusion of European and African languages

– developed on the slave plantations throughout the Caribbean region as a linguistic means by which the slaves could communicate with each other in this 'new' world while preserving some words and phrases from the 'old' one. By speaking in this mode they were often able to disguise their intentions and at the same time to remind themselves that they had not yet fully yielded their identity. The evidence of the general process of creolisation – this synthesis of that which was African with that which was European to produce something new in skin coloration, music, food and literature – can be seen throughout wide tracts of the Americas from New Orleans down to Brazil. In Creole cultures one can always detect both the influence of the coloniser and the strength of the colonised.

The 'negritude' movement celebrated the creativity of creolisation, and pointed to the importance of the Creole folk tale. But things got still more complicated. These writers decided that while it would be 'legitimate' to recite these tales in the Creole language in which they had been conceived, they could only be committed to paper after they had been 'translated' into French. To write in Creole would be nonsensical, for, according to the Césaire faction, Creole was not formally a language. But French was most certainly a language; it was *the* language. The embracing of folk tales gave the followers of Césaire's movement the opportunity to be modernists in the French tradition and revolutionaries in their own culture by virtue of this affirmation of their own native art form; but the revolutionary bugle ceased to sound as soon as the question of tampering with the French language became an issue. 'Negritude', although clear in its desire to promote the idea of an African past, stopped well short of proposing the severence of links with France, political or otherwise. This reluctance to break clean away from the metropolitan centre won the movement as many critics as it did supporters. One critic was Glissant, who preferred to view himself within the specific framework of the French Caribbean and resisted what he viewed as the somewhat obsequious gestures towards Paris that Césaire and others seemed only too keen to indulge in. During the past decade there has been a rebirth of literary activity in the French Caribbean region, which has witnessed both the reappearance of journals in the general tradition of *Tropiques* and the publication of a spate of novels and theoretical essays by a wide range of writers. The most prominent among these new writers is Patrick Chamoiseau, for whom the Creole language, and the role of the Creole storyteller in the narrative tradition, are the central concerns of his work.

Chamoiseau was born in Fort-de-France, Martinique in 1953 and both grew up and was educated in the *département*. He is the author of a collection of Creole folk tales; three novels, including *Texaco* (1992), which won the Prix Goncourt; two volumes of autobiographical writing, *Antan d'enfance* (1990) and *Chemin-d'école* (1994); and two volumes of 'theory', *Eloge de la Créolite* (1989) with Raphaël Confiant and Jean Bernabe, and *Lettres Créoles* (1991) with Raphaël Confiant. *Lettres Créoles* begins by describing the dynamics of French colonisation, and it chronicles the manner in which the 'cries' and the 'silences' of the African oppressed eventually evolved into the Creole folk tales told by 'the storyteller'. The book develops into a full-scale investigation of the emergence of a written literature in both French and Creole between 1635 and 1975, and a critical evaluation of the contribution of this literature to the general creolisation of the French Caribbean.

As one might imagine, Chamoiseau the literary theorist seeks to practise what he preaches when he turns his attention to writing fiction. As a writer he consciously associates himself with the man on the plantation, who, after the white master has gone to sleep, creeps out into the night and begins to tell tales. Chamoiseau the novelist is trying to make the oral (Creole) tradition of stories associated with Africa and slavery accessible to the written page, and at the same time he is trying to re-establish the central importance of the figure of 'the storyteller' in the narrative life of the French Caribbean. As he observed in 1988 in an essay called 'Les Contes de la survie':

'Our stories and storytellers date from the period of slavery and colonialism. Their deepest meanings can be discerned only in reference to this fundamental epoch of French West Indian history. Our storyteller is the spokesman of a fettered, famished people, living in fear and in the various postures of survival.'

The novel *Texaco* spans the years 1823 to 1980 and is divided into four 'epochs', which represent the 'African' Martiniquan building materials of the period: straw, crate wood, asbestos and concrete. The novel opens in the city of Saint-Pierre, the old cultural capital of the island, which was destroyed by a volcanic eruption in 1902. The location shifts to a place called Texaco, a classic shanty town of the African diaspora, peopled by former plantation slaves who are searching for urban employment. The township is located in the capital, Fort-de-France, near a petrochemical installation owned by the Texaco company. Texaco is considered an eyesore and an embarrassment by the authorities, who wish to evict the squatters and raze the place.

Chamoiseau situates himself as the recorder of the memories of Marie-Sophie Laborieux, a Creole woman largely responsible for the creation of the township. Utilising a playful, witty device that is part of the folklore tradition, the author is variously addressed by Marie-Sophie as 'the Word Scratcher' ('le Marqueur de paroles') or 'Oiseau de Cham'. Marie-Sophie recalls over a century and a half of her island's history, beginning with the story of her father, Esternome, all the while weaving into the fabric of her story the central events of Martiniquan history, including the abolition of slavery in 1848, the Vichy period during the Second World War and De Gaulle's visit to the island in 1964. At various times the novel introduces excerpts from Marie-Sophie's notebooks, Chamoiseau's letters to his 'Source' (Marie-Sophie), and a government official's notes to 'the Word Scratcher'. Marie-Sophie struggles against the *beke* (white Frenchman born in the colonies) who owns the land, but eventually she triumphs and saves Texaco, extracting from the authorities the promise of decent roads and electricity for the township.

There are two refracting panes through which one can view this novel. There is the pane of allegory as Chamoiseau demonstrates a great loyalty to the superstitions and the ancestral voices of those of African origin whose stories, beliefs and myths underpin the narrative framework. And there is the pane of language, as the author seeks to make something new out of the distinct languages. Joined together, the allegorical and the linguistic at times mystify the reader. Moreover, as the novel continually unfolds in a seemingly random fashion one begins to search with increasing vigour for structural clues regarding closure. But Chamoiseau never promised a 'conventional' narrative. In fact, in the introduction to his collection called *Creole Folktales* (1995) he reminds us that conventionality is the last thing we should anticipate from him: 'I did not try to strip the tales you are about to read of all their mystery, nor did I append a glossary. Allow the strange words to work their secret magic, and above all, read these stories only at night.'

Chamoiseau is a follower of Glissant's theories of *marronage*, which hold that the runaway slave who opposes the system is the archetypal Caribbean folk hero. And yet, as has already been noted, on these small islands the 'maroon' can never truly escape and take to the hills and form self-determining, fully independent communes. The small-island rebel must remain, to some extent, dependent upon the 'plantation' for food, women and friends. Out of this complex, ambivalent relationship to the power structure, the only way effectively to resist and affirm identity is to work both with the system and against it at the same time, to undermine it from the inside *and* the outside. What writers such as Patrick Chamoiseau, Raphaël Confiant, Daniel Maximin and others are now proposing is that this act of *le petit marronage* involves more than the embracing of the 'amputated history' of Africa that was crucial for the avatars of 'negritude', and it involves more than a Glissant-inspired refocusing on French Caribbean history. The act of literary *petit marronage* involves nothing less than the restructuring of the French language. The 'revolutionary' theories of 'Créolite' advance the idea that French Caribbean national identity will be properly forged and preserved through a correct balance of memory and language.

Being bilingual, the French Caribbean has traditionally offered its writers two options. The writer may produce a novel in polished French, perhaps adopting some Creole for the dialogue to give a flavour of the region; this is the option favoured by 'mainstream' writers such as Maryse Conde or Simone Schwartz-Bart. Or the writer may choose to fully utilise Creole, as Raphaël Confiant has done in the past. By embarking upon this latter project the writer risks losing a large part of his or her 'metropolitan' readership, and perhaps local readers too.

It is the achievement of Patrick Chamoiseau to have provided a third option. He moves fluidly between both languages, within paragraphs, within sentences even, and thereby forges a new 'French' language out of the two, exploiting the space between the languages and developing illicit and unexpected fusions. Chamoiseau's language is oppositional and inclusive, and it depends upon a profound understanding of both French and Creole. Yet implicit in Chamoiseau's way is a full acknowledgement of the 'power' of language. Marie-Sophie's notebooks refer to this idea: 'With their words, they would say: *l'esclavage*, slavery. But we would only hear: *l'estravaille*, travail. When they found out and began to say *Lestravaille*, to speak closer to us, we'd already cut the word down to *travail*, the idea of plain toil . . . ha ha ha, Sophie, the word cut across like a weapon . . .'

Chamoiseau first demonstrated his new linguistic strategy in *Solibo Magnifique* (1988), the novel that preceded *Texaco*. The action begins in a square in Fort-de-France, where we find the central character, Solibo, talking to some people, among them the author. Suddenly Solibo drops dead. The police are called to investigate, two suspects die under torture and ultimately the cause of death remains a mystery. The conclusion of the novel is a narrative stream that flows without punctuation and recounts what Solibo was saying when he died. We 'hear' Solibo's words, but this is written literature, not oral literature, and Chamoiseau is a writer. His task is not only to make his cultural and political point about language and the role of the storyteller, it is also to convince us that he has found a style that is faithful to the oral tradition. His narrator hero reminds him of this problem: 'Solibo the Magnificent used to say to me: Cham Bird, you're a writer. OK. Me, Solibo, I'm a talker. Do you see the distance between the two? . . . I'm going away, but you, you'll stay behind. I was a talker, but you write, telling people that you come from speech. You shake hands with me across the distance. That's fine, but the distance remains . . .'

The traversal of that distance is Chamoiseau's quest, as he grapples with problems of narrative and form, and the nature of his struggle marks him out as a unique figure in French Caribbean literature. Chamoiseau's storyteller talks directly to the reader, insulting him, cajoling him, teasing him. He holds on to a rope that is looped through a ring in the reader's nose and he confidently leads him down an unpaved narrative highway. In the late nineteenth century storyteller/writers stopped talking directly to readers. Sometime in the early twentieth century such figures disappeared altogether and abandoned their stories to the unchecked consciousness of their fictional characters. Whatever one may think of Chamoiseau's revolutionary intentions, or his wisdom in dropping a depth charge into the heart of the French language, it is clear that this writer has not returned empty-handed to the oral tradition of Creole folk tales. He has returned with the full armoury of world literature and a comprehensive knowledge of what has happened to the form of the novel in the twentieth century.

Chamoiseau is 'postmodern' only in the sense that the techniques of modernism have provided him with the wherewithal for the creation of 'oral' novels such as *Solibo Magnifique* or *Texaco*. On closer examination, it is clear that both Joyce and Faulkner have shown him how to allow language to flow unchecked so that it smashes the narrative mould and overflows into something disturbing and new – into something neither 'written' nor 'spoken', but identifiable as both. And among his contemporaries, one cannot help but note the similarities in his writing to the work of Salman Rushdie. Like Rushdie, he has an ancestor named William Makepeace Thackeray. And, like Rushdie, he tells the history of his people in great polyphonic rushes of words and ideas, all the while revelling in name play, punning, parenthetical asides, strange but effective metaphors and a highly effective penchant for affecting the stuttering rhythms of speech.

> My first concern was to avenge my Esternome. In my mind (ejected from carefree youth), good Sir Lonyon was the source of the world's misery. He and his two Bosses carried the death of my Esternome on their shoulders. At the hour I found my Esternome lifeless I rushed to the coolie Silver Beak to seek revenge. Collapsing in his hutch, I howled like a Christmas pig, raking my lungs. The Quarter made a circle around my misery. They eyed my pain like a bad season. A few tried to take me elsewhere. I tore away from them to implore again at that inhuman door. Coolie Silver Beak was inside, but he didn't budge. They dragged me to my hutch where they attended to the body of my dear Esternome: bathing him, clothing, covering him with the ointments which best protect the body on that unknown journey.

Clearly Patrick Chamoiseau is as much a product of the library as he is of a shanty town named Texaco, or an island named Martinique.

Chamoiseau's language is a literary construction. No Martiniquan would speak exactly as he writes. Chamoiseau knows and acknowledges this. Solibo reminds him of it: 'That's fine, but the distance remains . . .' But the empirical basis of Chamoiseau's language matters little, for *Texaco* is an act of literary creation, not a pastiche of an earlier form or a documentary report. Chamoiseau's enduring achievement is to have stitched Creole into the heart of the French language, and French into the heart of the Creole language, and to have encouraged a modal exchange that is by turns subtle and alarming. Indeed, his world leaves one questioning the wisdom of Césaire's observation in 1978 that 'Creole cannot express abstract ideas, [it is] an exclusively spoken language'. Well, apparently not. Chamoiseau's work, particularly *Texaco*, is all the more remarkable given the traditional resilience of the French language to even the most minor of revisions. Perhaps this is why critics hostile to Chamoiseau have dubbed his language *français-banane*.

It is only proper, obviously, to honour the role of the translators, Rose-Myriam Rejouis and Val Vinokurov. Despite its huge success in France, and its international reputation, *Texaco* has taken five years to appear in English. This has been due in part to the difficulty of translating from two languages, the French and the Creole, and being faithful to the collage of meaning and counter-meaning in which 'Oiseau de Cham' revels. But the diligence of the translators has been amply rewarded, for they have provided a wonderfully fluid text, and by adding to Chamoiseau's own chronology and footnotes a glossary of French Creole terms, they have gone a long way towards resolving some of the many ambiguities of language in which this novel delights.

Patrick Chamoiseau has emerged at an important time in French Caribbean literature; or perhaps, as these things often happen, the emergence of Chamoiseau has made the time important. He has helped the writers and the intellectuals of the French Caribbean to recognise that the oral tradition is in mortal danger of being supplanted by the written tradition; that the world of Africa, in its creolised form, is continually in danger of being mediated to the margins by the world of France; that the Creole language too contains history and power and that it too is in danger of being displaced by the polished periods of French. If these aspects of the Créolite universe are allowed to disappear then all diasporan people of African origin will lose a little more of their identity.

It was Césaire who began this task of reclamation, and he was suceeded by Glissant. But it is Chamoiseau who is making the most audacious attempt at recovery. He has set out to rescue a tradition, to reconfigure language, and thereby to ensure that we continue to participate in that crucial act of memory.

> The sap of the plant becomes clear only once the roots have revealed their secret. To understand Texaco and our fathers' rush toward City, we'll have to go far, deep down my own family tree, for what I know of collective memory is only what I know of my own. Besides, my memory is only faithful when it tells the history of my old flesh.

An accomplished literary *petit marron,* Chamoiseau has demonstrated to the African people of Martinique and Guadeloupe, and to everybody who considers the problems of identity with moral and literary seriousness, that the writer should always create himself and his people before somebody else creates them.

1997

Following On: The Legacy of Lamming and Selvon

I am often asked by journalists which writers have most influenced me, or which books have meant the most to me. An impossible question in many ways, for the answer depends upon what I happen to be writing and, of course, what I happen to be reading at any given moment. However, these days I find myself mentioning two writers with increasing frequency: George Lamming from Barbados and Samuel Selvon from Trinidad. Two very different writers who, as fate would have it, arrived in England in 1950 aboard the same ship. I won't attempt to summarise their varied and remarkable careers. I will try instead to say a few brief words about why, as the years pass by, these two writers have become increasingly important to me.

When I first realised that I wanted to write I looked to books by authors who were, in terms of both subject-matter and visage, in my ballpark. Given the fact that in the 1970s there was not what we might term a black British literary tradition, I looked to the United States and to a familiar roster of writers: Leroi Jones (or Amiri Baraka), Ralph Ellison, Richard Wright, James Baldwin, of course, and to the poets Ted Joans, Nikki Giovanni, Don Lee, Sonia Sanchez. These were urban writers, and in some ways 'angry' writers, whose beat was the cold, concrete streets of the city, and whose voices were raised against poverty, prejudice, police brutality, racism and all the various evils that 'the man' was heaping upon our urban heads.

Although I was born in St Kitts, I had been raised and educated in the inner city, in Leeds, and I knew something about the reality of the cold, concrete streets of the city. I could connect with the frustrations of the African-American writers, and I could certainly identify with the dark faces that stared out from their book jackets. However, I was not only reading for inspiration and affirmation, I was also reading in the hope that I might one day become a part of this club of writers – albeit American writers. It never occurred to me that I might become part of the other club of writers; the British writers of the late 1970s, the John Fowles, William Golding, Iris Murdoch, Doris Lessing 'club'. Although these writers were all British, they seemed to me to inhabit an altogether different world from the world with which I was familiar. And then, in the early 1980s, I travelled to the United States.

I had first visited the United States in 1978 and it was there that I was initially fired with the ambition to write. Three or four years later I returned and in the interval I had familiarised myself with the work of many African-American authors. However, when I returned, now armed with this new knowledge, I became confused. I remember one hot, sweaty Saturday night sitting in a theatre somewhere off Broadway and watching the Negro Ensemble's production of Douglas Fuller's play *A Soldier's Play*, which featured a very young Denzel Washington. At the interval I finally figured out what was wrong with the relationship between this play and me; in fact, between all African-American literature and me. The simple fact was I was not an American. I could respond to the universal elements of African-American fiction, or theatre, or poetry, and I could recognise the roots of its indignation, righteous or otherwise. However, African-American writers, in spite of their chosen locales, which were recognisably urban, and their faces, which were undeniably black, left me with a feeling that there was still something missing. Like the British writers such as Golding or Lessing, they were, at least to my eyes, from a different world. On that hot and somewhat bewildering New York night I realised that if I was going to write I would have to find some other literature which I could both learn from and be inspired by.

At this stage, to my mind, Caribbean literature meant either V.S. Naipaul, whose politics I found difficult to digest, or books in the Heinemann Caribbean Series, whose texts had the annoying habit of continually making reference to fruits and flowers and trees which bore no relationship to those I grew up with in Leeds. The truth was, I would no more have known a breadfruit from a plantain, or a mango from a papaya. An hibiscus might well have been a flamboyant tree for all I knew, and a palm tree was a palm tree was a palm tree. Who cared that there were a dozen varieties of palm trees, all with their own specific names and histories. Caribbean literature in its broadest sense baffled me. And then I came upon Samuel Selvon and George Lamming.

Samuel Selvon's *The Lonely Londoners* was a revelation to me. I recognised the urban landscape, even though it was presented to me in the most striking Caribbean vernacular. However, more important than this, I also recognised the contradictory tension engendered by Selvon's attraction to and rejection by England. In Selvon's fiction there was a sense of being both inside and outside Britain at the same time. The literature was shot through with the uncomfortable anxieties of belonging and not belonging and these same anxieties underscored my life and the lives of many people of my generation in the Britain of the 1970s and early 1980s.

Selvon also wrote about love and the concomitant emotion, which is jealousy. What made his work painful to read was the love he expressed for a city which, deep in his heart, he knew would betray him, and others like him. The following is from Selvon's story 'My Girl and the City'. The narrator's girlfriend asks him the pointed question, 'But why do you love London?'

> Maybe I could have told her because one evening in the summer I was waiting for her, only it wasn't like summer

> at all. Rain had been falling all day, and a haze hung above the bridges across the river, and the water was muddy and brown, and there was a kind of wistfulness and sadness about the evening. The way St Paul's was half-hidden in the rain, the motionless trees along the Embankment. But you say a thing like that and people don't understand at all. How sometimes a surge of greatness could sweep over you when you see something.
>
> But even if I had said all that and much more, it would not have been what I meant. You could be lonely as hell in the city, then one day you look around you and you realize everybody else is lonely too, withdrawn, locked, rushing home out of the chaos: blank faces, unseeing eyes, millions and millions of them, up the Strand, down the Strand, jostling in Charing Cross for the 5.20.

Samuel Selvon's ability to paint a portrait of the gritty inner city, make it attractive, and at the same time people it with characters who were migrating from office to home, from desk to tube, from country to country, people on the move, in between, ambivalent, and lonely, eventually had a larger impact on me than the African-American literature that I had been reading. And then I happened upon the work of his fellow emigrant, George Lamming.

The first book of George Lamming's I read was a remarkable novel from 1972 entitled *Natives of My Person*. As densely textured as Faulkner, and possessing formal ambitions of Joycean proportions, it was clear to me that I need no longer be afraid of Caribbean literature alienating me on the grounds that I could not tell a mango from a papaya. This literature was drawing me in, teasing me with its deeply historical sensibility, challenging me with its structural gamesmanship. Lamming was in a different league from the vast majority of the other Caribbean writers whom I had been attempting to read. And then I came upon his book *The Pleasures of Exile*.

I recently rediscovered the now tattered paperback edition

of *The Pleasures of Exile* that I bought in the early 1980s. This nonfiction book – a volume which Lamming describes in the introduction as 'really no more than a report on one man's way of seeing, using certain facts of experience as evidence and a guide' – makes links between the Atlantic slave experience and the colonisation of language. It places the migration of Caribbean peoples to Britain into a global political and cultural context, and in this sense the book is – as I later discovered – in the tradition of the work which C.L.R. James had been pursuing for many a decade.

I want to quote from Lamming in *The Pleasures of Exile,* for it is not only essential to try to understand the effect that these writers had on their successors, spearheading, as they did, a genuine revolution in Caribbean writing in the second half of the twentieth century; it matters that we try to understand the effect that these writers and their writing had on contemporary English letters, and British society at large. Or, put it another way, did they have any effect? In 1960, in *The Pleasures of Exile,* Lamming wrote:

> An important question, for the English critic, is not what the West Indian novel has brought to English writing. It would be more correct to ask what the West Indian novelists have contributed to English reading. For the language in which these books are written is English – which, I must repeat – is a West Indian language; and in spite of the unfamiliarity of its rhythms, it remains accessible to the readers of English anywhere in the world.

It is difficult for somebody of my generation to know exactly what effect novelists such as Samuel Selvon and George Lamming had on English reading back in the 1950s and 1960s. I can hazard a guess, for I don't underestimate the impervious nature of British society, both then and now. However, in the 1970s and 1980s I know that these writers had a profound effect on my generation, the second generation in this country, who found themselves trying to deal with ambivalence and confusion with regard to their relationship to British society. During this period Allison & Busby reprinted much of Lamming's work, and new editions of Selvon appeared. In this period I am convinced that Selvon and Lamming had an effect on what Lamming calls 'English reading'. Those of my generation who were going to write found in the work of these two authors recognisable subject-matter and a restlessness associated with formal invention, which meant there was no longer any necessity for us to keep looking to New Jersey or Chicago or Detroit for our literary fixes. The groundwork had already been laid down by Lamming and Selvon and a generation of writers from the Caribbean, who had migrated to Britain during the 1950s and early 1960s. They were our literary antecedents, writers who knew not only the names of the flora and fauna, but also the pages of London's *A–Z*. They knew also the front door and the back door of the BBC. Particularly the back door.

I would like to conclude by pointing to just one more section from Samuel Selvon's exquisite story 'My Girl and the City'. If I were to direct a student towards writing which captures the rhythm, texture and tone of London just as the austere 1950s were about to give way to the swinging 1960s I would not send them to the plays of John Osborne or Arnold Wesker, or to the prose of David Storey or John Braine. For acuity of vision, intellectual rigour and sheer beauty of language they would have to be supplicants at the pages of Selvon and Lamming. If the answer to George Lamming's question is 'West Indian novelists contributed little to English reading habits of the time', then more fool the English reading public. This haunting extract from Sam Selvon's 'My Girl and the City' is part of what they were missing.

> Once again I am on a green train returning to the heart from the suburbs, and I look out the window into the windows of private lives flashed on my brain. Bread being sliced, a man

taking off a jacket, an old woman knitting. And all these things I see – the curve of a woman's arm, undressing, the blankets being tucked, and once a solitary figure staring at trains as I stared at windows. All the way into London Bridge – is falling down. is falling down, the wheels say. One must have a thought – where buildings and the shadows of them encroach on the railway tracks. Now the train crawls across the bridges, dark steel in the darkness: the thoughtful gloom of Waterloo: Charing Cross bridge, Thames reflecting lights, and the silhouettes of the city buildings against the sky of the night.

When I was in New York, many times I went into that city late at night after a sally to the outskirts, it lighted up with a million lights, but never a feeling as on entering London. Each return to the city is loaded with thought, so that by the time I take the Inner Circle I am as light as air.

At last I think I know what it is all about. I move around in a world of words. Everything that happens is words. But pure expression is nothing. One must build on the things that happen; it is insufficient to say I sat in the underground and the train hurtled through the darkness and someone isn't using amplex. So what? So now I weave, I say there was an old man on whose face wrinkles rivered, whose hands were shapeful with arthritis, but when he spoke, oddly enough, his voice was young and gay.

But there was no old man, there was nothing, and there is never anything.

1998

Britain

Introduction: A Little Luggage

The rush of migration from the Caribbean to Britain in the 1950s included my parents and me. We arrived in England during the summer months of 1958. My parents were a young couple with little luggage beyond me, their infant son. Only now do I look back and realise how profoundly disorientating and disturbing it must have been for them both, my mother just twenty and my father twenty-five. They disembarked into a grey, overcast world, hoping that their young son would be able to garner an education and, as he grew up, make some kind of a life for himself beyond the limitations of the Caribbean world. Of course, they also wanted this for themselves. All three of us stood in a family cluster and my parents looked about them. Despite the strangeness of this new place, they felt convinced that they had come to the right country.

Like most West Indian migrants, they were relatively inexperienced in the ways of the world. Immediately on arrival they made a second, equally bleak journey north to Leeds, where the accommodation they secured was typical of that occupied by West Indian migrants of the period. The house was overcrowded and the toilet was outside and at the end of the street. They soon found work, but they were isolated, lonely and vulnerable. The greatest blow to their soul was the 'news' that because of the colour of their skin, they would inevitably experience difficulty being accepted as British. This fact cast a particularly dark cloud over their lives, and over the lives of countless thousands of other West Indians who had arrived in the *mother country* clutching a British passport.

Postwar Britain was an austere and insecure place. British people knew that their role in the world was shrinking, and the years between the handing over of India in 1947 and the Suez crisis in 1956 were years in which the reality of Britain's increasingly limited role in world affairs was becoming painfully evident. As a result many Britons began to avert their gaze from the former Empire and concentrate upon the difficult task of rebuilding British industry and confidence. A huge percentage of West Indian people, including my parents, arrived in Britain motivated by a desire to contribute to this process of rebuilding. Their role in the Health Service, in transportation, and in a wide range of service industries, helped to stabilise the economy and eventually enabled the nation to enjoy what became known as the swinging Sixties.

However, my parents did not do much swinging in the Sixties. My parents, and other West Indian migrants, persevered in the face of much hostility and prejudice, particularly over housing and employment. By the 1970s their children's generation, my generation, was still being subjected to the same prejudices which had blighted their arrival, but we were not our parents. You might say we lacked their good manners and their ability to turn the other cheek. Whereas they could sustain themselves with the dream of one day 'going home', we were already at home. We had nowhere else to go and we needed to tell British society this. The 1976 and 1977 Notting Hill riots were born out of this frustration. By now my parents had witnessed their son grow up into a truculent, afro-sporting rebel. It is difficult to imagine what they saw when they looked at their stubborn, urban child, but it was certainly a young man wrought out of altogether different material from that which had shaped the children of their friends whom they had left behind in the Caribbean nearly twenty years earlier.

After three, often confusing, years at university, I began my life as a writer. I knew that this was not going to be an easy path to pursue. As far back as 1926, the American writer Langston Hughes had already articulated the anxiety that I now found coursing through my body. 'The Negro artist works against an undertow of sharp criticism and misunderstanding from his own group and unintentional bribes from the whites.' What kind of a writer was I going to be? A polemicist? An apologist? An interpreter? My early work in the theatre, while achieving some small commercial and critical success, certainly divided opinions along racial lines. To many I was not radical enough, while others wished to reward me with honorary membership of a club to which I had no desire to belong. The critic for the *Yorkshire Post* reviewed my first play, *Strange Fruit,* and made the following observation: 'Mr Phillips has pillaged the white man's theatre knowledgedly for a powerful, rangy, tragic play which is, ironically, about black men's roots.' 'Pillaged' the 'white man's theatre'? 'Knowledgedly'? I stopped reading reviews.

The subject-matter that presented itself to me, during the turmoil and welter of Britain in the late 1970s and early 1980s, was determinedly political. How could it be otherwise? I remember struggling to write a third play, with a postcard that I had bought in France lying face-up on my desk. It was of a white woman's face, probably that of a woman of thirty or thirty-five, who had just cried, or who would cry. Curled around her forehead, with just enough pressure to cause a line of folds in the skin above her eyes, were two black hands; obviously power and strength slept somewhere within them, but at this moment they were infinitely gentle, describing with eight fingers that moment when a grip of iron weakens to a caress of love. And on the man's third finger of his right hand a ring; he was not married, at least not to her. Perhaps neither of them was married. When, some months earlier, I had first seen the postcard it had taken me only a few Parisian seconds to decide that the next piece that I would write would be about this image.

So much of the 'racial trouble' in British life seemed to have occurred as a result of this one image, and the uncomfortable word that it brought forth; miscegenation. In 1919 there were race riots in Liverpool which were, according to a report in the *New York Times,* caused by 'the Negroes' familiarity with white women'. Within a few weeks of my parents' arrival in Britain in 1958, the Notting Hill riots erupted and again there could be little doubt as to the origin of the 'problem'. The *US News and World Report* was outspoken in a manner which complemented the coyness of the British press on this subject. It reported that in addition 'to friction over housing and employment' the riots were caused by 'the resentment of white men over Negroes associating with white women. In London and other industrial cities it has been commonplace to see young Negro men with white girls . . . the association of Negro men and white girls has stirred jealousy and resentment among young men.'

It was into this climate of proprietorial paranoia that my parents had migrated. I grew up in this claustrophobic environment, and fresh out of university I was now attempting to become a writer in a country that was suffering a profound identity crisis. I was living in a society which had, with the end of the Empire, imported its colonial practice of arriving in the tropics, raising a flag and constructing a club – which of course meant establishing rules of membership – into the domestic arena. The Britain that I recognised practised discrimination in education, in housing, in employment, in all areas of social life. Us and them. Lines were not to be crossed. Those who transgressed were to be severely punished by social ostracisation and random acts of violence. One day my immigrant father took his teenage son to one side and shared with him the whispered news that he should always be especially vigilant if out at night with a white girl. The son listened, but he had already discovered for himself the truth of this statement. In fact, he would forever wear a small scar on his face that was testament to the wisdom of his father's belated words. This being the case, there was little that the son could say in answer, beyond a grateful, surreptitious, nod. In a sense, Britain had come between them.

As a five-year-old I remember sitting with my parents and

watching the funeral of Sir Winston Churchill on television. A few years later, a shivering boy in shorts and long socks waited with his mother for what seemed like hours outside Leeds Civic Hall, hoping to achieve a glimpse of Her Majesty the Queen. In those days my parents and their young son lived in the same Britain. By the mid-1970s we lived in different countries. And to cap it all, now I wanted to be a writer, not a doctor or a lawyer, but a writer. They had brought me to Britain in the hope that I might make something of myself beyond the limitations of the Caribbean world. They had brought me to their imaginary world of British good manners and civility, and in the face of overwhelming evidence they continued to suspend their disbelief at what they had discovered in order to nurture the dream that I might succeed. But now they were watching pitched battles between their children and the British police, live on national television. When I began purposefully to put pen to paper they had to admit defeat. They now conceded that the Britain that they had imagined they were bringing me to back in the 1950s had, in all likelihood, never existed.

Today my parents' generation of West Indian migrants, who stepped gingerly from the ships in the 1950s, are now grandparents as a third generation has emerged. Some of these senior citizens have made arrangements to return to the Caribbean of their childhood. Since the early 1990s several hundred a year have been escaping the cold, the hostility, and trying to re-establish themselves at 'home'. But, of course, the Caribbean has also changed. It is expensive and the society is not always open to 'returnees'. Those who have stayed on in Britain remain determined and focused in the face of a sharp increase in racial violence and acts of intolerance. The homogenisation of Europe opens the door not so much to immigrants, but to nationalists who lament the erosion of racially inscribed 'traditional' values. But my parents' generation look on with stoicism. Their job is done. They worked with discipline and purpose. You still see them: the pensioner with her bus pass. The newly retired nurse at the post office. The old boy in the local with his pint and newspaper. They arrived with a little luggage. They have survived the loss of their imaginary Britain. Sadly, in some cases, they have also had to survive the loss of their children. But they have survived.

Ignatius Sancho: A Black British Man of Letters

The second half of the twentieth century has witnessed the decline of Britain as a power of global significance. Concomitant with this waning of international importance has been a redefinition of what it means to be British. In the 1960s comments by the Tory MP Enoch Powell, which sought to exclude black people from the national picture, reminded the populace that Britain possessed a racially constructed concept of nation. In the 1980s, with the emergence of a second generation of black people who were born in Britain, Mrs Thatcher redefined this concept actually to *include* some black people. However, this redefinition of nation was not a benevolent act. Mrs Thatcher's 'generosity' was directly connected to Britain's increasing sense of herself as somehow inadequate. In the 1980s and early 1990s, poll tax rioters, Clause 28 'Queers', Brussels bureaucrats and the perpetrators of 'race' riots all fed Britain's sense of herself as a nation in crisis. There was a perceived need to co-opt 'trouble-makers' from the fringes and make them feel a part of the centre. What Mrs Thatcher achieved by including black people in her concept of nation was to introduce the idea of divide and rule into the domestic arena, an idea that had long been used as a central tenet of Empire.

In 1983 the Conservative Party produced, with the aid of the advertising firm Saatchi and Saatchi, a now notorious election poster. It featured a black man who was smartly dressed in a suit and carrying a briefcase. The caption read: 'Labour says he's black, Tories say he's British.' Implicit in the new Thatcherite concept of nationhood was the idea that one could not be both black and British. Black equals bad, British equals good. We will take you as British as long as you look like you belong – no afros, no dashikis, no beads, no shoulder bags, only a suit, tie and briefcase, thank you very much. For the first time in British history, two types of black person were now being officially recognised: the 'good' and the 'bad' – the British and the black, the assimilable and the subversive. The nation had certainly moved on from the 'Powellite' model in which *all* blacks were to be excluded from the national narrative and encouraged to go 'back to where they came from'.

Two hundred years ago, towards the end of the eighteenth century, Georgian England was fast approaching a crossroads. The times were still characterised by leisure – slow wagons, peddlers in the street, spinning wheels – but already one could detect the strains of the industrial age that would quickly eradicate this bucolic Hanoverian era. England was beginning to be troubled by political disturbances, such as the Gordon riots. As if this were not enough, there was also a deeply ingrained fear of Catholicism and Irish immigration, and an open acknowledgement of the nuisance of free blacks and slaves who occupied both high and low stations in national life. Generally, there was a recognised confusion as to how this great nation might now comport itself on the threshold of modern times. There was no need to espouse a racially constructed nationalism, for it was understood that the nation was white and that the black presence, no matter how annoying and unseemly, posed no real threat, for it simply represented the unwelcome backwash of the nation's maritime adventures in the slave trade. The thousands of blacks who congregated in Liverpool, Bristol and London constituted a 'problem' that might be solved by such practical means as the founding of the colony of Sierra Leone and, if necessary, the wholescale deportation of the dark strangers.

Two hundred years later, despite the 'Powellite' cry to send them 'back to where they came from', Britain's black population is clearly a more permanent part of the national scene. The cultural impact of black people on British society has been considerable, and it is this cultural 'work' that has helped to move the nation from the Powellite notion of exclusion towards the Thatcherite model of limited inclusion. Musical groups such as Aswad and Soul II Soul have exerted a powerful pull on the British sensibility – both black and white – not just in terms of music, but also in terms of style. In literature the emergence of writers such as Salman Rushdie and Linton Kwesi Johnson meant that inevitably questions would have to be asked about what constitutes the nature of being British. In sport, Linford Christie, Frank Bruno and Ian Wright, to name three, have become national heroes, which means that Britain can no longer pretend to define her sense of nationality along strictly racial lines. These developments in the broadly 'cultural' zone have not been matched by similar developments in politics, business or government. That a handful of black MPs have begun to be elected suggests that black people have only just started to gain a foothold on the lower rungs of 'power'. Clearly the changing racial definition of nation owes nearly everything to the cultural response.

In the eighteenth century there was certainly a cultural response to Britain by the black community in terms of music, literature and the theatre. Black musicians and actors populated the land, and writers such as Olaudah Equiano and Ukawsaw Gronniosaw spoke eloquently and forcefully about their individual lives and the general nature of the black experience in Britain. However, while the odd musician such as George Bridgetower may have been outstanding, there was not enough evidence of excellence in the work of these artists to force British society to sit up and take notice. One also has to bear in mind the fact that during this period it was difficult for a British black person to gain information regarding developments in the diaspora. Two hundred years later the black community in Britain would gain some confidence by observing the processes of decolonisation in Africa, and the success of the Civil Rights movement in the United States. They were able to view their own interventions as part of a global stategy, whereas black people in eighteenth-century Britain largely perceived their own efforts as occurring in a national context.

Ignatius Sancho was born in 1729 on a slave ship that was crossing the Atlantic. He arrived in England aged two, finding himself in the austere household of three sisters in Greenwich. Yet from these unpromising beginnings Sancho went on to become a servant in the Duke of Montagu's household, which provided him with the opportunities to pursue an education and finally to leave service and open his own grocery in London's Mayfair. It was then that Sancho became a dedicated correspondent. A devoted husband to a black West Indian wife, Anne Osborne, and father to six children, most of Sancho's letters concern the domestic travails of a grocer in ill-health trying to keep together body and soul. However, Sancho also feels moved to comment upon both political and literary life in Britain, and he does so with a deep love of the country, and a thwarted desire to belong. In one particularly telling description he appropriates a Shakespearian image, and then undermines it with the reality of his own appearance. 'Figure to yourself, my dear sir, a man of convexity of belly exceeding Falstaff – and a black face into the bargain.'

It is easy to think of Sancho as obsequious, but such a description is far too reductive. True enough, Sancho adopts a deferential tone in his dealings with society, but the same could be said of nearly every 'novice' writer of the period. It was common practice to display a full command of etiquette and to bow 'excessively' before one's literary and social superiors. In this sense Sancho was merely acknowledging the convention of the times. Although writing at the height of the debate about slavery, Sancho chose not to rail and preach against the evils of the institution in as outgoing a manner as, say, Equiano. He did, however, bring up this very subject in his first letter to Laurence Sterne, encouraging the famous writer to wield his pen on the side of those lobbying for the abolition of the slave trade:

> – That subject, handled in your striking manner, would ease the yoke (perhaps) of many – but if only of me – Gracious God! – what a feast to a benevolent heart.

To view this family man as an 'Uncle Tom' is to misread both the historical period and the nature of the man. The journey from slave ship to Mayfair shop is a remarkable one. Ignatius Sancho was hyper-conscious of his unique role in London society, providing as he did an alternative mirror into which one might peer and spy a black man beyond the model of the stage fool, as perfected by such vagrants as Billy Waters, or the protester and pamphleteer, as perfected by Equiano and others. Sancho probably regarded himself as something of a role model, and his presence in literary London would certainly have complicated many individuals' ideas of blackness. In fact, a review of the 1782 first edition of the *Letters of the Late Ignatius Sancho* claimed that the book 'presents to us the naked effusions of a negroe's heart, and it shews it glowing with the finest philanthropy, and the purest affections . . .' Sancho's dignity and literacy were never going to be enough to force British society to reconsider the model of a racially constructed nation, but Sancho was the forerunner of the possibility of thinking about black people in assimilationist terms. He was a 'good' black.

The sociologist Stuart Hall has recently noted the extent to which American academics and scholars of the African diasporan world are turning their attentions towards both contemporary and historical Britain. It seems to me that this is largely because Britain provides the earliest model of vigorous interaction between those of the African diaspora and those of European origin. For much of the eighteenth century America remained a British colony and her relationship with her black population was not as complex as Britain's, where a black middle class had clearly begun to emerge. However, this black British middle class was only able to negotiate eighteenth-century society with some difficulty. The personal anxieties of such negotiations resulted in the development of a 'double consciousness' along the lines which the great American philosopher and writer W.E.B. Du Bois would later identify in the United States. There was among these pioneering black Britons a sense of both belonging and not belonging. A sense of being part of the nation and being outside it. It is no wonder that in order to understand the roots of their own African diasporan traditions Americans have begun to look at Britain.

Ignatius Sancho held the key to understanding British society through both his command of the language and his bearing. However, by virtue of his pigmentation and history, he was doomed to occupy a role both 'central' *and* 'peripheral'. In contemporary Britain Lord Taylor, a Tory member of the House of Lords who has recently had to settle for a seat in the upper house after being spectacularly defeated in the 'safe' Tory seat of Cheltenham, represents the idea of a British black man who occupies both the centre and the margin. Such 'doubly-conscious' men are the true successors to Sancho, but their lives are made considerably easier in societies which are now happy to subscribe to assimilationist strategies of nationhood. While these 'Uncle Toms' will never win the general applause of 'the people', or disrupt the nation's sense of race, they will, by virtue of their very existence, ask society to address itself to uncomfortable questions. What makes Ignatius Sancho's role in this strategy so intriguing is that, while the British nation was still mired in a guilt-free sense of itself as strictly white, and while there was an absence of cultural or political pressure to encourage the nation to adapt its image of itself, and while there was precious little reflected evidence of diasporan success beyond the shores of Britain, Sancho still persisted in ploughing his own unique 'doubly-conscious' furrow with a courageous dignity.

1996

Linton Kwesi Johnson: Prophet in Another Land

Linton Kwesi Johnson is a reed of a man, slim and little more than five feet eight inches in height. When he squares up to somebody, it is the force of his personality that counts, not his physical presence. The confrontation had been brewing for some time. Finally, after the gig at the Théâtre Elysée Montmartre in Paris, Linton and the musician had it out. During the set I had watched Linton turn to the violinist and make a comment that was clearly calculated to rein in this musician's excessive stage theatrics. A few minutes later Linton turned to him again, and this time let him know that his amplifier was too loud. Linton was right. From where I was standing on the balcony the violinist's scratchings and scrapings were dominating the other instruments. The violinist made no attempt to turn down his amplifier.

After the gig, I showed the security guys my backstage pass and entered a small, dingy corridor. Linton's dressing room was to the right, and beyond it was the dressing room of Dennis Bovell and his band. And then I saw Linton in the corridor face to face with the violinist. 'I'm telling you, you were too fucking loud.' The violinist tried to stare Linton down, but Linton kept repeating himself. 'Don't fuck about with me, you were too fucking loud.' As I backed away, I bumped into a blonde French woman in her early forties. I had already met Virginie. She handles Linton's business affairs in France. Virginie arched her eyebrows as if to ask what was going on. I said nothing, for the situation was self-evident. The violinist chose this moment to capitulate. He turned from Linton, then stormed past Virginie and myself and back out in the direction of the auditorium. Linton retired to his dressing room and slammed the door shut. Virginie swallowed deeply. 'There are some people from Warner Brothers who need to see Linton.' I smiled sympathetically.

Linton Kwesi Johnson was born in the small rural town of Chapelton, Jamaica in 1952. In 1963 an eleven-year-old Linton came to England to join his mother. He attended school in south London and as a teenager joined the British equivalent of the Black Panther Party. Soon he was not only agitating and demonstrating on the Brixton front line, he was also writing poetry. He left school at sixteen and went to work for the Civil Service, but in the evenings he studied for his A levels. In the early 1970s he went to London University's Goldsmith's College to study sociology, where he became one of the first black Britons to pass through the British education system and take a degree.

Upon graduating Linton began to write and record in earnest. His debut album, *Dread Beat 'an Blood* (1978), accurately captured the disaffection of a generation of black youths in Britain. The albums and books of poetry that followed only served to confirm his reputation as a cultural commentator of the first order. *Forces of Victory* (1979), *Bass Culture* (1980) and *Making History* (1984) explored the many iniquities and ironies of contemporary black British life. Linton was quick to remind his audience that Britain's first generation of black workers had been offered unskilled, exploitative jobs, while their children, the second generation, were being marginalised by the school system, harassed by the police and faced the seemingly lifelong prospect of unemployment.

In the mid-1980s Linton severed his ties to Chris Blackwell's Island Records, and began to hone his entrepreneurial skills by founding his own label and slowly building his own roster of artists. He also 'retired' temporarily from the recording scene, although he continued to give poetry readings. Britain in the late 1980s appeared to be changing, as a handful of black people were finally entering the mainstream in the media, in parliament and in sport. However, Linton Kwesi Johnson remained unconvinced and silent. In 1991 Linton eventually emerged from his 'retirement' with a CD entitled *Tings an' Times,* which was also the title of a new volume of verse. And now, seven years later, he has just released a new CD, *More Time,* which, like its predecessor, remains as politically impassioned as ever. However, as a third generation of black Britons emerges, a generation who are invested in Scary Spice and Sol Campbell as role models, what is the continued relevance of Linton Kwesi Johnson? And what on earth are the French supposed to make of him?

I put these questions to William Tanifeani, a journalist and activist who I had arranged to meet in a bar near my hotel in St Germain. He is a man in his early forties with the type of afro that we only see on old episodes of *Top of the Pops.* But William is not likely to sing. He is all business, from the glass of mineral water that he orders to the file of papers that he shuffles on the table before us. 'You see, Linton is, along with Bob Marley, the most important of the reggae artists that have come to France. People listen very carefully to his lyrics. When he sings "Inglan is a Bitch" or "Sonny's Lettah" French people know all the words.' William recounts for me his memories of seeing Linton playing at the Palais to the north of Paris in front of 6,000 people. He looks vaguely disapproving when I express surprise that Linton can command this kind of an audience in France. 'Perhaps the time is right for us here,' he suggests. 'Back in the Seventies when you were having a lot of trouble with the emergence of your second generation of black people, Linton was saying things that you needed to hear. But now? Well, maybe it is us who need to hear these things.'

We are joined by a friend of William's. Mogniss Abdallah looks slightly dishevelled in his crumpled jacket and trousers, open shirt, and scuffed shoes, but his manner is patrician and enhanced by a handsome pipe. Mogniss is in charge of an agency called IM Media, which seeks to expose the racist immigration practices of the French government, and highlight the issue of racist attacks, murders and police violence by organising events, making films and publishing magazines and journals. Mogniss opens his battered briefcase and pulls out a sheaf of ten-by-eight photographs of Linton speaking to some migrants in one of the vast, sprawling estates that surround Paris. 'You see, when Linton comes here he does not always have time to do this, but sometimes he will come and speak to the youth. For them it is something they will never forget.' I stare at the pictures of Linton surrounded by eager crowds of young French boys and girls of North African origin. Mogniss suggests that I keep the photographs, offering them to me as proof of the other side of Linton.

I leave Mogniss and William for an appointment with Hélène Lee. Linton's assistant in London had told me that she was a French journalist who was well informed about Linton and his work. I discover Hélène to be a petite woman in her fifties who, on this warm day, is wearing a fur-lined and fully zipped-up anorak. Under one arm she carries a copy of a book about Rastafarianism. We walk the short distance from my hotel to a small bar where, in a characteristically French manner, we sit outside and on the corner of the street so that we block the flow of pedestrian traffic. I soon discover that Hélène is working on her own book about Rastafarianism and she has just returned from six months in Jamaica. 'Yes,' she says, pointing to the anorak, 'six months in Jamaica can do this to you.' Like William and Mogniss she seems surprised that I do not realise how famous Linton is in France. 'You see, here he is regarded as something of a prophet. French people like music that teaches. And they like his modesty and his living the message as well as saying it. You will see at tonight's concert. All kinds of people will be there. Young and old, hard-core reggae fans and those just interested in the drugs and the drink. And black and white, of course.'

I ask Hélène if the French audience really understand what Linton is talking about, or if the primary appeal is the music?

'The basis of his support is his lyrics,' she says. 'He is considered one of the top conscious lyricists of reggae, although his lyrics have nothing to do with Rasta.' She pauses for a moment. 'Or perhaps because they have nothing to with Rasta.' Glancing at my watch, I realise that I will have to leave Hélène perched somewhat precariously on this busy Parisian street corner. But Hélène has a final point that she insists on making. 'Linton could have a much bigger impact in France, writing for magazines, going on talk shows, playing bigger venues, but he is content to speak through the music and leave it like that. He is radical in the work.'

Barbès-Rochechouart is an avowedly multi-racial neighbourhood. Before I even leave the Métro station I am accosted by men in North African dress eager to sell me cheap jewellery, ties, sunglasses, shoelaces, all of which are laid out for inspection on creaking tables. Out on the streets the throng of people represent a veritable United Nations of traffic. I slowly pick my way along the Boulevard Barbès-Rochechouart only to discover that the pedestrian traffic is surreptitiously being made increasingly impossible by the presence of scores of bewildered tourists trying to find their way to Sacré-Coeur. And then I see the Théâtre Elysée Montmartre.

I stand on a traffic island in the middle of the boulevard. From this vantage-point I can see that the theatre has long since passed its heyday, but its crumbling façade cannot completely obscure the suggestions of former glory. Built over a century ago, the theatre was originally an extremely popular music-hall venue. In the middle part of this century, music hall having passed its sell-by date, the theatre became an established venue for wrestling and boxing. Of late it has been a home for music concerts, primarily those originating in the world of reggae or rap. The red, green and gold posters announce LKJ and the Dennis Bovell Band, but I can also see the evidence of recent visits by Burning Spear, Culture and Dennis Brown.

Jamal and I crane our necks and stare down the street as we wait for the tour bus to arrive. Dressed in his Toronto Maple

Leafs sweatshirt and baggy jeans, I imagine Jamal to be in his late twenties. He is the tour manager and he has already informed me that, having played Rouen last night, the drive from their hotel to the Elysée Montmartre should take them about one and a half hours. Then Jamal suddenly stands up straight, one ear still pressed to his mobile phone, and announces that they will be here in five minutes. 'They are near, but stuck in traffic.'

I don't know why, but I had imagined that Linton and the band would be travelling around in a mini-bus as opposed to a large double-decker coach. They look like a football team arriving at Wembley on Cup Final day. However, as I peer through the window of the coach it soon becomes clear that this unblazered assemblage of young men are not prime athletes. In fact, they look like what they are: a group of musicians who are tired of touring around France doing one-night gigs.

Linton is the first off the coach. He has the enviable gift of appearing to be a man with no time to waste. 'Let's go.' I follow him through the throng of hangers-on and journalists who now litter the steps of the Elysée Montmartre, and on into the wide-open space of the auditorium. There are no seats, which surprises me, for I had assumed that a venue with this history would boast neatly arranged, velvet-clad rows of chairs. But there is nothing, just a bar at the back of the hall, and a large elevated stage at the front. Linton's dressing room features the normal rock star's necessities. The bottle of fine brandy, the bottle of whisky, the champagne, the cold roasted chicken, the fruit, cheese and plates of cold meat, the fridge stocked with beer and a neat pile of napkins, plastic forks and paper plates. Linton looks at it all somewhat contemptuously, then tumbles into one of the couches. He turns to me as though only now seeing me for the first time, and he laughs. 'What happen?'

'Just a few black MPs,' says Linton, crossing then uncrossing his legs, 'and a few people on telly, and people think that things have fixed up. But nothing has changed, just people's willingness to look at it.' He takes another sip of coffee. 'There's a break in continuity between the second and third generation. We were involved in building. They've inherited it and they've got no sense of urgency about taking it to another stage. Today bright young black people don't lobby the Labour Party, they join it.' But surely this is a good thing, I suggest. 'But you don't see, there's a real need for an independent black organisation to police the mainstream. Look at the lack of black British music played on the radio. They think that "UB40" is reggae. Or look at the disproportionate number of black first offenders who are given custodial sentences. And over fifty black people have died in police custody in the past fifteen years. And that's just the ones we know about.'

As I frame my next question, Linton pours us both a refill of coffee. I ask him what happened to the black radicalism of the 1970s and early 1980s. He shakes his head and sighs. 'They've all gone into Channel Four or parliament or got a television show. They're part of the establishment that is saying it's all right, no problem. Tell that to Stephen Lawrence's parents.' I suggest to Linton that the drive of an immigrant is different from the drive of a settled citizen, and he agrees. But he adds quickly, 'It looks like the price of this "success" might be our losing some kind of political identity and independence.' From the look on his face I can see how painful this notion is to him. The idea of being independent, of being his own man, is of primary importance to Linton Kwesi Johnson.

He slumps back into the couch, a tired figure in his baseball cap, which is emblazoned with the word 'Jamaica', his pink shirt hanging out over his trousers, and his feet wiggling incessantly in his checked socks and sandals. Clearly the tour is wearing him out, but he knows that this is part of the price he pays for being totally in charge. Linton was the first reggae artist to leave Island Records. By doing so he turned his back on one million dollars' worth of promotion that Chris Blackwell had promised to spend in order that he might transform Linton Kwesi Johnson into a major international reggae star. However, Linton has no regrets. These days if Linton makes a record and he likes it, he puts it out. He has no desire to be controlled by the corporate music world.

I ask Linton if he has any idea why he is so popular in France and he thinks for a moment. 'I don't know. I first came here in 1979 as the opening act for the movie *Rockers*. Blackwell had me singing to a backing tape with dancers. They didn't cue it properly so everything was totally out of sync for about three numbers. I came back in 1982 and played a big club, and it's been all right since then. Maybe it's just that this place is willing to listen because things have definitely got worse. I remember waiting to meet Mogniss outside this theatre a few years ago, and I watched some bouncers pick on an Arab youth and start to beat him up. On the same tour we played Solingen in Germany, near Cologne, and the day after we left the fascists fire-bombed a Turkish hostel and killed them.'

Linton then remembered the time he was arrested and beaten by the British police in November 1972. He was walking in Brixton when he saw three policemen 'choking a guy to death'. Although he didn't know the man he asked him for his name and address. 'I was trained by the Panthers to do this.' While Linton was writing down the man's name and address and the numbers of the policemen choking him, they turned on Linton and, calling him 'a fucking black bastard', arrested him. Linton had time to slip the piece of paper to another man before he was placed in the back of a police van with three others, two women and a man, who had been picked up on 'suspicion' that they were about to commit a crime.

Once the van doors were closed the police proceeded to attack the four of them, kicking them repeatedly in the head and body. All four were charged with assaulting the police. Linton advised his fellow detainees to say nothing until there was a lawyer present, and also to ask to see a doctor. Eventually, after a protracted legal case, the charges against all four were dismissed and the officers were transferred from Brixton police station. Having finished the tale, Linton stares for a moment into the middle distance. 'This stuff is still going on back in

Britain and here as well. I don't understand how people can say, "Everything is all right, it's all taken care of." Seems to me the only one saying anything is Bernie Grant.'

Dennis Bovell is a small, thickset man. He comes in and quietly breaks off a chicken leg. He offers me some champagne and then simply stands and looks at Linton. We are to understand that Linton is needed for the soundcheck. I tell Linton that I will come backstage after the gig and we can talk some more. 'All right,' says Linton, slowly levering himself to his feet. He rubs the back of his hand into his face, then stretches and rolls forward on to the balls of his feet. He stifles a yawn as he speaks. 'I check you later.'

In the evening I push my way through the massed crowds and into the theatre. On entering the auditorium I am greeted by the sight of hundreds of people sitting cross-legged on the floor rolling joints and drinking beer. The vast majority, perhaps 90 per cent, are white, but while many look like students it is clear that, as Hélène Lee had predicted, this audience represents a wide social spectrum. Dennis and the band are already playing, so I buy a beer and make my way up to the balcony. 'Mesdames et messieurs, bonsoir.' Linton is dressed in a smart suit and tie, his trademark porkpie hat, and a handkerchief tucked nattily into his breast pocket. The evening is to be a retrospective of Linton's work over the past twenty years, and naturally enough he begins with selections from *Dread Beat 'an Blood*. As ever, he does not sing; he simply recites with rhythm over the sound of the band. Linton explains the historical context of the songs as he announces them, so that references to Blair Peach, the Notting Hill riots of 1976 and 1977 and Toxteth are all clarified.

The ecstatic audience are clearly knowledgeable. 'Here's an old anti-fascist number that is even more relevant today than it was when I wrote it back in the Seventies,' says Linton. There are huge cheers, for the audience know that he is going to sing 'Fite dem back'. Halfway through this rousing anthem, Linton snaps out his handkerchief and mops his brow, neck and face, without disturbing his hat. And then, the retro part of the evening over, Linton launches into the songs from the new album.

The single from the album, entitled 'Liesense Fi Kill', is particularly haunting. Linton introduces it by suggesting that 'the police still think that it's all right to kill black people with impunity'. Halfway through the number the violinist launches into a haunting funereal solo that is only marred by his prancing about the stage, to Linton's obvious displeasure. The song receives a huge ovation, so much so that Linton cannot continue for some minutes. After five more tracks from *More Time,* it is all over. 'Mesdames et messieurs, bonsoir. I always have a great time here. I'm glad you could join me on the anniversary of my twentieth year as a reggae recording artist.' And then he is gone. When I first listened to *More Time* on CD, I thought that I detected a new lyrical and musical sophistication to Linton's work. Having now heard the tracks live, I am sure that this is Linton's best album. I am particularly struck by 'Reggae Fi May Ayim' and 'Hurricane Blues', poems in which Linton writes about love. While over the years there has been no mellowing of Linton's political agenda, these days he seems more tolerant of those who might live by the heart and not only the head.

Backstage I stand with a distraught-looking Virginie, who, having caught the tail end of Linton's confrontation with the violinist, is unsure of what to do with her Warner Brothers executives. I suggest that she wait a few minutes, then bring them to Linton's dressing room. As Virginie goes to seek out her guests, Linton pops his head out of the dressing room and motions me to come in. 'I told you, man. You have to deal with people's egos. Everybody thinks they know better than you. I kept telling him, but he don't listen.' He goes to the fridge, takes out two beers, opens them both with his teeth, then hands me one. 'I don't get this bloody hassle when I'm doing a straight poetry reading.'

Five minutes later Virginie and her five Warner Brothers executives crowd into the dressing room. Linton makes sure that Jamal brings in enough chairs for everybody and then he starts to hand around food and drink. It is clear that Virginie wants Linton to sign a licensing deal with Warner's, but although Linton appears affable and relaxed it is apparent to me that he is deeply vigilant. The Warner publicist suggests some recordings with French rappers and Linton nods without committing himself. Then Linton pitches a few questions to let them know that he is well versed in the business side of the music industry. Heads nod, smiles are pasted to lips and promises are made. Eventually they leave, but only after Virginie has orchestrated a toast to 'Linton and Warner Brothers'.

Now that we are alone I can see again how tired Linton is. He opens another two beers, hands one to me, then thumps himself down into a hardbacked chair. He sits with his elbows resting on his knees and his beer bottle dangling between both hands. There is a knock at the door. It opens and two French girls put their heads around the corner. 'Wrong door,' says Linton without looking up. They quickly shut the door. 'Other dressing room,' he whispers. Linton's Marxist training may have given him a solid grounding in the realities of politics, but I doubt if he ever imagined just how high a price he might have to pay for controlling the means of production. Earlier in the day I had hovered at the back of the hall while Linton was going through the sound check with Dennis and the band. He looked tired then, but he was as polite as ever and remained the consummate professional. When the soundman asked him to say something for balance, Linton stepped forward, leaned into the microphone, and intoned, 'This is not cash, this is a check.'

1998

The Pioneers: Fifty Years of Caribbean Migration to Britain

I

I have imagined the scene many times. We are in the late 1940s, or in the 1950s, or even in the early 1960s. Crowds of young West Indians are peering from the deck of a ship, eagerly securing their first view of the white cliffs of Dover. Before them lies a new land and a new future. At the moment of that first sighting I imagine that their dominant emotion would have been that of a profound sense of loss, for clearly they knew that it would be many years before they would return home to loved ones and familiar landscapes. A significant page in the narrative of their young lives was being turned; people and places were being confined to an earlier chapter. These emigrants were chained now to the future. A future in Britain. And, of course, they expected.

These young men and women had been raised and educated on the many scattered islands of the curved archipelago which constitutes the English-speaking Caribbean. The very language which sat on their tongues, the bibles tucked away in their hand luggage, the belated hand-me-down colonial fashions which draped their shivering bodies, all bespoke a profound affiliation to the land which lay before them. They expected from Britain in the same uncomplicated manner in which a child expects from the mother. They expected to be accepted, but they hoped to be loved. They expected to be treated fairly, but secretly they yearned for preference. They were coming to the 'mother country' to impress and be impressed and they had much to offer. From the deck of the ship their first glimpse of the white cliffs of Dover suggested a homecoming of sorts. The weather was a little chilly, but having reconciled themselves to the fact that the Caribbean was behind them, over the horizon and out of sight, they hoped now that everything would be just fine. Sadly, they were soon to discover that the chilliness did not just refer to the weather.

2

> *'Tis said there is a great number of Blacks come daily into this City, so that 'tis thought in a short time, if they not be suppress'd, the City will swarm with them.*
>
> (London) *Daily Journal*, 5 April 1723

Sixty-five years later, in 1788, the same drum was still being banged. Philip Thicknesse, a contemporary observer, noted that 'London abounds with an incredible number of these black men ... in every country town, nay in almost every village are to be seen a little race of mulattoes, mischievous as monkies and infinitely more dangerous.' Eighteenth-century Britain, at the height of the slave trade, and at a time when it was fashionable for the well-heeled to employ black servants, was a vibrantly, if not altogether successful, multi-racial country. As countless critics have pointed out, one need look only to the work of Hogarth and his contemporaries, or glance at the literature of Fielding or Thackeray for confirmation of this fact. However, during the nineteenth, and particularly in the early part of the twentieth century the number of black people in Britain fell rapidly. The abolition of the slave trade in 1834 accounted for much of the numerical decline, and intermarriage and mortality only served to speed the process.

Of course, this does not mean that racism and prejudice also subsided. Far from it. Consider, for example, the recently researched case of Britain's first black outfield soccer player. Walter Tull was born in 1888, the son of a joiner from Barbados, who had come to Britain in 1876. By the time Walter was ten years old both parents had died and he was placed in a Methodist orphanage in London's Bethnal Green. In 1908 he signed professional forms with Tottenham Hotspur as an inside-left, and he quickly established himself as a player whom the *Daily Chronicle* described as 'very good indeed with a class superior to that shown by most of his colleagues'. However, in 1909 Tottenham Hotspur played a game at Bristol City and the racial abuse was such that the chief football magazine of the day called the language 'lower than Billingsgate'. Tull was subjected to racial chanting and monkey noises, precisely the same type of abuse that is still showered upon the modern black player. Racism was rooted into British society long before the era of the slave trade, but it was practised with a particular vigour during these years. However, after the abolition of the slave trade in 1834, racism survived, and it was there not only to greet poor Walter Tull but to welcome postwar Caribbean migrants to Britain.

3

In 1941 George Orwell sought to capture what was essential about the British character in an often-quoted essay entitled 'England Your England'. In it he stated categorically that British people had no desire to view themselves as a nation of immigrants, and that a sense of continuity with the past was a crucial determinant of national identity. This would have come as something of a surprise to Daniel Defoe, who, two and a half centuries earlier, in his poem 'A True Born Englishman', had pointed to what he termed 'the mongrel condition' of the proud nation which, much to its chagrin, had long been subject to continual waves of migration. However, in 'England Your England' Orwell was merely restating what most British people *wanted* to believe. That their traditions, hobbies and pastimes – their culture, if you will – was not only deeply rooted in a continuous historical past, but was impervious to pollution by foreign sources. It was to be understood that the British needed neither to learn from, nor be subject to, other people's decidedly inferior cultures. Britain was mature and fully formed. British influence *upon* others was the norm; after all, was there not an Empire to prove this?

The nineteenth-century imagined community of Empire did much not only to legitimise British racism, it also entrenched the very ideas of Britishness that Orwell explored in his essay. After all, if Britain was a club whose members were scattered across the globe doing fine and necessary work, it made sense that one should at least clarify the rules of membership. In the nineteenth century the details and minutiae of being British took a firm grip on the national imagination, and writers and thinkers began to betray a powerful interest in British (which generally meant English) culture. Orwell's 'England Your England' was merely an extension of this obsessive British desire to define the culture and thereby achieve some form of closure around the concept of identity. In his essay Orwell determines that England is

> The clatter of clogs in the Lancashire mill towns, the to-and-fro of the lorries on the Great North Road, the queues outside the Labour Exchanges, the rattle of pin-tables in the Soho pubs, the old maids biking to Holy Communion through the mists of the autumn mornings . . .

But Orwell does not stop here. 'How', he wonders, 'can one make a pattern out of this muddle?' He tries again. This time English culture is

> somehow bound up with solid breakfasts and gloomy Sundays, smoky towns and winding roads, green fields and red pillar-boxes. It has a flavour of its own. Moreover it is continuous, it stretches into the future and the past, there is something in it that persists, as in a living creature.

Well, this second attempt to achieve closure does not entirely satisfy Orwell so he tries again. This time he appears to be clutching at straws when he declares, 'We are a nation of flower-lovers, but also a nation of stamp-collectors, pigeon-fanciers, amateur carpenters, coupon-snippers, darts players, [and] crossword-puzzle fans.'

In the end the only conclusion that Orwell can reach is the somewhat unconvincing one that because there has always been an England, there always will be an England. In the final sentence he declares that England has 'the power to change out of recognition and yet remain the same'. In other words, having failed to achieve a proper definition of English culture, Orwell decides to have it both ways. Perhaps his desire to define and fix 'Englishness' was prompted not only by the fervour of war, but by a knowledge that change was on the horizon; that the 'so-called' barbarians were at the gates. A mere seven years after the publication of 'England Your England', on 22 June 1948, the SS *Empire Windrush* docked at Tilbury and discharged 492 Jamaican migrants. The modern phase of postwar Caribbean migration was beginning. As Orwell's essay suggests, a people who had no desire to witness the national character of Britain 'polluted' by foreigners, was about to come face to face with a people who fully expected to be welcomed as British subjects.

4

One hundred and twenty-five thousand people came from the Caribbean to Britain between the years 1948 and 1958. Between 1959 and 1962 approximately another 125,000 arrived, making a grand total of about 250,000. With the passing of the 1962 Commonwealth Immigrants Act, this flow slowed to a trickle. Further legislation in 1968 made immigration from the Caribbean virtually impossible. A great number of the pre-1962 migrants were actively recruited by British companies such as London Transport, or Wall's Ice Cream, which, like countless other companies in the immediate postwar years, were in desperate need of labour. Some migrants arrived with the altruistic purpose of helping the 'mother country', but everybody wanted to better themselves, both financially and in terms of their experience of the world. There was, of course, also the hope that their children might have a first-class education, and if this could be achieved then whatever difficulties they might endure in Britain would be worthwhile. Sadly, it did not take long for these difficulties to make themselves known. White British attitudes towards Caribbean migrants were palpable from the start. Hundreds of testimonies by these pioneer migrants speak to the indignities that were heaped upon them.

Wallace Collins, who migrated to Britain from Jamaica as a twenty-two-year-old in 1954, eventually left for Canada in 1966, where he wrote a book about his experiences in Britain. In *Jamaica Migrant* Collins remembers his first Saturday night in England. 'A big fellow with sideburns' spotted Collins and another Jamaican friend and shouted across to them, 'You blacks, you niggers, why don't you go back to the jungle?' The big fellow then lunged at Collins with a knife and Collins ran for his life. This type of verbal and physical abuse was the norm for Caribbean migrants to Britain in the 1950s, particularly if they were young and male. Blatant discrimination in housing and employment was also a given, although the Caribbean sense of humour often found ways of stanching the pain. A character in A.G. Bennett's book *Because They Know Not* sums up how many migrants dealt with the prevailing atmosphere. The character comments:

> Since I come 'ere I never met a single English person who 'ad any colour prejudice. Once, I walked the whole length of a street look a room, and everyone told me that he or she 'ad no prejudice against coloured people. It was the neighbour who was stupid. If we could only find the 'neighbour' we could solve the enter problem. But to find 'im is the trouble! Neighbours are the worst people to live beside in this country.

The problem, of course, was that the Britain to which Caribbean people had migrated was not the Britain they expected to find. In 1955 the Trinidadian Learie Constantine, who had been in Britain since the early 1930s as a revered cricketer in the Lancashire league, wrote about his adopted home:

> After practically twenty-five years' residence in England, where I have made innumerable white friends, I still think it would be just to say that almost the entire population of Britain really expects the coloured man to live in an inferior area devoted to coloured people, and not to have free and open choice of a living place. Most British people would be quite unwilling for a black man to enter their home, nor would they wish to work with one as a colleague, nor to stand shoulder to shoulder with one at a factory bench. This intolerance is far more marked in lower grades of English society than in high, and perhaps it disfigures the lower middle classes most of all, possibly because respectability is so dear to them. Hardly any English women and not more than a small proportion of Englishmen would sit at a restaurant table with a coloured man or woman, and inter-racial marriage is considered almost universally to be out of the question.

5

In the postwar years British insecurity was everywhere in evidence. Deeply anxious about her rapidly changing role in the world, and disturbed by the rapidity with which the rapacious Empire was becoming the toothless Commonwealth, Britain was having to adjust to a new relationship with countries such as India and Pakistan. The humiliation of the Suez crisis in 1956 suggested both to Britons and foreign observers that Britain's importance as a global power was also waning. The seemingly all-pervasive influence of American mass culture simply added to Britain's increasingly desperate self-questioning. What did it mean to be British in this postwar world of decline and retreat?

Clearly in such a climate mass immigration from the colonies served only to exacerbate the anxiety that was already gnawing away at British society.

Eventually, and predictably, there was civil disturbance as the number of unprovoked physical attacks against Caribbean migrants grew and the arrivants began to defend themselves. White Britons were offered precious little explanation of the fact that these 'foreigners' were in fact British, that they had come to help, and that astonishingly enough for a migrant group only 13 per cent were unskilled labour and that 87 per cent had an often highly developed trade. Instead the British public were informed by a leading daily newspaper that yet another boatload of 'West Indians' had arrived 'whose calypso flamboyance could not be chilled even by the frosty air of an English winter'. The British government, who should have been making some concerted attempt to clarify what was happening in British society, colluded in this media-driven campaign of disinformation and obfuscation. Violence was hardly surprising when one learns (from Harold Macmillan's memoirs) that in 1955 the Conservative government actually considered using the phrase 'Keep Britain White' as an electoral slogan. This fact is made all the more disturbing when one realises that this was the political party which had been actively responsible for recruiting Caribbean labour to Britain.

When one looks back at the comments made by white Britons of this period about the pioneer generation of Caribbean migrants, it is clear that white British hostility was rooted in a physical distaste for black people. In other words, it was a most primitive form of racism. Undercutting white people in the job market; the living arrangements of Caribbean migrants, with many people sharing a single room; Caribbean people's ignorance of customs such as lining up in an orderly manner at a bus stop; their insistence on wearing loudly coloured shirts and ties: complaints such as these are commonly directed towards new groups of immigrants in any place at any time. By contrast, the particular focus of white British hostility was unashamedly racial. The comments of a personnel officer at a London-based factory are typical; when asked about coloured workers he replied:

> We've found them slow and there've been complaints from the other men over their toilet habits. I'd rather have a strapping Irishman any day than a darkie, even if the Irish don't stay long. After the last redundancy, it would cause a lot of trouble among the men if we took on any more coloured men or even swarthy British subjects from Egypt, so we're not doing so.

A personnel officer at a south London garment factory was equally explicit:

> We require ability or a capacity for training, and also a smart appearance. From coloured applicants, after long experience, we also require intelligibility and an appearance attractive enough not to give offence to the rest of the staff. By this I mean that they should not be unkempt or too dark or negroid-looking.

6

Across the centuries British identity has been a primarily racially constructed concept. The situation has been complicated by the fact that in Britain it has been the habit to conflate race and ethnicity so that one can still be white and excluded. Therefore, although race has been used to define who is British and who is an 'alien', it is also true to say that 'ethnicity' has also been a determinant. So at certain times in British history being Jewish, or Catholic, or speaking with an Eastern European accent automatically stamped one as alien. Race and ethnicity are the bricks and mortar with which the British have traditionally built a wall around the perimeter of their island nation and created fixity. On the inside reside patriotic Britons, who are British by virtue of their race (white) and their culturally determined ethnicity. On the outside of the wall are the foreigners with their swarthy complexions, or their Judaism, or their smelly food, or their mosques, or their impenetrable accents, or their unacceptable clothes, or their tongue-twisting names, or their allegiance to Rome.

The difficulty that postwar Britain had with Caribbean migrants, as opposed to immigrants from the Indian subcontinent or from Africa, is that as an ethnic body Caribbean migrants were far more in tune with what Orwell might have understood to be the British character. They were English-speaking Christians, who had studied their Shakespeare and Wordsworth at school, and while they might like saltfish and ackee, or curried goat and jerk chicken, they seemed able to synthesise these peculiar ethnic aberrations with a broad understanding of the ways of the British. In other words, to many white Britons these Caribbean migrants were uncomfortably and surprisingly British, and in order properly to exclude them and reinforce their alien status white Britons needed to accentuate the one aspect of their identity which these people could do nothing about – their race – which, of course, accounts for the perversely physiological racism to which Caribbean migrants were subjected. For white Britons the equation would henceforth be simple and blunt. British people are white. Even the hitherto unacceptable Jew, Irishman or Pole, whose ethnicity was certainly not British, would now be acceptable, for the battle was to 'Keep Britain White'. Despite the evidence of the British passport in the hand of the Caribbean migrant, the nation could certainly agree on one thing. A black man could never be a British man.

It was precisely this point that Enoch Powell, the paterfamilias of modern British racism, was trying to make in 1968 when he made his now infamous series of speeches, in which he tried to give racial prejudice a veneer of intellectual respectability. Powell claimed that Westminster was 'betraying the nation' by permitting immigrants to settle in Britain, for, by virtue of their race, they could never be admitted as full members to that closed, fixed, club called Britain. He was furiously attempting to convince the British people that a guilt-free nationalism which was racially constructed was synonymous with Britain's best interests. I quote Powell. 'The West Indian or Asian does not by being born in England become an Englishman. In law he is a United Kingdom citizen, by birth; in fact he is a West Indian or Asian still.' Why should this be the case when it would not be the case for a Spanish Jew or a French Canadian? The answer is simple. Because the West Indian or Asian is black, and people such as Powell were clinging on by their fingertips to the idea that Britain would always be white. As long as Britain could define membership of the British nation along racial lines then she could continue to reside in the past and snuggle up against the cushion of her imperial history. The Powellite strategy was simple and transparent. Appealing to the lowest common denominator in British society, he wished to stigmatise Caribbean migrants as 'alien', as impossible to assimilate, as genetically 'foreign', then organise a campaign to send them back.

There is no doubt that Powell's ugly proclamations were endorsed by a large section of the British population. Almost overnight he became an icon for millions of British people who were either too shrewd or too embarrassed to approve publicly of the crude racism of self-proclaimed fascists or ignorant skinheads. When the leader of the Opposition, Edward Heath, removed Powell from the Shadow Cabinet, the nation's dockers and London's Smithfield porters downed tools and marched to the House of Commons in his support. They were supporting a man who had said, 'In fifteen or twenty years' time, the black man will have the whip hand.' He went on to quote a letter he claimed to have received about an elderly widow living in Wolverhampton: 'She finds excreta pushed through her letter box ... she is followed by children – charming, wide-grinning, piccaninnies. They cannot speak English, but one word they know. "Racialist," they chant.' Powell's various speeches during 1968 were vulgar, incendiary and calculated to cause the maximum possible damage to the lives and interests of non-white British citizens. We know now that the social catastrophe which Powell predicted never came to pass: we know that he was not only wrong statistically, but he clearly misjudged Britain and the British character. History has taught us that this was a temporary alliance of patrician eloquence with gutter racism, but back in 1968 neither black nor white Britons could be sure of what might befall them in the years to come.

7

In 1968 I was ten years old, and the school I attended was on the Whinmoor estate in the northern part of Leeds. One morning my friend Terry Neat came up to me in the school playground to tell me a joke. He claimed his dad had told him it. He said it goes like this, 'Two Pakis walking down the street singing "We Shall Overcome".' That was the joke. I don't know if I laughed. Terry definitely laughed, but I didn't get the joke. I don't think Terry did either, but clearly his father did. This was not only the year of Powell's terrible speeches, it was the year of the death of Martin Luther King Junior and the end of a key period in the Civil Rights struggle in the United States. Clearly there was some conflation of these two events in this joke. Our friendship survived, but the ground beneath my feet became increasingly unstable. Like all non-white children in Britain during this time I tiptoed somewhat cautiously through life, knowing full well that Britain's ambivalence towards me and my parents' generation could cause a stranger, a friend, or even a teacher to turn on me when I might least expect it.

The key issue for me and my generation – the second generation, if you will – growing up in the Britain of the late 1960s and 1970s was identity. We spoke with the same accent as the other kids, we watched the same television programmes, we went to the same schools, we did the same exams. Surely we were

British. Well, of course, we were and eventually we insisted that we were even in the face of a nation which continued to invest in a racially constructed sense of itself. We endured discrimination in schools, in jobs, in housing, the same discrimination that was earlier visited upon our parents. However, our response was different from that of our parents, who often held their tongues in order that they might protect their children. We were invested in British society in a way in which they were not and it was clear to us that a British future involved not only kicking back when kicked, but continuing to kick until a few doors opened and things changed. We, the second generation, had to change British society with our intransigence, or what the police force called our 'attitude', because British society was certainly not going to change of its own volition.

The inner-city disturbances of the 1970s and early 1980s were largely born out of frustration with this situation. That they occurred principally in the cities of London, Liverpool and Bristol should come as no surprise to anybody who understands the complex relationship of the past on the present. These were the three chief slaving ports of Britain during the eighteenth century and the injustices perpetrated in these three cities had caused discontent to simmer for decades. During the late 1970s I was a student at university, and I remember every night being exposed to images on the television screen and each morning reading stories in newspapers, all of which depicted black youths who looked just like me as a disciplinary problem in the heart of Britain. Very seldom did these reports mention the truly appalling police harassment, the continued discrimination in housing and in the workplace, and the institutionalised racism to which we were all subjected. For a moment my generation flirted with the idea of making being 'black' the basis of our identity, as African-Americans had done in the 1960s and 1970s, but mercifully this unsatisfactory notion never really took hold. In the end what the second generation were actually saying, brick, bottle, stone or book in hand, was, we are British, we won't allow you to harass and marginalise us, and we are not going away. In fact, we don't *have* anywhere else to go. And then came Mrs Thatcher.

8

It did not begin well. In 1978, a year before Mrs Thatcher was elected Prime Minister, she claimed that 'the British people who have given so much to the world' were understandably fearful of being 'swamped by alien cultures'. Once again a British politician was attempting to invoke a racially constructed sense of Britain, for there was no doubt that the 'swamping' cultures she was referring to were colour-coded. In the wake of the Falklands War her victory address at Cheltenham on 3 July 1982 clarified further her imperial mindset:

> We have learned something about ourselves, a lesson which we desperately need to learn. When we started out, there were the waverers and the fainthearts ... The people who thought we could no longer do the great things which we once did ... that we could never again be what we were. There were those who would not admit it ... But – in their heart of hearts – they too had their secret fears that it was true: that Britain was no longer the nation that had built an Empire and ruled a quarter of the world. Well, they were wrong.

This was not a comfortable speech for many Britons to listen to. For Britons, such as I, whose heritage was blighted by the inequities and cruelties of Empire, this was a disgraceful speech, and one which served only to remind us of our tenuous position in British society.

Mrs Thatcher's Britain was invested in images of Britain as a colonial power – 'Put the "Great" back into Great Britain again' was a popular Tory Party campaign slogan. However, alongside her desire to evoke an imperial past, Mrs Thatcher was also interested in hurrying the demise of the 'well-born' as a ruling force in British society. The self-made businessman, the upwardly mobile person who has no time for patrician codes of behaviour, or blue-veined privilege, or bumbling one-party Toryism, this would be the type of Conservative who would win favour under Mrs Thatcher. Her desire to modernise the nation by dismantling the Welfare State and selling off state-owned industry meant that economic considerations began to play a large part in her perception of who and what was British and patriotic. And, ironically enough, despite her imperial sensibility, it was Mrs Thatcher who eventually took the first real step in moving Britain away from a primarily racially constructed definition of British nationality and belonging.

In 1983 the Conservative government produced an election poster which featured a full-page advertisement of a nattily dressed young black man in a suit, with his arms folded, staring confidently into the lens of the camera. The slogan beneath it read, 'Labour says he's black, Tories say he's British.' Suddenly there were to be acceptable 'aliens', such as profitable Asian businessmen and upwardly mobile black men in suits, which meant that there would also be unacceptable 'aliens', presumably those who still had the temerity to go to the mosque or wear dreadlocks. However, Mrs Thatcher's new idea of British nationality, with its dependency on economic virility and on codes of behaviour, was clearly to be culturally and not racially constructed. Her new nation of hard-working, ordinary people, who were being encouraged to forget their 'place' and 'make it' in what she called her 'property-owning democracy', was to include non-white Britons, for Mrs Thatcher had more invested in the *realpolitik* of the City than she had in the racism of her Home Counties electorate.

During the 1980s television stations and local councils began appointing executives whose special duty was to cater to this newly recognised, and now to be tolerated, constituency of non-white British citizens. It was during this decade that the first black Members of Parliament were elected and non-white faces began to play for and even captain national sports teams.

In music and fashion black became synonymous with style, and although the racism which had greeted the pioneer generation of Caribbean migrants still existed, it was impossible not to recognise that for the black British community things had changed for the better. Mrs Thatcher still continued to identify enemies within – the IRA, the 'loony Left', scroungers, do-gooders and trades unions – but even as she rewarded the working classes with neo-Georgian doors, double-glazing and carriage clocks with which to adorn their newly purchased council flats and houses, she was also creating a space for the black community in Britain to begin to come of age.

9

So fifty years after the SS *Empire Windrush* unloaded 492 Jamaicans at Tilbury docks, what kind of society do we have in Britain today? Most would probably claim that we have a multicultural society, but do so without stopping to think what they really mean by multicultural. The word can, of course, refer to a society that is composed of many different cultures all living side by side. Or it can refer to a society whose common culture is composed of an amalgam of the interests and origins of its constituent members. The first alternative, while implying a healthy respect for the cultures of different people, can never really work. In such societies there will always be one dominant culture and a hotchpotch of others which are, by definition, lesser; cultures which will be merely tolerated until some parent leads a boycott against the local school because it encourages its children to recognise *divali*; or until some police cadet finally sniggers out loud when being shown how the Sikh community tie their turbans.

A truly multicultural society is one which is composed of multicultural individuals; people who are able to synthesise different worlds in one body and to live comfortably with these different worlds. In order for a society to tolerate such individuals the society must by definition be open, fluid and confident. In other words, the society must be everything that Britain was not when the first Caribbean migrants stepped off the ships in the 1940s and 1950s. This pioneer generation met a Britain that was no longer sure of herself, a Britain which sought to define herself by strategies of exclusion, a Britain fearful of her shrinking role in the world. Should these same Caribbean migrants step from the transatlantic ships today they would meet a different Britain in which a government who would discuss using 'Keep Britain White' as an electoral slogan could never hope to be elected, and would probably be violating the law of the land. While things are still far from perfect, and while Stephen Lawrence's killers still walk free, and while there is still huge under-representation in government, in the city, in the universities, in all spheres of power in Britain, then the dream which those pioneer Caribbean migrants carried in their hearts will have to be deferred. However, there is no doubt that in the past fifty years Britain *has* changed and it has changed radically.

Most Britons are no longer interested in the aimless navel-gazing of a George Orwell. And those who persist in defining British nationality in terms of race must become terribly confused when Paul Ince leads out the England soccer team, or Linford Christie does a lap of honour draped in the Union Jack. Young British people, both black and white, are these days increasingly invested in cultural plurality as a signifier of their identity rather than crude notions of race. They are able to synthesise Wordsworth with Jamaican patties, or *Romeo and Juliet* with the music of Bob Marley, and happily many of the pioneer generation who stepped from the ships in the 1940s and 1950s have lived long enough to see these changes. This pioneer generation should take heart in their achievement, for the re-imagining of Britain is the logical extension of their arrival in the country. Because they refused to be beaten into submission by a country which patently had no desire to welcome them, and because they refused to disappear conveniently, to slope off back to where they had come from, British concern with a continuous past, with fixity, with a racially conscious rigidity, is these days playing an increasingly small part in how the nation thinks of itself.

10

So how should Britain define itself as a nation? A synthesis of Indian takeaways, baked beans, soccer, Jamaican patties, St Patrick's Day, pub on Saturday, Notting Hill Carnival, church on Sunday, mosque on Friday and fish and chips? I say emphatically, yes. The inability to achieve proper closure around a culturally, as opposed to racially, defined concept of nation will inevitably cause more closed-minded citizens some problems. But better an open, fluid definition of nationality than a return to a situation where race and nation are perceived of as being synonymous. Should this happen then we will once again find ourselves surrounded by people like Norman Tebbit, the former chairman of the Conservative Party. In November 1997 he stood up in the House of Lords and said that 'different cultures will splinter our society'. And of course, being staunchly of the old school, by different cultures he meant different races. A day or so later the *Daily Telegraph* felt it necessary to admonish one of their own. 'Norman Tebbit was not quite right about multiculturalism . . . A child with a Welsh father and a mother from Ulster can eat Indian food, listen to reggae, and watch Italian football without experiencing cultural confusion and political alienation.' Precisely.

I would argue that whereas George Orwell claimed that 'It needs some very great disaster, such as prolonged subjugation by a foreign enemy, to *destroy* a national culture', the truth is that it needs some very great fortune such as continual waves of immigration to *create* a national culture. And one of the most important waves of migration in the second half of the twentieth century has been the arrival of Caribbean migrants to Britain after the Second World War. Not only did they help to rebuild Britain with their labour, they made Britain think beyond Derby Day, Wensleydale cheese and the Boat Race as signifiers of national identity. As a nation Britain is now reluctantly postcolonial, but stubbornly pre-European. While it was the pioneer generation of Caribbean migrants who helped to introduce Britain to the notion of postcoloniality, it is their children's and grandchildren's generation who will help Britain cross the Rubicon of the English Channel and enter the European age of the twenty-first century. But this will be a different story. Fifty years ago the SS *Empire Windrush* dropped anchor at Tilbury docks and discharged 492 Jamaicans. It is these individuals, and the quarter of a million who succeeded them, who deserve our acknowledgement, respect and gratitude, for as they stood on the deck of the ship and stared out at the white cliffs of Dover, they carried within their hearts a dream. And like all great pioneers, in the face of much adversity and innumerable obstacles, they remained true to their dream. Without them Britain would be a poorer place.

1998

White Teeth by Zadie Smith

Today's media are dominated by the debate around what is perhaps best described as 'identity politics' in British life. Do we want a multicultural society? Do we already have one? If so, is its existence an affront to the 'native British', whoever they may be? Modern postcolonial Britain has constituent parts that have originated in the Caribbean, in the Indian subcontinent, and in Africa; in fact, in all corners of the globe. It is precisely this helpless heterogeneity that Zadie Smith recognises and celebrates in her wonderfully poised first novel, *White Teeth*.

The novel follows the fortunes of the families of two best friends: Archie Jones, a white working-class man who works in a mail-order delivery firm, and who is married for a second time to a Jamaican woman, Clara. And Samad Iqbal, a Bangladeshi who is married to Alsana and who works in a restaurant. As the hinge of generation turns, their children begin to complicate the lives of these two men. Samad has twin boys, Magid and Millat, and Archie has a daughter, Irie. Naturally enough, the children become friends and they create a dazzlingly complex world of cross-cultural fusion in modern-day London.

Samad is concerned at the way in which his sons are growing up in Britain (Magid has taken to being addressed as 'Mark Smith'), so he dispatches Magid back 'home' to be brought up by relatives. After Magid's departure, Millat Iqbal and Irie Jones befriend a boy called Joshua and a third family, the Chalfens, take centre-stage. Marcus Chalfen, an eccentric scientist and university lecturer, and his wife Joyce, a mother and author of

The Inner Life of Houseplants, have four children, including their eldest, Joshua.

The Chalfens are a quintessential liberal, pseudo-Marxist, white, middle-class family who, as one might expect, welcome this 'exciting' rush of hybridity into their lives. Eventually, Marcus becomes penpals with the orientally exiled Magid, and on Magid's return to Britain it is Marcus who meets him at Heathrow and begins to make plans for this now level-headed, polite young man to study law. Meanwhile, Millat has renounced 'white birds' and joined 'the Cricklewood branch of the Keepers of the Eternal and Victorious Islamic Nation', which Irie points out has an 'acronym problem': KEVIN.

Samad and Archie 'observe' events from the vantage point of their retreat, O'Connell's Café on the Finchley Road, a place run by Abdul-Mickey, the son of an immigrant named Ali. All five sons were named Abdul, but Ali took the precaution of attaching an English name as a gesture to the clarity demanded by the new country. O'Connell's Café offers Samad and Archie a place from where they can view the interaction between the various families, as the novel ranges back and forth in both contemporary and historical time. This multi-layered, deeply plotted novel resists easy categorisation, which is precisely the author's point.

Britain has perennially sought to define herself and her character by defining others. Naturally enough, the country finds itself in great difficulty when presented with those who seem keen to resist definition. These 'in-betweens'; these Abdul-Mickey's, or his brother Abdul-Colin; these working-class white men, like Archie, who marry Jamaican women twenty years their junior; these non-believing 'Muslims' such as Millat; these 'white birds' who go weak at the knees for people like Magid; such people present Britain with a problem of categorisation. For those of a colonial mindset, this swirling postcolonial world is blurring distinctions and challenging received wisdoms at an alarming rate. It is uncomfortably clear to those of the 'old school' that the hitherto familiar cultural signifiers of belonging are no longer the preserve of one group to the exclusion of another. One only needs to overhear a conversation on practically any London street corner.

> 'For your information,' snapped Irie, moving the nut out of Millat's reach, 'old people *like* coconuts. They can use the milk for their tea.'
>
> Irie pressed on in the face of Millat's retching. '*And* I got some crusty French bread and some cheese-singlets and some apples –'
>
> 'We *got* apples, you *chief,*' cut in Millat, 'chief', for some inexplicable reason hidden in the etymology of North London slang, meaning 'fool', 'arse', 'wanker', a loser of the most colossal proportions.
>
> 'Well, I got some *more* and *better* apples, *akchully,* and some Kendal mint cake and some ackee and saltfish.'
>
> 'I *hate* ackee and saltfish.'

However, it is not only those of a colonial mindset who must open themselves to change. When 'nature' visits Britain in October 1987, in the form of a hurricane, the Iqbals' world is shaken up. While Samad and Millat hurry to flee the house, Alsana sits stubbornly on the sofa confident that nothing will happen because 'Mr Fish', the BBC weatherman, has assured her that all will be fine. When she finally relents, and gets in the car and drives from the house with 110-mile-an-hour winds howling all around, she confesses that her world has changed.

She is of an immigrant generation that expected to encounter a benign Britain; a 'civilised' Britain as characterised by BBC announcers in dinner jackets, crumpets for tea and the comforting thwack of leather on willow. Quite probably a Britain that never existed, but nonetheless – in her mind – a more reliable Britain than that to which she is currently being exposed.

> 'England, this is meant to be! I moved to England so I wouldn't have to do this. Never again will I trust that Mr Crab.'

> 'Amma, it's Mr Fish.'
> 'From now on, he's Mr Crab to me,' snapped Alsana with a dark look. 'BBC or no BBC.'

The depiction of the dysfunctional Chalfen family, while often very funny, finally seems too cartoon-like. Marcus and Joyce Chalfen tolerate the abusive, foul-mouthed Millat, who rolls joints at their table, drinks their alcohol and generally calls the shots around their house.

> 'Oh, Millat, *don't* smoke that stuff. Every time we see you these days you're smoking. It upsets Oscar so much. He's not that young and he understands more than you think. He understands about marijuana.'
> 'What's mary wana?' asked Oscar.
> 'You know what it is, Oscar. It's what makes Millat all horrible, like we were talking about today, and it's what kills the little brain cells he has.'
> 'Get off my fucking back, Joyce.'

It is frustrating not to have a more 'substantial' white family at the heart of the novel, for Irie, Millat and Magid are treated by the Chalfens with a degree of patronage that is both familiar and unsurprising. Their son, Joshua, has a more complicated response to the situation, for Irie is the object of his desire. However, his two-dimensional parents do little more than enliven the more farcical elements of the narrative.

There is, of course, nothing farcical about the pain of wanting to belong. In this respect *White Teeth* is full of false smiles and contrived faces; masks that are repeatedly donned in order to better hide the pain. The 'mongrel' nation that is Britain is still struggling to find a way to stare in the mirror and accept the ebb and flow of history which has produced this fortuitously diverse condition, and its concomitant pain. Zadie Smith's first novel is an audaciously assured contribution to this process of staring into the mirror. Her narrator is deeply self-conscious, so much so that one can almost hear the crisp echo of Salman Rushdie's footsteps. However, her wit, her breadth of vision and her ambition are of her own making. The plot is rich, at times dizzyingly so, but *White Teeth* squares up to the two questions which gnaw at the very roots of our modern condition. Who are we? Why are we here?

2000

Extravagant Strangers

The British character, like that of most nations, has been forged in the crucible of hybridity – of cultural fusion. And, of course, it is not just what the Americans term 'people of colour' who have contributed to this process of 'mongrelisation'. One immediately thinks of Defoe and his satirical poem 'The True-Born Englishman', a poem levelled against the English for their mistreatment of the Dutch who arrived on these shores with William III. Defoe catalogues the various groups who have made up this heterogeneous thing, the Englishman. He identifies Romans, Scots, Picts, Irish, Welsh, Saxons, Danes and a whole variety of French people. Clearly, over the centuries, British life at all levels, the royal family, the musical heritage, parliament, military, sport, entertainment and the city have been invigorated, shaped and to some extent defined by the fortuitously heterogeneous nature that is the national condition.

However, in the face of overwhelming evidence, the mythology of homogeneity not only exists, it endures. It also excludes and prevents countless numbers of British people from feeling comfortable participating in the main narrative of British life. At certain periods in my life I have been one of these people. I have, at times, recoiled in horror at the very notion of having my name yoked together with that of this nation. I have resisted allegiance to flag and to country. I have spectacularly failed Norman Tebbit's cricket test – simple-minded as it is – and, in common with thousands of others, I have had to learn to come to terms with a country that partly defines its historical sense of self by first identifying, and then excluding, the 'other'.

A large part of my British education has involved learning to recognise when fellow citizens are viewing me as little more than the 'other'.

For many British people, the idea that Britain has a history that has, over the years, been characterised by much ethnic, linguistic and cultural diversity, would be to undermine their basic understanding of what it means to be British. As a writer I am interested in the way in which this continual influx of the 'other' into Britain – of colour or otherwise – has impinged upon the literary culture. Two years ago I began to look in earnest at the English literary canon, paying particular attention to those writers who might in some way be defined as the 'other'. And then, about a year ago, I realised that the writers I was most interested in were those who might be regarded as the 'other' in the most radical way. They were, all of them, not even born in Britain.

The earliest group of 'outsiders' writing in Britain were all by-products of the slave trade. The very existence of black writers in Britain in the eighteenth and nineteenth centuries goes some not inconsiderable distance to dispelling the widely held notion that black people have not chronicled for themselves the nature of their existence in this country. These writers – often through no choice of their own – found themselves domiciled in Britain and, naturally enough, their writing – mainly journals, diaries and autobiographies – mimics the style and manners of the literary movements of the time. It is, however, what they had to *say* about their precarious position in British society that marks them off as 'different' from their British-born contemporaries. Perhaps the two outstanding 'outsider' writers of the late eighteenth century are Ignatius Sancho and Olaudah Equiano. Both writers were enslaved in childhood, yet survived to regain their freedom and learn to read and write. Whereas Equiano's autobiographical writing is charged with an anti-slavery zeal, Sancho's writing – in the form of letters – reflects more fully the anxieties of the 'outsider' writer trying to work in Britain. Right here, near the very head of the tradition of writing by those not born in Britain, one can detect an ambivalent relationship with Britain. Sancho despairs at the decline of his beloved Britain, but at the same time he realises that he is forever doomed to be an outsider.

> L[or]d S[andwic]h has gone to Portsmouth, to be a witness of England's disgrace – and his own shame – In faith, my friend, the present time is rather comique – Ireland almost in as true a state of rebellion as America – Admirals quarelling in the West Indies – and at home Admirals that do not chuse to fight – The British Empire mouldering away in the West, annihilated in the North – Gibraltar going – and England fast asleep. What says Mr B – to all this? he is a ministerialist – for my part, it's nothing to me, as I am only a lodger, and hardly that.

If one examines the work of other writers of the eighteenth, nineteenth and twentieth centuries who were not born in Britain, it is interesting to note that they too often display an ambivalence towards Britain not too dissimilar to that expressed by Sancho. However, ambivalence takes different forms. The controversial jingoism of a Rudyard Kipling, the social commitment of a George Orwell, the political 'extremism' of a Wyndham Lewis, all seem to me connected to their particular sense of being British. To be born outside a country which places so much import on identifying the 'other', will inevitably result in writers such as Kipling, Orwell and Lewis; and Jean Rhys, and E.R. Braithwaite, and Ruth Prawer Jhabvala and many others feeling a discomfort towards Britain. These writers may not feel as great a sense of alienation as Sancho, but all will certainly recognise themselves as 'different' because of the accident of their birth. Race seems important to me only insofar as one has to acknowledge that being *visibly* the 'other' will only serve to intensify the feeling of being outside. It is, of course, in British society, possible to feel alienated by dint of accent, by class or even by regional affiliation. In short, race is simply the most *visible* sign of alienation and one which, unlike the other forms, cannot be denied. There is little that Henry Higgins could have done for a black Liza Doolittle, and a black Jimmy Porter would not, I suspect, be railing against society. His discourse might be more resigned whimper than tub-thumping oration.

There is, I think, another element beyond that of subjective ambivalence towards this country, which is common to the work of many British writers who were not born in Britain. This relates to form and structure. Many of the early writers were, like Sancho, little more than formal imitators, but their timidity had more to do with their own problems of literacy than with any stylistic conservatism. Beyond the work of these writers, most 'outsider' writers seem to have zealously embraced formal innovation.

Joseph Conrad, T.S. Eliot, Lawrence Durrell, Doris Lessing, Wilson Harris: five of the most radical innovators of form in English literature and none born in Britain. Many reasons have been proposed as to why this might be, including Terry Eagleton's assertion that writers with 'access to alternative cultures and traditions' have an opportunity to respond in a more vigorous manner. The problem with this statement is that Terry Eagleton never makes it clear just *what* it is in British society that the writer with 'access to alternative cultures and traditions' is responding to. Eagleton claims that such writers have a 'broader framework' to operate within, which is perhaps the case. Access to alternative cultures and traditions does give one a 'broader', though by no means better or more important, framework to operate in, but again the critical question of just *what* it is that such writers are responding to in British society is never really tackled.

My own hunch is this: that the British writer born outside of Britain is always, to some extent, going to feel something of a discordant relationship with this country. This is clearly evident in the work of writers I have already mentioned. However, what stirs the writer into feeling that their relationship with

Britain is discordant is Britain's desire to promote herself as a homogenous country whose purity is underscored not only by race and class, but, perhaps more importantly, by a sense of continuity. The sentiment is as straightforward as this: we are who we are because we've always been who we are. The end result of such thinking is that writers born outside Britain – of all backgrounds – are tossed together as disrupters of this greatly cherished continuity.

Many of the writers who were born outside Britain display a tendency to both experiment with discontinuities of time, and revel in the disruption of conventional narrative order. We can clearly see this in the work of the five mentioned above: Joseph Conrad, T.S. Eliot, Lawrence Durrell, Doris Lessing and Wilson Harris. Their work reflects their own condition as disrupters of national continuity. This formal response to a country's perception of itself is not confined to Britain. The formal strategies of the writers of Latin America and writers from the former Eastern bloc, such as Kundera, Márquez, Grass, Carpentier – the list is almost endless – clearly reflect a lack of faith in traditional notions of time or linear narrative. These are the countries in which one can never assume that tomorrow will be like today, or today like yesterday. Their writing is a forceful response to their own country's condition. Similarly, the work of many 'outsider' writers in Britain contains a formal response to Britain's perception of herself. The specific factor that Terry Eagleton imagined the 'outsider' writer responding to in a 'vigorous manner' is Britain's comfortable notion of herself as a country with an untroubled continuity to both the details of her history and the make-up of her people. And it is the formal nature of the response that is most arresting.

If one pursues this hypothesis, it is possible to see how British writers not born in Britain, who might otherwise appear to have little in common, suddenly became explicable as 'partners'. Take the case of two authors: one who constructs the anarchic form of the novel *Vanity Fair*, with its blank pages, drawings and bizarre plot. And the other whose playful, exuberant inventiveness results in *Midnight's Children*. 'Partners?' one might ask. Allowing for differences of social background and times, the fact that both of these British authors were born in India seems to me a factor to be included into the equation rather than a coincidence to be quickly passed over in the search for more explicable reasons for their 'challenge' to form. Eventually *every* writer discovers that his or her main struggle is with this one word: form. Plots are relatively easy to acquire, and characters will, if one is both patient and lucky, eventually show themselves. But form, how to tell one's story, is the ultimate challenge. By virtue of the accident of their birth, 'outsider' writers have to continually define and redefine their position in relationship to Britain. They cannot accept the 'comfort zone' of continuity, for this is to exclude themselves from a full participation in British life. Their work is therefore necessarily characterised by constant questioning and reinvention of the most vigorous type.

The same questioning and reinvention is, of course, present in the work of some British writers born in Britain. Indeed, Virginia Woolf really was born in London, not in Bombay or Barbados. However, the discontinuities of time in her work seem to me related not so much to her place of birth, but to a deeply felt response to being marginalised on account of her gender and sexuality. As I hope I have already established, this feeling of being 'outside' the mainstream of British society can be implanted in a person's soul by a variety of factors. Virginia Woolf's sense of being 'outside' is no less real than George Orwell's, but at the moment I am principally interested in those who were not born in Britain. Further, I have not mentioned the work of the Irish writers such as Joyce or Beckett, writers without whom it would be difficult to imagine modernism. I have left them out, remembering Seamus Heaney's riposte to Blake Morrison and Andrew Motion when they included him in their 1982 Penguin *Anthology of British Poetry*. Heaney responded in verse.

Be advised my passport's green
No glass of ours was ever raised to toast the Queen

It is in the last fifteen years that we have witnessed the full flowering of the tradition of the 'other' voice in British literature. Suddenly, with the decline of the Empire, and postwar migration into Britain, the barbarians from all corners of the globe have assembled within the gates. And the writers among them have produced a sustained challenge to the English literary tradition in both content and form. It is hard to imagine recent British literature without V.S. Naipaul, Salman Rushdie, Kazuo Ishiguro and Ben Okri, all writers whose ambivalence towards Britain is expressed in their choice of subject-matter, and whose narrative techniques involve disrupting the continuum of time. The 'vigorous manner' has of late been growing increasingly vigorous. The times more desperate. So much so that even V.S. Naipaul's two most recent novels, *The Enigma of Arrival* and *A Way in the World,* are beginning not only to play with time but to call into question the very notion of the novel as a legitimate form of literary communication. This is an altogether different spirit of literary adventuring from that which produced the excellent, but conventionally linear, *A House for Mr Biswas.*

I would like to mention the work of some of my British-born contemporaries who have been writing fiction in the Thatcherite and post-Thatcherite 1980s and 1990s. Their work has been described, by the critic Patricia Waugh, as 'post-consensus fictions'; fictions which seek to respond to the radical changes wrought in the heart and soul of this nation by a political revolution, the full magnitude of which many of us have still not grasped. This period produced writers such as Graham Swift, Jeannette Winterson and Peter Ackroyd, to name but three. Writers who all challenge form, disrupt linear narrative and explore primary historical ruptions in British society – both past and present – around issues of gender, class and sexuality. In other words, these British-born writers seemed, in this 'post-consensus' phase, to be responding to the vagaries of Thatcherite Britain as if they were 'outsiders' in Britain. To some extent they formed an unconscious alliance with their contemporaries who were not born in Britain. The result of this teamwork is that for the past fifteen years it would be fair to say that the only truly functional multicultural and multiracial area of British life – aside from the national athletics team – has been the literature.

Writers respond to the societies they find themselves in and, either consciously or unconsciously, they reflect the health or sickness of these societies. Which brings me back to Defoe, and his satirical poem 'The True-Born Englishman'. I think it would be true to say that the British have little idea of who they are. This is not surprising. They are spoonfed a vainglorious history and they swallow. Perhaps the British are unique among European nations in that they are not in any way ashamed of their national history. They have no memory of jackboots tramping down their streets. The British have no memories of the awful mutability of national boundaries, a mutability that can serve seriously to corrode a people's sense of who they are. They have no memory of death camps on their soil, or hands raised in pathetic gestures of defeat. It is a history to be proud of. And, if the times are right, revel in. But such a history is dangerous, for it supports myth-making.

Defoe's poem points to a failure of historical memory which continues to this day. British people find it difficult to support the idea of assimilation, for this word necessitates admitting that the British character can be enriched and thickened – to borrow an analogy – like stock, 'with new ingredients from somebody else's garden'. On the other hand, to yield – I choose the word carefully – to multiculturalism one needs to be confident about one's own identity.

In his poem, Defoe defined the mongrelised 'mixture' underpinning the heterogeneous British tradition as follows:

> The Scot, Pict, Briton, Roman, Dane, submit,
> And with the English-Saxon all unite;
> And these the mixtures have so close pursued,

> The very name and memory's subdued.
> No Roman now, no Briton does remain . . .
> Fate jumbled them together, God knows how;
> Whate'er they were, they're true-born English now.

In the three hundred years since this poem was written, one can add to the 'mixture' the Pole, American, Nigerian, Jamaican, Hungarian, Indian, Pakistani, Trinidadian, Canadian, and so on. As Defoe said, 'they're true-born English now', their contribution to British society extensive and important, their contribution to English literature undeniable.

But Britain remains a country for whom a sense of continuity with an imagined past continues to be a major determinant of national identity. Even if one speaks the language, attends the church, writes the books, builds the roads, bridges, cathedrals, one's right fully to participate in this society is always under threat from somebody or some institution which determines that you don't look, or act, or behave in a British-enough manner. If I had a pound for every time I've been told to go back to where I came from, I'd be a rich man. One's right to participate is always under scrutiny in ways as crude and as simple as the sentence a British diplomat in Portugal once shared with me when, having lost my passport in Lisbon, I was trying to obtain emergency papers to return home to Britain. 'Mr Phillips,' he said, 'you don't even look British.'

British writers not born in Britain will, as long as this situation goes unrepaired, continue to feel a personal ambivalence towards Britain. And as they settle at their desks to explore their ambivalence, they will discover new formal strategies which will expand our understanding of what is possible in literary form. This is a process which, as we stand on the threshold of a new century, shows no sign of letting up, for, despite Defoe's plea, Britain continues to display little interest in viewing 'outsiders' as the 'true-born Englishmen' that Defoe claims them to be. The richness of the British literary tradition may be an ironic by-product of this failure of national imagination. Personally,

I would rather have a less vigorous literature, and a healthier nation in which the process of moving along the road from the 'outside' to the 'inside' was not burdened with so many psychological obstacles. Writers are generally able to negotiate these obstacles and even flourish while hurdling them. But, in case we forget, most of us are not writers.

1995

Leeds United, Life and Me

My father has never understood my relationship with Leeds United. In 1958 he came to England from St Kitts, with a young wife and me, his baby son. As far as he was concerned the word 'sport' was synonymous with cricket. We settled in Leeds and my earliest memories are of my father and his various drinking pals all huddled around the radio listening to the Test Match. When I was five, and ready to go off to primary school, my father was disappointed that I was not displaying even the slightest interest in cricket. I did, however, love football. I remember my teenage babysitter quizzing me on the names of the teams in the English First Division. I could recite them all and this feat soon became a party piece, which my baffled but proud parents were encouraged to have me perform whenever relatives came to visit. What strange changes this new country had wrought in their five-year-old son.

This was in 1963, the season that Leeds United won promotion to the First Division, the season in which they began to display the form that would result in their decade-long domination of the English game. I persuaded the babysitter to take me to Elland Road to watch my first game (Leeds 3 Leicester City 1), and I'm now sure that I was probably the youngest fan in the stadium and undoubtedly the only black one. And I was, of course, immediately hooked. I was 'Leeds', and with this firm declaration of faith the cultural gap between my parents and myself opened still further, a gap that has never been truly closed.

Being a Leeds fan during the 1960s and 1970s meant

coming to terms with a number of facts. First, one had to learn to hate Manchester United, Arsenal and Chelsea. I found this very easy, and pleasurable, to accomplish. Second, one had to accept that one would be hated by all so-called 'purists', who regarded the manager Don Revie's style of play as 'dirty' and tainted with gamesmanship. Finally, one had to get used to being the runner-up. Between 1963 and 1975 we were bridesmaids in the League on more occasions than I care to remember, runners-up in the FA Cup final three times, runners-up in the European Cup final, in the European Cup Winners Cup final: the list is painful. We twice won the League title, we won the FA Cup, the League Cup, the Inter City Fairs Cup (the forerunner of the present-day UEFA Cup), but even now the thought of what might have been sends me spinning into despair.

Being a black Leeds fan during the 1960s and 1970s meant coming to terms with an entirely different set of facts. The same people who would hug you when Leeds scored (which we often did), would also shout 'nigger' and 'coon' should the opposing team have the temerity to field a player of the darker hue. I remember West Ham's Clyde Best coming in for some particularly vicious stick, and being astonished that the Leeds fans around me had no idea of the multiple ironies of my own situation. The sight of fans in the Leeds Kop swaying and singing 'I'd rather be a nigger than a scouse' was a little difficult for me to compute. However, it was in the late 1970s, during the sad post-Revie slump, that I realised enough was enough.

My brother and I had travelled from London to see Leeds play Fulham at Elland Road, and because we were aware of the reputation of Leeds fans as being among the more vicious racists in the country, we had taken the precaution of sitting in the family stand among those we imagined to be tolerant and sensible people. How wrong we were. When a black Fulham player scored a late equaliser, not only were we subjected to torrents of abuse, but sharpened pennies were thrown at us. After years of unquestioning loyalty, I came to the sad conclusion that it was simply crazy to subject myself to the trauma of going to see Leeds United play.

For a few years I flirted with the notion of 'coming out' as a Queens Park Rangers fan. In the early 1980s I lived five minutes from their ground in London and I began to wander over there on a Saturday afternoon. Terry Venables was the team manager and the Rangers were lively and entertaining. More importantly, the crowd seemed remarkably passive and good-natured, unlike the baying hounds of Elland Road. However, my adrenalin never pumped with the same intensity as it did for Leeds. If QPR lost I never endured the same post-match, weekend-long, depression that I did if Leeds lost. Quite simply, I never suffered for QPR and I knew that I never would. I soon found myself surreptitiously turning to the Leeds match reports in the papers and then I started to turn up at their London fixtures, and by the mid-1980s I came to regard QPR as a dreadful, and somewhat embarrassing, illness from which I had now fully recovered.

In the magical year of 1992, when we were challenging for the League title, I was living in the United States. At precisely 11.40 a.m. east-coast time on every Saturday morning, I would call England for the football results. When there was a key match my brother in London would prop the phone by the radio or television so that I could listen to the commentary. Visits to England were now scheduled around League fixtures and invitations to give readings or lectures would be accepted or rejected depending upon where in the country Leeds United were playing. And to this day the situation remains the same.

I am writing this in New York City, where I currently spend most of the year. Here in New York I don't miss the English pubs because you can buy English beer anywhere. I don't miss the newspapers or the television because with new technology I can easily walk down the street and buy an English paper on the same day that folks in Britain read it, or I can turn on the television and watch the nine o'clock news from the BBC. I don't even miss the games because there is a two-hour programme every Sunday with highlights of all the Premier

League games, and if I want to watch a live game at a weekend I can just call 'pay-for-view'. What I do miss is the thrill of actually being at Elland Road.

I miss parking the car as close to the ground as possible. I miss walking towards the ground and seeing the huge cantilevered stand. I miss being able to turn to my best friend, John, and say (yet again), 'There's the cathedral.' I miss being able to read the programme and drink bad Bovril and wonder who's going to play today, and who might be injured, and then quickly flick to the page in the programme with the League tables so that I can check out exactly where we are. I miss talking to the old guys next to me in the stands, who always wonder if I've been before. I miss being able to say to them, Sprake Reaney Cooper Bremner Charlton Hunter Lorimer Clarke Jones Giles Gray. I miss being able to look over at the spot in the Lowfields Road stand where my dad and I sat in the early 1970s when he came to his one and only game (Leeds 5 Derby 0). As we left the ground, my dad turned to me and said, 'Bremner, he's a dynamo.' That's it, Dad. You're getting it. But he never did. To this day he still listens to cricket on the radio.

Leeds United reminds me of my father. Leeds United reminds me of my best friend, John. Leeds United reminds me of the moment my mother caught me crying as a teenager because in 1972 Leeds had lost the game that would have given them the double. Leeds United reminds me of who I am. All together now, 'We are Leeds, We are Leeds, We are Leeds.' Somewhere, thirty-five years ago, a small black boy in the company of his white teenage babysitter stood on the terraces at Elland Road and muttered those words for the first time. And I say back to that child today, 'And you will always be Leeds, for they are a mirror in which you will see reflected the complexity that is your life.'

1998

Conclusion: The 'High Anxiety' of Belonging

For much of the past year, a short story and an essay have been sitting on top of my desk. Hardly a week has passed by when I have not picked up one of them and read it through. Joseph Conrad's 'Amy Foster', and George Orwell's 'England Your England' are both concerned with the idea of 'home.' Their concern provides me with a mirror into which I can peer and see reflected my own fascination with this word. If, as the poet Robert Frost once suggested, 'Home is the place where, when you have to go there, they have to take you in,' then both Conrad and Orwell – in their short story and essay – seem to me to be examining the criteria for membership that will allow them to be taken in. I wonder if I gave up trying to do this some years ago.

I grew up in Leeds in the sixties and seventies, in a world in which everybody, from teachers to policemen, felt it appropriate to ask me – some more forcefully than others – for an explanation of where I was from. The answer 'Leeds,' or 'Yorkshire,' was never going to satisfy them. Of course, as a result, it was never going to satisfy me either. I soon recognised that no sooner had the words 'Leeds' or 'Yorkshire' fallen from my lips then a corollary question would be asked. My interrogator would paste a smile of benign patronage to his face. 'No lad, where are you *really* from?' Things are different now: Britain appears to have yielded to the inevitability of a multi-cultural, multi-racial society. Back then, however, the banal rallying cry of 'send them back' could be heard emanating from all levels of society, while politicians from the far left to the far right knew that they could mine votes by promising to hurry through legislation that would prevent more of 'us' from coming in.

Today there is a tacit understanding that Britain has changed. It has been a few years now since a Briton had the temerity to ask me, 'where are you from?' I take this as a sign of progress. Sadly, however, I am coming to understand that despite these welcome changes, the constant questioning of those early years, and concomitant undermining of my sense of belonging, has inevitably affected my ability to embrace Britain as 'home' with the degree of vigour that I might wish. Two years ago my lawyer asked me if I had any thoughts about how to 'dispose of' my body. A chilly question, but I answered without hesitation. 'I wish my ashes to be scattered in the middle of the Atlantic Ocean at a point equidistant between Britain, Africa and North America.' He looked puzzled, but I instantly understood that this watery crossroads lay at the centre of a place that had become my other 'home'; a place that, over the years, I have come to refer to as my Atlantic home. But why the desire to actively cultivate a plural notion of home?

For the past thirteen years I have lived in London, and 'elsewhere' – most consistently in the United States. I have, in the past, felt the desire to abandon Britain altogether. This feeling surfaced most powerfully in 1987 when Mrs. Thatcher achieved her third successive election victory. Her government's continued incantation of a discordant, neo-imperial, rhetoric of exclusion led me to the conclusion that I simply did not need the grief. I did leave Britain, albeit briefly, but I quickly rectified what I soon understood to be a mistake. I felt that I had a responsibility to address British society from within. A decision was made to retain a British passport, to pay British taxes, to remain a British citizen. I believed then, and I continue to believe, that as long as there remain people who are incapable or unwilling to uncouple nationality from race, then my continued presence has virtue in so far as it might serve to confound, or perhaps even educate, such people. But, as I have already confessed, I do have another 'home.'

After thirteen years of compulsive itinerancy, I know my Atlantic 'home' to be triangular in shape with Britain at one apex, the west coast of Africa at another, and the new world of North America (including the Caribbean) forming the third point of the triangle. If one draws a line between these three points, I regard the area of Atlantic Ocean that is described to be a much travelled pond. Across the centuries, countless millions have traversed this water, and unlike myself, these people have not always had the luxury of choice. They have felt alienated from, or abandoned by, the societies that they have hitherto known as 'home'. They have hoped that somewhere, over the horizon, there might be a new place where they might live and raise their children. These are the people that I have written about during the course of the past twenty years, and as one book has led to another, I have grown to understand that I am, of course, writing about myself in some oblique, though not entirely unpredictable, way.

All journeys have a beginning. Mine began on the west coast of Africa in a slave fortress. Perhaps it was Elmina Castle in Ghana. This would make me happy for Elmina Castle is probably the most beautiful building that I have ever seen. Set on a promontory jutting out into the Atlantic Ocean, it was built by the Portuguese in 1482 to help facilitate trade with the Africans in the immediate vicinity. The castle was captured by the Dutch in the seventeenth century, and eventually became British in the nineteenth century. Initially, the goods traded and bartered were muskets, cloth, liquor and brass, in exchange for gold. (The British named the whole region the Gold Coast, a name which remained in use until 1957 when Ghana achieved her independence.) However, at some point in the sixteenth century Elmina Castle was adapted to accommodate the storage of new goods – human beings. Elmina Castle, constructed a full decade before Columbus set sail in search of the New World, was very quickly transformed into a place of unspeakable misery and cruelty, yet it remains a building which fascinates me. Aside from the aesthetics of line, and the human ambition which informed its construction, I remain mesmerized by the multiple contradictions of Elmina Castle. I will relate just one such contradiction.

The massive structure has recently been renovated so that it might form the centrepiece of an ever-expanding diasporan tourist trade. African-Americans have, in the wake of the book and television series *Roots,* discovered cultural tourism. There is, in the United States, a whole network of agents and airlines ready to facilitate the anxious desire of African-Americans to return 'home' to Africa in order that they might discover their ancestry. A building like Elmina Castle offers great possibilities for making money if one can attract tourists to it. And, sure enough, this is happening. Modern four- and five-star hotel facilities are springing up in the small fishing village of Elmina and its environs so that African-Americans, and others of the diaspora, can return 'home' in relative comfort.

Inside the castle itself there are guided tours on the hour, and – of course – a gift shop. The problem is the gift shop, which is located in what used to be a female dungeon. Tens of thousands of African women were shackled in this space, held naked and shivering, awaiting the final journey through the door of no return and into the hold of the slave ship. Thereafter, they were forced to endure the unspeakable horrors of the middle passage as the ship slowly crossed the Atlantic Ocean from east to west. Today the gift shop sells postcards, books and trinkets. The local vendor is making money. Visitors, particularly those from the African diasporan world, are indignant when told about the 'history' of the gift shop. On the other hand, the great majority of Ghanaians simply do not understand what all the fuss is about. For them, the building holds little romance. It does not suggest a departure or a journey. It is not emblematic of 'home' lost or found.

History is contained in buildings. Their names mean something. We have clues to our past, our present and even some idea of our future if we study buildings and their origins. I first visited Elmina Castle in the late eighties. As a man of African origin, I was coming face to face with a part of my Atlantic history. It was disturbing, but I wished neither to look the other way, nor to romanticise the encounter. I wished simply to understand. This place, after all, was where my journeying in the Atlantic world began. When faced with our own histories in the form of places and buildings, we all respond differently. A holocaust survivor wanders the ruins of the Warsaw ghetto and then breaks down and cries. Ronald Reagan idly sips a pint of beer in an Irish pub and smiles for the cameras. We respond in different ways. The half-crumbling sugar mills which litter the landscape of the Caribbean islands are an eloquent and painful reminder of Caribbean history. But what to do with them? Pull them down and make room for a condominium development? Leave them in their state of dereliction? Or rebuild them and charge tourists ten dollars to walk around them, and then offer these same people the opportunity to buy some molasses, or some sugar, or some local rum? What to do with our buildings? The answer is often to be found nestling neatly between two questions. To what extent do I belong to this place? How much do I want to forget? On coming face to face with our history the vexing questions of belonging and forgetting rise quickly to the surface. And near-cousin to the words 'belonging' and 'forgetting' is the single word, 'home.'

As a young boy growing up in Leeds, I was both confused by, and afraid of, the word 'home'. Fear and confusion are fertile soil in which to plant the young writer. Over the years I have written about my relationship to the word 'home' and I have also read and reread literature which bears some relationship to this word, including Orwell's essay, 'England Your England' and Conrad's short story, 'Amy Foster'. For the past year this essay and short story have been the literary poles around which I have danced. I have read both pieces more times than I care to admit. In the case of Orwell's essay, I have tried, by some process of literary osmosis, to enter England, to *feel* England, to feel *for* England to the exclusion of the Atlantic world, but I have failed. Something in me rejects the idea of standing alone with Britain as my sole 'home'.

Conrad's 'Amy Foster' intrigues me. A mysterious man from central Europe is castaway in an English coastal village. Nobody knows who he is, but he tries to make himself at home in this strange place. Sadly, he fails. He is not at home. But then neither was Conrad or Orwell. Both were British, but both were born elsewhere, Conrad in Poland and Orwell in India. As I oscillate between Conrad and Orwell I realize that for me – also born elsewhere – there will never be any closure to this conundrum of 'home'. My continued sense of alienation in a British context is hardly original. The roots are racially charged, but others have felt similarly excluded on grounds of class, gender or religion. Others have been subjected to questioning that is designed to undermine their sense of belonging. The end result of such questioning is the engendering of feelings of rejection and distrust. Some people have little choice but to live in this state of high anxiety. Some others hurry to make plans to leave. I have chosen to create for myself an imaginary 'home' to live alongside the one that I am incapable of fully trusting. My increasingly precious, imaginary, Atlantic world.

Two years ago I travelled to Lens in France, to watch a crucial World Cup soccer game between England and Colombia. The atmosphere inside the stadium was impassioned. As the strains of 'God Save the Queen' began I rose and, together with the thirty thousand other English fans, I belted out the words to the national anthem with a vigour that shocked me. For a moment the cloud of ambivalence was lifted. I belonged. Why not, I wondered, submit to the moment and cease struggling? After all, what is wrong with a tee-shirt emblazoned with the Union Jack? The sixties and seventies are over, I thought. Come on, move on. However, for me, the unequivocal answer to such private urgings is contained in the one word; 'vigilance'. History has taught me that for people such as myself the rules will change. The goalposts will be moved. A new nationality act will be passed. And another. For people such as myself, the complex troubled history of Britain suggests vigilance. Mercifully, not everybody suffers the same degree of anxiety over this question of belonging. Most people live secure lives in a place that they recognise as their own. I understand that to such people my ambivalence will probably appear to be at best slightly cranky, at worst, paranoid. But then most people did not grow up in Leeds in the sixties and seventies having to endure a daily chorus of 'Why don't you fuck off back to where you come from?' Whenever I stand on the ramparts of Elmina Castle and gaze out at the Atlantic Ocean, I know exactly where I come from. I can look to the north and to the west and see the different directions in which I have subsequently journeyed. And, on a clear day, I can peer into the distance and see where I will ultimately reside.

2000

ALSO BY CARYL PHILLIPS

THE ATLANTIC SOUND

Liverpool, England; Accra, Ghana; Charleston, South Carolina. These were the points of the triangle forming the major route of the transatlantic slave trade. And these are the cities that Caryl Phillips explores—physically, historically, psychologically—in this wide-ranging meditation on the legacy of slavery and the impact of the African Diaspora on the life of a place and its people.

History/0-375-70103-6

THE EUROPEAN TRIBE

In this richly descriptive and haunting narrative, Caryl Phillips chronicles a journey through modern-day Europe, his quest guided by a moral compass rather than a map. Seeking personal definition within the parameters of growing up black in Europe, he discovers that the natural loneliness and confusion inherent in long journeys collide with the bigotry of the "European Tribe"—a global community of whites caught up in an unyielding, Eurocentric history.

Essays/Memoir/0-375-70704-2

EXTRAVAGANT STRANGERS

This exciting anthology is a collection of writings from thirty-nine British authors who were born outside of Britain and therefore see it with clear and critical eyes. Caryl Phillips has included selections by Thackeray, Kipling, Conrad, Orwell, Naipaul, Rushdie, and many other "extravagant strangers" who prove that English literature has been shaped and influenced by outsiders for over two hundred years.

Literature/Anthology/0-679-78154-4

ALSO AVAILABLE:

Cambridge, 0-679-73689-1
Crossing the River, 0-679-75794-5
The Final Passage, 0-679-75931-X
Higher Ground, 0-679-76376-7
The Nature of Blood, 0-679-77675-3
The Right Set, 0-375-70646-1
A State of Independence, 0-679-75930-1